A Name for Herself

A Name for Herself

A Dutch Immigrant's Story

K. A. Van Til

RESOURCE *Publications* · Eugene, Oregon

A NAME FOR HERSELF
A Dutch Immigrant's Story

Copyright © 2020 K. A. Van Til. All rights reserved. Except for brief quotations in critical publications or reviews, no part of this book may be reproduced in any manner without prior written permission from the publisher. Write: Permissions, Wipf and Stock Publishers, 199 W. 8th Ave., Suite 3, Eugene, OR 97401.

Resource Publications
An Imprint of Wipf and Stock Publishers
199 W. 8th Ave., Suite 3
Eugene, OR 97401

www.wipfandstock.com

PAPERBACK ISBN: 978-1-7252-7538-6
HARDCOVER ISBN: 978-1-7252-7539-3
EBOOK ISBN: 978-1-7252-7540-9

Manufactured in the U.S.A.   07/02/20

To Kathy, who let me write this book,
when I should have gotten a job.

These too lived by faith . . . of whom the world was not worthy.

Hebrews 11.

Contents

Preface | ix
Acknowledgments | xi

Introduction: Visiting Grandma | 1
Going Dutch | 3
Becoming Americans | 9
Amsterdam Comes to Chicago | 15
Proving Ourselves as Farmers | 24
Midwest Industry Calls | 32
Spies in the Land | 40
Homesteading in Montana | 47
More Dutch Immigrants: The Zwiers | 56
Love in the West | 64
Family and Gangsters in Chicago | 75
Now Everyone is Poor | 84
Sundays in Lansing | 92
A Woman's Work is Never Done | 115
A Dogs' Vocation | 125
The War | 132
A New Post-War World | 140
Finally, My Own House! | 147
My Sweet Pete | 153
Such A Good Son | 161
Coping After Al | 171

Irene Moves Back West | 178
Don: Christian, Agnostic, Jewish, Divorce | 188
Lin Completes the Circle | 197
Taking Care of the Next Generation | 208
A Few Trips of My Own | 217

Epilogue | 219

Preface

GRANDMA WAS A REMARKABLE woman. At ninety she was as sharp as one of the pins she used to hem her dresses. While serving tea and cookies in her little senior apartment one day, she abruptly turned to me and said, "Well, I sure haven't made a name for myself; maybe one of you grandkids will."

That struck me forcefully, for two reasons.

First, why would a poor immigrant woman with an eighth-grade education even think she *could* have made a name for herself.

Second, grandma and millions of women like her *should* have made names for themselves. They were pioneers and saints who made America what it is today. Like many, she was born abroad, labored, struggled, prayed, loved, laughed, bore children, cared for others' children, tilled virgin soil, sent sons to war, was widowed, and much, much more.

This book is my small effort to honor her name, and that of others like her. I hope that contemporary readers who not have "made a name for themselves" may also take comfort and inspiration from the story of her life.

Acknowledgments

To Stanley Zwier, Irene Zwier DeVries, and Linda Zwier Van Til for writing out the answers to many annoying questions about their mother, providing photos, and responding to phone calls.

To Donald Zwier, posthumously, for photos.

To Daniel P. Zwier for transcripts of his grandfather's sermons.

To Roxanne Zwier Swanson for writing material about her parents, and for taping an interview with Minnie Zwier.

To historian Robert Swierenga for providing and pointing out historical resources on Dutch immigrants.

To Nancy and Gayle Recker for writing and permitting me to use material from "Spirit Trained Eyes: The Western Adventure."

To Melanie Van Til for taking pictures of old photos and getting them prepped for reproduction.

To Emily Van Til Mendez, Marie Van Til, and Anna Van Til DeYoung for proofreading the manuscript.

To novelist Rhoda Janzen for writing and publishing guidance.

To poet D.L. James for editorial work.

To editor Michael Thomson for connecting me to Resource Publishers.

To journalist Mark Lewison for editing and publishing guidance.

To Reinder Van Til for previous editing and publishing guidance.

To family historian Andy Voss (husband of Jane Zwier), for the genealogy and story of the Zwiers of Opperdoes, as well as related photos.

To Herb Brinks, for his collection of Dutch letters in "Write Back Soon."

Introduction
Visiting Grandma

"You must have the 'Q.' There are only four letters left on the table. I've got a U that I can put over here and make "LUNE." That should give you space to use your Q. If you can get a six-letter word, you'll hit the double word score and get yourself a nice bunch of points."

She was demolishing me at Scrabble again. Once she had put the game well out of reach, she switched to the role of coach. It was 1988. Grandma was 89, and I was 29, in grad school. I had stopped by her little apartment in Lansing, Illinois, to see her, as my mom insisted. Grandma was always glad to see me, brewing the obligatory Lipton tea, and serving a few homemade chocolate-chip cookies. Then she got down to business.

"How are you doing? What are you learning at the seminary? How's my nephew Rob doing there?"

After these and many more questions she addressed me with a sly grin.

"Wanna try your luck at Scrabble?"

She knew she would cream me. If there would have been professional Scrabble tournaments at the time, she'd have entered, and won.

"OK, but go easy on me."

She never did. She had spent a lifetime devouring books, and it showed in her vocabulary. I always wondered how such a smart woman only got through the 8th grade.

"Hardly anyone went on to High School in those days," she said when I asked. "I would have liked to have gone on to college and been a teacher but couldn't. I had to help support the family. Can you imagine how wonderful it must be to teach children to read, and then help them understand what they've read?"

"I'm sure you'd have made a good teacher, maybe High School English or History."

"Well, your mom and uncle Don are both teachers, and good ones. I guess they got some of those teaching genes from me."

"You didn't get to be a teacher, but you sure have led an interesting life, coming to U.S. as an infant, moving out west, living through the Depression in Chicago, and two World Wars."

"Interesting? Ha! I would say more like 'poor and unremarkable.' No, I've done nothing special; I've made no name for myself."

"But Mom told me you use to ride horseback with the Indians out in Montana."

She sat back in her chair and smiled.

"Well, there might be a few interesting parts. I'll tell you what I remember."

Going Dutch

I REMEMBER PA TELLING of the day he sat in the Unemployment Office in Amsterdam asking for help. He'd never taken a guilder from the government, or from anyone else, so it was the most shameful day of his life. The employment officer asked him all the usual questions:

"Name?"

"Ahlrich Recker."

"Address?"

"Korteprinzengracht Straat 192, Amsterdam."

"Occupation?"

"Carpenter."

Then came the question that introduced a note of injury and outrage to Pa's voice whenever he told the story, even decades later. The employment officer didn't miss a beat. Without looking up from his notes, he asked

"Have you ever been in jail?"

"Why no! I've never been in jail. I've never even broken a law."

Pa was an organist and professing member of the Christian Reformed Church. Every Sunday he played for services in which the Ten Commandments issued forth from the pulpit. Breaking those Commandments was unimaginable to him.

"Ah, that's too bad; we have a nice job program for prisoners returning to society."

"You mean if I were a criminal you'd have a job for me?"

"Ya."

"How can that be? I've never committed even a minor offence, but you tell me you'd have a job for me today if I were a felon? That's crazy!"

"Maybe so, but that's the way it is," the officer mechanically retorted.

Pa slowly left the employment agency. His feet seemed to move by themselves, heavily, and aimlessly. He was six feet four inches tall, but when he walked home that day he must have hunched down to about five feet six. He was a serious man in his thirties, with a long mustache that covered his mouth and draped over each side of his chin. Though serious, he also had a sneaky wit that he used when sparring with friends. But there was nothing funny about the pickle he was in now. He had a wife and three young children to care for, and no job. He trekked down the worn, rutted, brick paved streets where thousands of Dutchmen had clomped before him. What was he going to do?

Pa was born on May 12, 1865, at about the time the U.S. Civil War was winding up. He too was familiar with military life, having served in the Dutch Army. Though he was in the Army, he spent most of his time aboard a ship in the Dutch East Indies, now known as Indonesia, helping to transport troops from one island to another. I guess when you are a sea-faring nation like Holland even the soldiers had better know their way around a ship. He was honorably discharged on May 12, 1892. He returned home to "Halfweg," a village "half way" between Amsterdam and Haarlem.

He was carpenter. He specialized in making carts, wagons, and wheelbarrows for farm use. Vegetable vendors pulled two-wheeled hand carts for their goods to sell around the neighborhood, and most farmers needed a horse-drawn wagon of some kind for crops or hay. There was considerable demand for Pa's wagons, since Amsterdam and Haarlem were surrounded by little farms. Most of them were small, family affairs, maybe five or ten acres, so each family needed its own wagon. Pa would build carts to specification for a farmer or make a general purpose one to rent or sell. In the Netherlands everything was regulated, so he paid for a permit to be a carpenter, another to be a wheel-right, and another to make wagons, etc. His special love was making baby strollers. He would talk with the young mothers and fathers about their baby or pregnancy. He would then use a typical design, and add a little change to the handle, or a curve in the sides to make each carriage unique. On the bottom or side of the cart he would carve his initials: "AR," for Ahlrich Recker, and the year.

The economy in the Netherlands was not good in the 1890s, so Pa's business was slow. One day he rented out a new hay wagon he had just finished building to a farmer from out of town.

"So you want to rent that wagon?"

"Ya, it's a nice new wagon."

"Where are you from?"

"Up toward Haarlem."

"You need it for haying? How long will you need it?"

"Should be about two weeks."

Pa took down the man's name and address, and got a deposit, as was his usual practice. But when neither the wagon nor the farmer came back two weeks later, Pa went to find the man. He went to the address and found a rye field. He went to talk with the neighbor nearest the address but was told, "I've never heard of that man." So Pa was stuck with a big loss. That hay wagon represented about one months' work and one months' wage. Pa just assumed that everyone else in the Netherlands was like him—honest to a fault. How could a fellow Dutchman take away his living? That theft is what had sent him to Amsterdam to work as a shipwright, and the loss of that job led to the Unemployment Office.

Ma and Pa lived near the very center of Amsterdam, the Dam Square, the royal palace, the gothic Nieuwe Kerk, and the upscale department store "De Bijenkorf." The Amsterdam city registry even states that they lived in the middle of two floors "een en een half hoog." There must have been an interior stairway that led to an intermediate floor where they lived. Why the city hall of Amsterdam would keep a record about a "half floor," I don't know. Dam Square had developed from the first dam on the Amstel River, giving the city its name of Amsterdam. Originally built in 1270, it brought together communities from either side of the river. In the Middle Ages it was a fish market, but developed into the town center after centuries of use. Pa and Ma would often take walks in central Amsterdam, look at the great stone lions on Dam square, and peer into the shops. The Rijksmuseum was a short train ride from their flat, so Ma and Pa were able to see some great Dutch art on a regular basis.

In the 17th century, Amsterdam had been the most prosperous, free, and important city in Europe; and hundreds of years later the Dutch still thought of themselves as leaders in both democracy and commerce. The 17th century was the Golden Age of the Netherlands, and Amsterdam was the goose that laid its golden eggs. It was the center of trade and finance for all of Europe. Ships from the Netherlands traveled as far as China and the Dutch East Indies. It was also the center of high art, with painters like Jan Steen, Rembrandt van Rijn, and Johannes Vermeer chronicling Dutch life in glorious detail. Who knows, those very Dutch Masters might have walked the same streets that Pa now trudged.

Pa and those painters seemed to share the same Calvinist ethic. The old Dutch Masters often showed the Dutch hard at work, celebrating their sober yet prosperous lives. Some paintings made biblical references, like Rembrandts' "The Prodigal Son," or "Moses Smashing the Ten Commandments." Others, like Pa's favorite "The Milk Maid" by Johannes Vermeer had a more subtle religious message. The title isn't accurate, since the maid is not milking the cows: she's pouring milk from a pitcher into glasses in an ordinary Dutch kitchen. You can see the Delft tiles and the Dutch oven behind her. Vermeer depicts this modest household and modest girl. Neither the home nor the bread on the table is luxurious; at best it's middle class. Pa remarked:

"Look at her," said Ma, "She's not a beautiful girl, pretty ordinary looking, don't you think, and even a bit squat."

"But look at the light from the window pouring in on the maids' face," said Pa. "It's as if a holy angel were shining light on this plain working girl."

"Ach, you're too sentimental."

"No, no, I'm sure Vermeer is trying to show that even the everyday work of this Dutch housemaid is glorious."

"Glorious? Housework?"

"Ya, she's heavenly, she looks blessed from above."

"Ach, now you're a great art critic? It's just a painting."

Pa saw his own work in the same way. He was not merely making carts and carriages because that's the job he was stuck with. He was making carts and carriages for God, in order to sell and lend them to others. They, in turn, would use the wagons to serve God in their own work. But now, he had no work. It must have weighed on him emotionally and spiritually, as well as financially. His job let him do God's work.

Many Dutch chose their names on the basis of their profession. Kuyper, for example, is a cooper, or barrel-maker, Smit is a smith, and so on. Other Dutch names often reflected our connection to the sea. For example, the well-known Dutch name, van Dyke, means that the Van Dykes' had been born by the dike. Other names with the "van" prefix also told you where its owner came from. Gerrit van Amstel, for example, was born near the Amstel River. And Henk Van der Zee was "from the sea." The Dutch were forced to choose last names when Napoleon Bonaparte invaded the Netherlands in the early 1800s. He needed tax revenue for his war machine and laid a heavy burden on the Dutch. But when the French revenuers went out to collect, they had a problem: most of the people had only first names, and many of them were the same. So when "Jan" was called on to pay up, he would protest that he'd already paid, and point to the name "Jan" in the collector's book. And sure enough, there was the name "Jan". The French were not fooled for a minute.

"Which Jan are you? Choose a surname!"

So the Dutch were compelled to choose last names; the Groningers (from the province of Groningen) often chose simple ones that started with "van" like "van Amstel" or "van Dyk" to say where they were from. Plenty of Frisians chose "DeVries" (the Frisian). Others apparently thought that the whole business of last names was a big joke and took on names that were none too serious. So, a peasant named Jan, who had one pair of shoes and hadn't eaten meat since last Christmas called himself, DeGroot "The Great." Another Jan thought to distinguish himself by noting he was "Nagteboorn" (born naked). And then there was the Jan who thought the whole surname business was an immense French farce, and so chose the surname "Vlaardingerbroek."

"Vlaar" is flame.

"Dinger" is fart.

"Broek" is britches.

So roughly, Vlaardingerbroek is "a flaming fart in the pants." They sure showed that old Napoleon a thing or two. Thankfully most Americans don't understand all these names, lest today the descendants of the original Vlaardingerbroek's, would be walking around shame-faced.

Pa was quite tall, but Ma was only four feet eleven inches. She always claimed that missing inch as her own and rounded up to five feet. She walked with a limp, since she was born with one leg shorter than the other. She was serious too, and did not possess the fountain of mirth deep inside that spontaneously bubbled up in Pa. They looked kind of comical walking together down the street together. He was a lanky, heavily mustached man, walking with great long strides, and she a stout little teacup of a woman, tilting quickly from side to side. Pa's family, the Reckers, had come from Germany some generations back. In fact there's a little town in the Palatinate called Reckershausen that we suspect was his family's origin.

They married on May 15, in 1890 in the Christian Reformed Church of the Netherlands. He was 21, and she, Boudewina Kok, was 18. Just like her height, however, she inevitably mentioned that she was really 18 and a half. That half year apparently gave her far more legitimacy as a young bride than a mere 18 would have. The Koks had been residents of the Halfweg area for generations.

By the time Pa went looking for a job in Amsterdam, they had been married for eight years. A year and a half after their wedding, Boudewina (Ma) gave birth to their first child, Hilkelina (called Lena). Two years later brother William was born, and in 1896 they added Ahlrich Jr. So when Pa went to the Unemployment Office in 1898 they had two and four year old sons, and a six year old daughter. As a bonus, Ma was pregnant with me. Ma and Pa were in a tough spot. They had always lived in the Netherlands and had family there. They loved their country and its people. But Pa figured that if the only way to get a job in Holland was to commit a crime, he would move somewhere else. The two options were *Amerika*, or *Sud Afrika*. The Dutch had been migrating to both for centuries. Pa praised the South African option.

"The Boors down there are very prosperous, he argued, "They have good farms and even diamond mines."

"Ya" said Ma, "they also have the English on one side and the Africans on the other. And neither one is too friendly. I won't go to Africa."

Though she was much smaller than Pa, she was in some ways stronger. Her will prevailed. They would go to America.

At the time these discussions were going on, I made my appearance in this world. On December 2, 1898, I became the youngest of the four Recker children. I was baptized as "Hermina," two weeks after my birth in 1898. I can't remember ever being called Hermina though; I was always "Minnie," an abbreviation of the last part of my name—"mina." Only four months later I would be carried aboard a boat headed from Amsterdam to New York. I would be an American.

Becoming Americans

IN THE 17TH CENTURY Holland was the most highly developed and wealthiest country in Europe. The Dutch East India Company traded throughout the world, and when its ships arrived in America it quickly recognized the importance of the Manhattan harbor. Dutch traders sailed to the area and moved up the Hudson River. Early in that century it looked as though America could become a Dutch-speaking country, but the Dutch only traded in America, whereas the English brought families and settled, so their population overtook ours. Though the English took control of New Amsterdam (Manhattan) in 1664 and renamed it after the English city of York, many Dutch customs carried on, including political and religious freedom.

At that time Holland enjoyed more religious freedom than any European country. The English Puritans, for example, first moved from England to Holland to escape persecution before immigrating to America. They were accepted by the burghers of Amsterdam, who told them, "You are welcome to live here as long as you obey our laws." They stayed in the Netherlands for a few years but didn't like their children learning Dutch instead of English and so sailed for America. Jews too lived at peace in Holland, having fled persecution in other countries. Many Jewish bankers and diamond merchants moved to the Netherlands from Spain and Portugal during the Spanish Inquisition, literally enriching Holland. The Dutch understood that ethnic and religious discrimination was bad for business.

The Dutch also believed more strongly in universal education than did the English. For example, the Dutch of New Amsterdam quickly established a school for their children, whereas it took the founders of Plymouth over fifty years to do so. They also brought their church to America, the Dutch Reformed Church, which later became the Reformed

Church of America which is the oldest, continuously existing denomination in America to this day.

In the 19th century Netherlands, all you had to do to find out about America was to open a newspaper or magazine. Hearing about the "Wild West" was a romantic tale about a land of untamed beasts and men. European circuses even featured real Indians and the cowboy shows of "Buffalo Bill Cody." They did amazing tricks on horseback, such as leaning off the side of a speeding horse to scoop their hats off the ground. Wild Bill even shot a quarter out from between a lady's fingers.

Most Europeans had heard of America's developing wealth and its freedoms. It was well known that anyone from Europe could go to America, if you were healthy when you arrived at Ellis Island. Ads for voyages to America filled the newspapers. Trans-Atlantic shipping was a competitive business, and shipping companies regularly advertised their fares and destinations. By the late 1800's most Dutch families knew someone who had immigrated to the U.S. Friends of my parents shared this letter from one Dutch farmer who had:

> *You seem curious to know how farmers live here. Presently we are harvesting the crops which we planted in April. Crops grow rapidly here and produce large amounts . . . Many farmers raise two crops each summer here: cabbage, onions, carrots, beets and pickles—also many beans. They plant the potatoes between the beans. There is not much dairy farming here . . . Most of the farmers here sell their crop in the large city of Chicago, which is the largest city in the area. I have been there four times, and it is really a sight. It has more wealth and treasure than the whole of Germany. Some houses are located on lots larger than two acres. It is impossible to imagine unless you have been there.*
>
> *Generally, American farmers are lazy and careless about farming. They could raise much more than they do. Still, there is no poverty here. Much of the crop goes to waste in the fields. Concerning potatoes, they harvest only the large ones and leave the rest to rot . . . When they have enough, most American are lazy and indifferent about such waste.*
>
> *Every day long trains go past my house loaded with meat and bacon. The meat goes to New York, and from there much of it goes to Europe. But the poor people of Europe hardly see any of it, while here everyone eats as much as he wishes. So it should be easy for you to understand that we enjoy life here . . . With my two boys I earn $80 per month—so you can well imagine that, if we remain*

healthy, I will be a man of means in a few short years. Thus, anyone who despises my new fatherland is no friend of mine.

You can see why Dutch farmers would think they could do much better for themselves in America, especially since the farms in Holland had been divided and subdivided down through the generations, many to only a few acres. We Dutch are proud of our work ethic and efficiency, so reading a letter like this confirmed what we had long suspected—we could do very well in America. In addition, so many Dutch had immigrated to the United States over the years that it was certain that a friend, cousin, or fellow church member was already there. On my mother's side, the Koks had immigrated to New Jersey a generation earlier.

When preparing to board we had to pack light. Our friends the Brinks shared a letter from their son, who advised what to bring on the journey:

> *Don't take any old clothes, because you can only carry 100 pounds along without extra charges—that is 80 Dutch pounds. Make small trunks, able to be handled by two men. From the baker you should get rye and wheat bread, slice them thick and let them dry. Take along 50 pounds of buckwheat meal, 60 pounds of bacon, 1 piece of dried meat, 5 pounds of sugar, 1 bottle of brandy, a small keg of beer, butter, coffee, tea, shelled barley, rice and beans. You must get all of these things because everyone must have 200 pounds to feed themselves aboard ship.*
>
> *When you reach New York, don't sell the remaining food because you still have a long trip ahead of you. My sister should not cut her hair this winter because women wear long hair here. But you can sell your silver caps; they are not worn here, so take along some yarn for stockings, also 5 cubits of black cloth for clothing, 4 cubits of coat material, and 6 cubits of skirt material. You can buy all of this in any Dutch city. Take along your church books, one Bible, and one New Testament. You should also take both volumes of Brakel along. Take a copper kettle and also a waan . . .*

The first links in the chain of Dutch immigration had been moored in America for centuries. Since so many had gone before us it seemed far less risky forming part of that long chain than striking out on our own.

In Holland we were part of a minority church group. The state church was the Dutch Reformed church, which received tax money and was closely tied to the government. In fact, the government asserted its control over the *dominees* and the seminaries that trained them. It was a religious monopoly. This meant that if you were born in the northern

Netherlands you were automatically baptized into the state church. As a result, many Hollanders were Christian in name only. To be Dutch Reformed merely meant you were from Holland, like the Irish were Catholic or Greeks were Orthodox. This thin veneer of Christianity was not enough for my parents. They were Christians from the inside out, not just people who happened to be born and baptized in the Netherlands. So, they joined a group of churches that had seceded from the national church in 1834. That church did not get government money, and had been harassed by the government. Thus, in addition to receiving economic benefits, moving to America would rid us of this problem. In America you could join whatever church you wanted, free from government control.

For centuries ships had been sailing from the great Rhine port of Rotterdam to the Americas, and by the 1890s they were leaving from Amsterdam as well. These ships were not usually filled only with Dutch people but with people from all over Europe who had travelled to the Atlantic coast in order to immigrate to America. Thousands of Germans, Poles, Czechs, etc., came to the Dutch ports to make the Atlantic voyage to the U.S.

We left for America in the spring of 1899. Like many Dutch, we boarded the *Holland America Line* that had been running from Rotterdam to New York for decades. Of course I have only been told this, since at the age of six months I could hardly have been expected to remember it. I've also heard that Ma was seasick for most of the two-week-long journey, so my big sister Lena held me and took care of me. There were nearly 2,000 passengers aboard, a few in first class, a few more in second class, but the vast majority in third class, or "steerage," like us. Steerage was the ship's lower level in which poorer passengers stayed. The lines running through there from the captain's helm to the rudder gave this deck its name. Steerage provided no privacy or separate rooms and only two bathrooms, one for the men and another for the women.

There were small port-holes, but not enough, so even daylight hours were dark, especially in the cloudy spring weather of the North Atlantic. With little ventilation, the smell must have been terrible, which in addition to the waves probably sickened my mother. Women put benches together to sleep on, and the men lay on the floor, spreading out coats or cloths to soften the crush of body on boards. Each person got three quarts of fresh water per day, so while we had enough to drink, there was little if any left over for cleaning, a severe hardship for my "cleanliness is next to godliness" believing mother. Thankfully, no disease broke out on our voyage. On many previous voyages some families had lost half their children; we all arrived safely, after two weeks, in America.

The lines at customs and immigration on Ellis Island reminded Pa of the stockyards in Holland. People were moved from stall to stall. When our turn finally came it lasted only a minute or so: we were all healthy (seasickness excluded) and had the Kok family waiting for us. Other families didn't make it through so easily. If you had cholera, tuberculosis, scarlet fever, or glaucoma you were put in quarantine. If you didn't recover, the shipping company that brought you to the U.S. would have to take you back at its own expense.

Each family had to register its name at the immigration office. We had no problem, since the name Recker is pretty tough to mangle. If you remove the "c" you even have a palindrome—*RekeR*. But many names did get changed. For example, there is a cute story about a little Chinese man named Ole Olafson. He was often asked, "How did a Chinese man like you get such a Swedish sounding name?" and he would answer, "I don't know. I was in line at Ellis Island behind a bunch of Swedes. When I got to the front of the line, the agent asked my name. I said, Sam Ting. For some reason he wrote down Ole Olafson."

Another equally fictitious story tells of a man, Mordecai Wiesenstein, who immigrated to the U.S. at about this time. In line, when a fellow countryman asked his name and Mort told him, his friend said,

"You don't want a name like that in the U.S. Try one like Carnegie or Rockefeller or even Smith."

By the time Mort got to the front of the line he had been waiting so long that he'd forgotten the strange-sounding names his friend had suggested. So when the agent asked for his name, he clasped his forehead and said,

"Ich hab dass vergessen" (German for "I forgot it").

The agent said, "Very well. Welcome to the U.S., Mr. Ichabod Fergusson."

The Dutch have been fortunate immigrants to America. We were part of the earliest European migrations to the U.S. and are close in appearance and culture to the English, who had become the dominant group. I know some immigrants like the Irish and the Italians were not liked at first, and of course the Negroes were brought over as slaves. But we Dutch never really faced discrimination from those who came before us. We fit in pretty well. We were Protestant and white and behaved much like the English. The only major difference was our language. So we talked Dutch at home and quickly learned English in the streets and schools.

The Koks had moved to America a generation earlier and settled in New Jersey, around Patterson. Ma had sent a letter to them, letting them know which ship we would be on, so they were there to greet us when we arrived and helped us get settled in the U.S. We stayed with them for a day or two but soon left New Jersey for Chicago by train. It was over 700 miles from New York to Chicago via the Pennsylvania Railroad Company, and the train only went about 25 miles an hour, so that trip added another three days to our journey. We were headed to Roseland, a Dutch enclave on the south side of Chicago. In 1853 a Hollander wrote this to a Dutch newspaper:

> *Come to live with us here in Roseland. Here we have freedom, equality, brotherhood—these are no idle words. Anyone who wants to work and is able to do so can easily earn a comfortable living—can live peacefully and enjoy life. People who are farmers one day become shopkeepers the following day and on the next day something else, because if one thing doesn't work, people quickly turn to something else. Here there is not the least difference between farmers, city dwellers, or gentlemen. People from the poorest day laborer to the President are addressed as "Mr."*

Ma and Pa would soon be called "Mr. and Mrs. Recker," Americans.

Amsterdam Comes to Chicago

In 1846 six Dutch families purchased parcels in a low prairie south of Chicago. They started farming there, and naturally planted flowers around their houses, as good Dutch folk always do. When others came and saw the little village, they noticed the thriving rose gardens, and named the settlement Roseland. These Dutch farmers brought their onions, cabbage, and peppers up the road to Chicago on horse-drawn wagons. The Dutch colony later expanded west and south, and into Northwest Indiana. They eventually drove their wagons up from South Holland, Illinois, and even Munster Indiana, selling produce at the South Water Street market in Chicago.

By 1870 Chicago had a population of about 300,000 and was the second largest city in North America. It was a transportation center; in fact, at that point it held the world's largest railroad station. It was also a powerful manufacturer of agricultural machinery such as the McCormick reaper, and International Harvester. Good jobs drew thousands of immigrants to Chicago.

In 1871 the Great Chicago Fire destroyed most of the downtown, saving only the Water Tower and a few other stone buildings. But this meant that the whole city center could be re-built, with bigger, better, and taller buildings. Chicago grew dramatically. Between 1880 and 1890 it doubled in size, from a half-a-million, to a million. Almost all of this growth was from immigration. In 1890, four out of five Chicagoans were foreign born, so the city we came to in 1899 was a tossed salad of ethnicities—Dutch, Poles, Swedes, Germans, Greeks, Italians, etc.

In a way, we brought Amsterdam with us to Chicago. Roseland was probably about half Dutch when we arrived in 1899, with Swedes, Scots and others making up other portions of the local population. By the time we arrived, the Dutch "kolonie" in Roseland was well established. There were literally thousands of Dutch in Roseland by the time we arrived, and thousands more would come over in the next 20 years. For our family it felt as though we had transplanted Holland to Chicago. We went to a Dutch speaking church, spoke Dutch at home and with our neighbors, went to Dutch owned stores, and even attended a Dutch speaking gradeschool. While some of the Dutch left Roseland and integrated with the broader population of Chicago, most stayed together, living in the same neighborhood, and attending the same churches.

Ma and Pa bought a house on 10631 Wabash Ave. in Roseland, Illinois. It was typical of the houses there. It was made of wood and had indoor plumbing, but no electricity. There was no insulation in the walls then, so things got pretty cold in the winter. The main floor had dividers in it, but not separate rooms with doors. There was one bedroom on the main floor, plus the kitchen and dining room. It had an attic, or second floor which was just some plywood nailed over the ceiling joists. A set of open-air steps went up to the attic, which served as another bedroom for my brothers. They aimed the feet of the bed toward the corner of the attic, since the slope of the roof made the sides of the upstairs room pretty narrow. There was a basement too. It included the furnace and its coal but was uninhabitable. We used it for storing canned vegetables, and as a laundry room.

After paying for transport across the Atlantic, plus train tickets for five from New Jersey to Chicago, there wasn't much money left, but since both Pa and grandpa Kok sold everything they had in Holland we could afford to buy and furnish a house. Moving to Chicago was quite an act of faith on their part. Roseland was a separate town when we arrived in 1899; but in 1909 Chicago annexed it, making it part of that great city. For decades though, Roseland was a Dutch "Kolonie."

A few rich people in Chicago had gotten telephones by 1900, but neither we nor anyone we knew had one. The first bathtub appeared in Roseland in 1888. If you didn't have one you had to bathe in a tub in the laundry room or give yourself a sponge bath. Our house didn't have a bathtub so Ma would scrub us raw from head to toe every Saturday night, so we'd shine like new dimes for church on Sunday morning. Some members of both the Kok and Recker families were already in Roseland so we quickly made friends at church and school. Pa was a friendly man and would often invite people over to our house.

"Why hello Reimer, they tell me you came from Holland just last year too."

"Ya, from Groningen."

"Why don't you come on over; we can enjoy a cigar and a little 'slukje'"

"Slukje" was a Dutch liqueur, made from raisins. Reimer would come over, and they would sit on the porch, smoke big cigars, and talk after work.

"Ya, it's not so easy here, but you can get work."

"Ya, back in the old country they were charging me a fee for everything but my shoelaces; we had to get out."

"True; here you can start over."

Pa bought a Lyon and Healy pump organ. He had been a church organist in Holland, and wanted all of us to be able to read and play music. He was our first and only teacher. "Sit down with your belly-button in front of middle C. Middle C is the one right below the two black ones. On the page, the middle C is the one in the middle of the two staffs, the treble and the bass. It has a line through it." Etc. We didn't have any beginning student piano books, unaware even of their existence. Pa diligently sat with each one of us, evening after evening. We wanted to please him, so we tried hard. The first song we learned was the hymn "Jesus Lover of My Soul." It was in the key of F major, with one flat. It repeated an F chord four times before moving to a C chord. The whole thing then modulated between F and C. Not tough, nor exciting.

Ma and we kids loved to walk up and down nearby Michigan Avenue. There were lots of shops there, and we liked to see the American styles. I was just a little girl, but I still remember holding Ma or Lena's hand, and walking down the street. Many of the neighborhood shops were owned by Dutch who had come earlier, so we always found almond paste, King Peppermints, and windmill cookies. Mom could make the wonderful pastry from Holland called "banket" with the almond paste. The almond paste was wrapped into soft and crumbly dough, and then rolled into skinny loaves like bread. She baked it till the dough was crisp and the almond paste inside had hardened; then she sliced it into about two-inch squares.

I still make it. Here is the recipe:

Ingredients:

- 2 cups all-purpose flour
- 1 cup butter
- 1/2 cup water
- 1 1/2 cups almond paste
- 2 eggs
- 3/4 cup white sugar
- 1/4 teaspoon almond extract
- 1 pinch salt
- 1 egg white, beaten

Directions:

1. In a large bowl, cut cold butter or margarine into flour until the mixture has a crumb-like texture. Make a well in the center, add cold water. Mix together until the mixture forms a ball. Do not over-mix. Chill dough.
2. Preheat oven to 450 degrees F (225 degrees C). Grease cookie sheets.
3. In a medium bowl, blend together almond paste, eggs, 3/4 cup sugar, almond extract and salt.
4. Divide dough in 4 parts and roll into 15 inch strips. Place filling along the center of each long strip of dough. Roll up and pinch the ends to seal. Place strips 2 inches apart on cookie sheet. Brush with egg white, and sprinkle with the remaining sugar.
5. Bake for 15 to 20 minutes, or until golden.

Try it!

She also made "Oliekoeken," which is a deep-fried ball of dough with spices, raisins and currants in it.

Our grandfather William Kok was a widower who had immigrated with us. But only three years after coming to America he died. I was only four at the time, so have but one memory of him. He was taking sod off an empty lot nearby and laying it in our yard. He carried the pieces in a wheelbarrow, and I followed him. The second trip he made, he said something to my mother, and I had to stay home. Maybe I was getting in the way, or he was afraid he might run me over with the wheelbarrow. His funeral and burial were in Roseland. So at the end of his life he was an American, buried here, like Sarah in the cave of Machpelah.

Pa and Ma had three more children in Roseland, natural born citizens of the United States: little brother Dick, and two sisters—Alice and Christina. I think they wanted their U.S. born children to have good American sounding names. My name, "Hermina" is not exactly a common in the U.S. so I was forever known as "Minnie." Later, we called Christina "Tini," so she and I were Mini and Tini; the wee little Recker girls. Tini genuinely was teenie and grew only to Ma's height of 4' 11", but I was not truly "mini," as I eventually achieved five feet and five inches.

When we looked out our windows, we could see all the Dutch women bustling about their little homes and gardens. Saturdays were big workdays for the women since everything had to be prepared before the Sabbath. The food had to be ready to cook, and no washing, or baking, or chores were permitted on the Lord's Day. So, Saturday saw the women peeling potatoes and putting them in the pot, thawing the meat for the large Sunday meal, and making delicious pies for desert. That way the Sabbath would be a true day of rest. The church bells of the local Reformed and Christian Reformed Churches rang at 6 PM every Saturday evening. They chimed, "Prepare your hearts for the Sabbath, and purify your souls to take Holy Communion."

But boy did those ladies get back at it on Monday. They had an unofficial contest as to who could get the laundry out first on Monday morning. At dawn or before, the women would wash the clothes and sheets from the previous week. This meant putting the largest kettle you had on the stove, and then pouring the hot water into a tub. The clothes were thrown into the tub with a good dose of lye soap. Then, with a stick, or some sort of plunger they vigorously stirred, prodded and sank each piece of clothing. Especially worrisome stains might require soaking overnight on Sunday. Since this was not really Sunday work, but preparation for Monday work, it was permissible. They then wrung the clothes through a hand wringer and dashed to the yard to hang them out to dry. Of course, everyone could look across the back yards and see whose wash was out first, second and third, etc. I still remember hearing Ma and Lena.

"Lena, get up, it's time for the laundry."

"But Ma, it's still dark out. Can't I sleep?"

"No, no, get going. Last week Mrs. Ridderbos had her laundry out almost a half an hour before me." I don't know whether Ma won any of those contests, but I'm sure she didn't come in last. She was a little fireball. Don't let the fact that she did not quite achieve five feet in height fool you; she was a force to be reckoned with.

George Pullman had started a railroad car factory near Roseland in 1859. Earlier, he had taken a train ride to Chicago and tried to sleep in his seat but couldn't, so he decided to make sleeper cars that were not only comfortable, but luxurious. He paid his workers well and hired Negroes to work as porters on the trains. He also set up an entire town for his workers; in it he permitted no taverns or houses of prostitution, etc. But he also permitted little freedom of speech or political activity; if you complained about Pullman, you were out. He even threw out renters who didn't maintain their houses as well as he thought they should.

In 1894 the economy in the U.S. was bad. Pullman cut back on wages and increased working hours in order to maintain his profit margins. He had promised his financiers a 6% return on their investments, and squeezing his workers was the only way he could do it. He did not, however, lower the rents on their houses, or let his workers seek other housing. He paid them $9.07 every two weeks and charged a monthly rent of $9.00. What's more, he ran a "company store," where people could buy on credit against their next paycheck. The store held few bargains, but it was the only store Pullman allowed in his town. The workers attempted to form a union and went on strike. Lots of Dutch Reformed guys worked for Pullman. They went to their pastors and asked what they should do. They certainly wanted a raise but were skeptical of the unions. The preachers advised, "You can't join a union, it's a secret society and demands an oath. You may only take an oath of allegiance to God." So most of our guys became "scabs." They crossed the picket lines, while the union guys threw bottles at them, and tried to stab them.

Pullman refused to enter negotiations with the strikers and instead called his friend Grover Cleveland, then President of the United States, to send in federal troops to put down the strike. Some 30 people were killed. This was national news, and one sad chapter in the history of unions in America. One lasting result of this strike affected long-term politics for the Dutch. Most of the strikers, it seemed, were Democrats and Catholics. Most all of them also seemed to be heavy drinkers and members of clubs and lodges. We Dutch Reformed refused to take the membership oaths of to any of these "secret societies," so we joined the Republican Party, and stayed away from the largely Democratic unions. For such reasons, Pullman liked the Dutch, and hired as many of us as he could. He died only three years after the strike, and the city of Chicago soon annexed the town Pullman had created.

Roseland was right next door to Pullman, so when Pa, the carpenter/carriage maker looked for work he didn't have far to go. Right next door they were making luxurious sleeper cars. Other Hollanders in Roseland had been working for Pullman, and quickly got him a job. The first day on the job, Pa was given an assignment to build a railing for one of the cars. He looked around, and could only find some crooked, knotty, pine planks. He searched for better wood. What he found instead was a gaggle of Swedes, laughing up their sleeves, "Hyar, Hyar." They had grabbed all the straight, knot-free lumber for themselves. Pa had to make do with the knotted pine that day, but the next day he and some other Hollanders got there early enough to grab some good lumber.

It was in Roseland that Ma and Pa became citizens. I was too young to go along and hear Ma and Pa make the Pledge, but they received their United States citizenship in Chicago on October 20, 1904. They stood up with all the immigrants and pledged their loyalty to the new land.

> *I hereby declare, on oath, that I absolutely and entirely renounce and abjure all allegiance and fidelity to any foreign prince, potentate, state, or sovereignty, of whom or which I have heretofore been a subject or citizen; that I will support and defend the Constitution and laws of the United States of America against all enemies, foreign and domestic; that I will bear true faith and allegiance to the same; that I will bear arms on behalf of the United States when required by the law; that I will perform noncombatant service in the Armed Forces of the United States when required by the law; that I will perform work of national importance under civilian direction when required by the law; and that I take this obligation freely, without any mental reservation or purpose of evasion; so help me God."*

Quite an oath! At least this oath was not secret though, and it recognized that there is a God. The country they were renouncing, Holland, was every bit as free and democratic as the one they were joining. But they were proud to be Americans. We all were. It was a new land, and we would make it our land. The new country accepted us, even though we spoke a different language and came across a great ocean to get here. That is the splendor of America. It welcomes people from all over the world, without regard to their religion or politics. You just come, proclaim your allegiance to this beautiful country, and go to work.

We were still newcomers to the U.S. though, as our neighbors would sometimes remind us. Brother Bill had a special Princess Wilhelmina bowler hat that he had brought with him as a prized possession from Holland. When some American boys saw him coming, they would steal his hat and the roll it down the street or send it flying through the air. Meanwhile they would taunt:

> *Dutchman, Dutchman, belly full of straw;*
> *Crying like a donkey,*
> *Hee Haw, Hee Haw, Hee Haw!*

Maybe "Hee Haw," is the way our Dutch sounded to the Americans. To me, Dutch sounds more like we are clearing our throats than saying "Hee Haw." But this little poem stung and stuck with Bill, who remembered it years later. We had been welcomed here as immigrants, so we never disparaged or looked down on other groups who came behind us. We were proud to be Americans, and happy to see others come and fill this great big land. It seemed clear that the United States was a place where people of different lands and languages could live together.

By the time we arrived, our church, the Christian Reformed Church of Roseland, had established Roseland Christian School on nearby 108th St. Roseland Christian School was not a little Bible club; it had a full-fledged curriculum and taught all the subjects. History was literally God's story. Science was the exploration of God's world. Art was a means of understanding and creating beauty. Music was the chief means of giving praise to God, etc. It was a very good school. Lena and Bill both graduated from there, and I went there from first to third grade. Upon graduation from 8th grade, most of the children went to work, proudly bringing their paychecks home. After her graduation, Lena served as a maid for a nearby American family.

"Here's the money for the week, Ma."

"Thank you, Lena, we sure do need it."

"Ma, do you think I could have a dollar to buy a bolt of cloth down at Marshall Fields?'

"A dollar?"

"It's a beautiful print cloth, and I want to make a dress of it."

"A dollar is a lot of money for one bolt."

"I know."

"What if you took 50 cents and find out what you can get for that?"

After graduation Bill found work as a lumberjack in Wisconsin. There were many stands of forest still open there, so he moved around with the lumber camps, from little town to little town with the other young men. He learned how to swing a two-sided axe, and how to keep it sharp. He once told us of one of a man who never learned how to use an axe properly and ended up with his head split open.

Pa and Ma took a daily paper in Dutch, *Onze Toekoemst*. It was about 16–20 pages long. Pa would read it carefully, and then point out articles for Ma or the older children who could read.

"Look at this, Dale Carnegie is in Chicago. He said that transferring money to the poor would be a terrible waste."

"Hey Ma, look at the new stoves they are making here in Chicago."

Ma would look at the ads for furniture and clothing, and Lena would look for recipes and fashions. It was in that paper that Pa found an ad for a farm in Wisconsin.

Proving Ourselves as Farmers

PA WAS A GOOD carpenter, but the work at Pullman was arduous and repetitive. And he was paid by the piece of railing or seating that he made, so he always came home tired and tense, worried that he hadn't done enough, so when he saw an ad in *Onze Toekoemst* for an 80 acre farm in Wisconsin, he was interested. He had always been of a rather independent mind, and having a family farm was attractive. The older boys, Bill and Al, were excited about the possibility too. They wanted to prove themselves as farmers in America. So, in 1907, after eight years in Roseland we sold the home, packed up all our earthly goods, gathered up seven children, and got on a train to Ringle, Wisconsin. Ringle was about as different from Chicago as possible. It was barely a town; rather, it was a train stop en route to Wausau, itself hardly a great metropolis.

Another family had homesteaded the farm but hadn't finished the work. Half of the eighty acres was cleared, but the back forty was still in timber. Even the cleared area was studded with tree stumps. Cutting down a tree is relatively easy but getting the stumps out in order to plant crops is a big chore. Pa and the boys pulled stumps from one forty-acre section and cut trees in the other. They had to dig around the stump, then chop some roots, then dig some more, and chop more roots. Finally, when they thought it was loose, they would get Barney (Our big Frisian horse) and hook a line from him to the stump. They tied the stump up as best they could and then had Barney pull. Often, it only came partially out, so they would have to dig and cut some more. They only had time to do this after the crops were in for the fall, and before they had to plant in the spring. They would go out in the cold Wisconsin winters with their saws and axes, and shovels, and Barney pulling a bob sled. Once they had the stump out, they would put it on the sled, bring it to the barn, and cut it up for firewood.

Then there were the stones. The land was filled with them. Like most of the land around Lake Michigan, the geology can be explained by glaciers that once extended far beyond the current shores. When those enormous icebergs receded, they left stones behind. But you can't farm stones; they have to be moved to get down to the soil. We collected the stones and used them to build fences, or wind rows. The guys hooked a sledge to the horses and threw or rolled the stones on it. The horse then pulled the sledge to the line where they wanted a fence. Then the guys had to take those same stones off and pile them up on top of each other, in as orderly as possible a row to make a fence. They made a big wind-block on the north side of the house to keep out the cold, nasty winter currents. What a lot of heavy work!

The fireplace and the stove were the sources of heat for the house. Every day and night of those long Wisconsin winters the men would feed them firewood. At night, the fireplace would be filled with wood, and the fire in the stove stoked. But by three or four in the morning most of that wood was gone, down to only embers and ashes. We were getting cold, even in beds with comforters, and two thick blankets. Pa would then put on his clothes, get some more logs from the wood pile, and add them to the fire. In the morning, one of us would get wood for the stove. We all left our clothes out overnight next to the stove, so every morning we raced into the kitchen area in our pajamas, tore the pajamas off as quickly as possible in the kitchen, and then dove into the clothes that had been laid out by the fire. We had a mini contest every morning to see who could go from pajamas to clothes the quickest. The loser paid the price of being cold the longest.

Pa and the boys would rise at 4:30 to go out and do chores, and then come in a couple of hours later for a big breakfast of eggs and bacon, or sometimes pancakes or oatmeal before going back out into the field.

Lena and Bill had finished eighth grade in Roseland, and did not go on to High School, which was normal in those days. In 1910 for example, only ten percent of the children in America graduated from High School. The ones who did go to High School usually came from wealthier families who didn't need them to bring home money, like Bill and Lena. Al, Alice, Christina and I all attended a one-room school-house in Ringle. We walked the quarter mile or so to school. Some days we managed to catch a ride with one of the men pulling a logging sled.

There was only one other girl in my grade—fourth. We used slates for our work, writing our work on chalk and then erasing each assignment;

paper was scarce and too expensive. One day she—Sarah, suggested that we exchange slates (each of us had our names engraved in the top of the slate), so I said sure. We were doing an English lesson, learning a story from the McGuffy Reader. Our teacher, Mrs. Schneider asked us a few questions about the story, and told us to put our answers on the slate. I turned in Sarah's slate with my answers. Mrs. Schneider looked at me with bewilderment.

"Why didn't you answer the questions, Minnie?"

I was aghast. I had certainly answered the questions, but on Sarah's slate. I assumed that Sarah was going to do the same with my slate. But she hadn't! There was my slate, with nothing on it. I had to stay late after school that day to finish that assignment, again. I couldn't understand why Sarah would play a trick like that, but I couldn't tell on her either.

I continued in school there through the 8th grade. By then Sarah had moved on, so I was the only eighth-grader in the class. In fact, since I was by then the oldest one in the class I became, in effect, the teaching assistant. I would help the younger kids, including my little brother and sisters with their work. I taught the littlest ones how to read by helping them sound out words. I taught history lessons for the ones in the middle grades. There was no graduation ceremony. I didn't know if I had passed my final tests until that summer, when my signed diploma came in the mail.

Education was different in those days. We did considerable study of history and literature, which I loved. Having good penmanship was important. We also memorized quite a bit of poetry. I still remember a poem by Ralph Waldo Emerson called *The Snow Storm*.

> *Announced by all the trumpets of the sky,*
> *Arrives the snow, and, driving o'er the fields,*
> *Seems nowhere to alight: the whited air*
> *Hides hills and woods, the river and the heaven,*
> *And veils the farm-house at the garden's end.*
> *The sled and traveler stopped, the courier's feet*
> *Delayed, all friends shut out, the housemates sit*
> *Around the radiant fireplace, enclosed*
> *In a tumultuous privacy of Storm.*

I always loved literature; it stirs my soul. Sure, the facts of math and science are necessary to use in life, but literature and history told me how people lived, and what they thought. Through literature I could travel to

India with Rudyard Kipling or visit the Industrial Revolution in England with Charles Dickens. Reading is a gift I have always cherished.

Back then the average school year was about 150 days, or about five and a half months. People needed kids to help on the farm, so the school year started only after the crops were in by late October, and ended in April, when we were again needed for spring cultivating and planting. Even so, that was too much time away for some kids; their families couldn't afford to bring them to school when farm work needed to be done. The teachers were almost always women. Teaching grade-school was women's work. They were often local High-School graduates who came back to the same school they had gone to as children. The earned about $400 a year, and worked hard for their money.

I dearly wanted to go to High School and become a teacher myself. But that was not to be. My help was needed back at the house. And, when I asked my parents about it, they said, "No, Minnie, we have heard that when Christian girls go on in school, they come back with lots of strange ideas, and even lose their faith." That sure hurt. But I later learned this was a pretty common attitude among poorer, Christian people. Since the county High-School was miles away, instead of just down the street I just kept reading on my own. The little library in Wausau was available to us, and we went there as kind of an outing. We all liked to read, especially Bill and me, so we would go to the library in a horse drawn wagon, and come back with our prizes—books

Every day, regardless of season, the cows had to be milked. There were only four of them, but each produced four or five gallons of milk every day, so we had about sixteen gallons of milk daily. I had to get up at 4:30 every morning with Pa, to do the milking by hand. I sat on a stool next to a cow, cleaned the udders and began to pull, or strip the milk from the teats. The milk squirted out into a bucket. When full, I carried the bucket to some steel jugs where the milk was kept. It was then Al's job to bring the milk to town. Every morning after milking he put the large jugs on the back of the wagon and hooked up the mule. He first went to two neighbor's houses and picked up their milk, and then on to the cheese factory. The neighbors had agreed to a certain price for each jug of their milk, and they paid Al a little something for the transport. This money wasn't Al's, it went back to Ma, the family financier. All this was no doubt done with no more than a handshake; I doubt anything was ever written down. In fact, I'm sure that if Al had suggested they write up a contract there would have been problems.

"What, you don't trust us to pay you for hauling the milk? Why would you question my word?" And they were right. No one questioned another's word. If we made a promise, we kept it. If they made an agreement, they honored it. Pretty simple.

Back home, Ma and Lena and I would take some of the milk and churn it for butter. What a long job that was. You could sit and turn the crank on the churner for half an hour before you saw any butter forming. When it was my turn, I always had a book in one hand and the butter churn handle in the other. When the right hand got tired of churning, I would switch to the left and hold the book with my right. Ma would sell off the extra cream that came off the milk, and also make buttermilk. We drank the buttermilk or sometimes made "soup and bri" with it.

In the summer we could go berry picking. We found strawberries in the early spring, scattered among the hay fields, and raspberries later in summer among the trees. Sometimes we would run across mulberries or blackberries. It seemed like every opening in the field or woods had a few berry bushes. We would go out to pick with lard or syrup pails, and usually come back with them filled. Ma would either can them or make preserves. When they were fresh, she would sometimes make pies. By adding some of our cream and a bit of sugar we had some very tasty deserts.

Lena kept her eyes open for different recipes, and sometimes shared them with our American neighbor ladies. She would come home all excited to try out some new recipe that she had gotten from them. Pa would look at her in mock earnestness and say,

"But Lena, is this really a tried and true recipe, like the ones from the old country?"

Lena, smiled. "I guess we'll have to find out!"

The baking and cooking were always a bit of a trick. We had no thermometer for the wood stove, so we had to maintain the temperature by keeping an eye on the fire. You couldn't just put something in the oven and let it go. You had to constantly check the fire to see if it needed more wood, or a bit of stoking. Getting the baked goods to come out just right was quite an art.

In July the men cut the hay, both timothy and clover. Pa and Bill would use the scythe to cut between the stumps, while Al and Dick turned over the swaths. When dry they raked it up in stacks and then picked it up with a horse and a hay rack. They would haul the rack to the barn and pitch the hay up into the loft so it could be used to feed the cattle during the winter. Pitching hay into that loft in July or August was a hot job. They came home with shirts drenched with sweat. Only the ends of the shirtsleeves were still dry, the sweat having poured out of their torsos throughout the whole long day of haying.

Some evenings, and every Sunday we would visit with our friends from the Forestville Reformed Church, usually at each other's houses. Almost all the houses had a piano or an organ, even if the kids had only two pairs of trousers. Pa would usually be called upon to play. We would sing some old hymns from Holland, or sweet melodies from popular songs in the U.S. like "Pack up Your Troubles in your Old Kit Bag," or "It's a Long Way to Tipperary," or "By the Light of the Silvery Moon." Pa would play holiday music for Christmas, Easter, and even the 4th of July. On winter days, the evenings would end with some good Dutch hot chocolate. And of course, we had to have cookies.

At Christmas, the Sunday-School kids would put on a program. It was the same program that Sunday Schools always put on. Dress up a few of kids like sheep, a couple like shepherds, find an honorable and cute little Mary to wed a confused young Joseph, and then put a white sheet over a tall boy who would play the role of the angel Gabriel. My little sister Christina got to be Mary; I was a shepherd. I can still remember the line given to me—Shepherd Two: "Come, let us go see this thing that the angels have foretold." After the program we got a piece of candy and an orange.

We could all play and sing a bit. Lena and I learned to play the piano and the organ. Bill and Al, and later Dick got some instruments to play, a trumpet and a baritone horn. Some of the other kids from church could play too, so we had quite the concerts out there in the northern woods. As I look back on it, I recognize how lucky we were. Out there in the woods making music! Music has always been valued in our family, and it's a gift we pass it on from one generation to the next.

Every night at dinnertime we were together. Ma and we girls made the meals. It was usually a meat dish with some potatoes and vegetables. Sometimes we made a stew with all the things we could find in the garden—peppers, tomatoes, onions, green beans, etc. We usually had some meat that had been frozen or dried. Pa opened the meal with prayer:

> *Our Gracious God and Heavenly Father,*
> *We come to you in the evening hour of this day to thank you for your many blessings. We thank you for the food that you have so bountifully provided, and for the hands that have so lovingly*

prepared it. We pray that you keep us from harm and danger, but above all from sin. We pray in the precious name of our Savior, Jesus Christ.

After the meal we would have a Bible reading, usually a Psalm but sometimes other passages. At the end of the reading, Pa would turn to us, and we were expected to say the last word of the Psalm, or more if we could. Pa would read Psalm One, for example, which ended with the verse

"For the Lord knoweth the way of the righteous: but the way of the ungodly shall perish."

So we would chime in with "perish." But that got to be too easy. One of us would say,

"the ungodly shall perish."

Another who was paying especially close attention would say,

"but the way of the ungodly shall perish."

Occasionally, one of us would get the whole verse, "For the Lord knoweth the way of the righteous, but the way of the ungodly shall perish."

That's not so easy to do, since you don't always know in advance which verse is going to be the last. It was a good way to keep us alert during Bible reading, and when we were able to say the whole verse, we got a very approving look from Pa; sometimes even a peppermint.

Since we read so much of the Bible, we occasionally got to some funny or strange passages. I remember when we kept going after the Psalms into the Song of Solomon. Oh boy did my brothers have fun with that one. Song of Solomon 4: 5 reads,

"Thy two breasts are like two young roes that are twins, which feed among the lilies."

Well that was just too much for my nine and thirteen-year-old brothers. When Pa read that at the dinner table, they burst out laughing.

"Ha, breasts like little fawns, bouncing around among the lilies."
"Whoa," they roared.

Ma severely stared at them and said,

"Some people think that the love between Solomon and his betrothed means that God loves the church; and God sees the church as a beautiful bride."

"But breasts, like fawns?" my brother Al cried.

"Maybe the church has breasts too," suggested Dick. "Ah, ha, ha. We should look for them next time we go to church."

Lena and I, who had only recently developed our own breasts, looked at each other with mild embarrassment.

"Now boys," said Pa, trying very hard to keep a straight face.

"I've never seen the church's breasts" said Al, "we could probably paint some on the walls of the sanctuary."

Pa could no longer keep a straight face. "Ya, I should probably take that up with the consistory."

Ma was not happy. "You boys shouldn't even know what breasts look like yet!"

"But we go to the library and see the National Geographic pictures" protested Al.

"And there are all those bra ads in the Sears catalogue," added Dick. "We know how they look, Ma."

Now Pa could hold it no longer. He burst out laughing. "Ma, I guess the boys are old enough to know about breasts. And since they are right there in the Bible, we can hardly forbid it."

Finally, the girls could laugh and smile too. But Ma was not happy. The fact that the Holy Bible talked about fawn-like breasts was clearly not to her liking.

As usual, we were working hard, and not having much to show for it. At first Lena worked at home, but couldn't find a job in that little town, so she started looking around. Like most girls her age, she sought a job as a live-in housekeeper. We stayed in contact with family and friends in the Chicago area, and one of them offered her a job in Highland, Indiana, a town just across the state line from Illinois.

Midwest Industry Calls

Lena turned sixteen and needed to help with the family budget, but there was really little for her to do in tiny Ringle. So Ma got in touch with some family members back in the Chicago area who had moved to northwest Indiana, around Highland and Munster, just south of Lake Michigan. Munster hugged the state line with Illinois, and the area came to be called "Illiana." Ma's cousins, the Kortenhovens, farmed in Highland and needed someone to work around the house. It was common in those days for girls who were finished with school but not yet married to work as live-in housekeepers, and since the Kortenhovens were family, Ma and Pa were sure they'd treat Lena well.

Thousands of years ago Highland and Munster had formed the southern edge of Lake Michigan. You could tell right where the shoreline had been since the sand was still piled high there. A paved road now ran over that old dune and was named "Ridge Road," since it rose above the low, swampy area along the nearby Little Calumet River. It had previously been a well-traveled Indian trail used by the Potawatomi, Illinois, and Miami tribes before they were pushed off by white settlers. You could sometimes still find arrowheads or pieces of Indian jewelry hidden in the sand.

When Bill was about sixteen, he too moved from Ringle to Highland, thinking it would be easy to find work in the huge, recently built steel mill in nearby Gary, Indiana. The mills in those days drew immigrant workers from all over Europe—Poles, Czechs, Italians, Germans, Irish, and us Dutch. Gary itself was named after Mr. Elbert Gary, the first president and co-founder of U.S. Steel along with J.P. Morgan. Bill went to labor around the enormous smelting furnaces that produced steel for buildings, railroads, and Henry Ford's cars. In 1908 Mr. Ford started building the Model T, so the mills shipped the steel to make them, up Lake Michigan, then down Lake Huron to Detroit.

Many Dutch had moved to the Highland/Munster area. Land in Roseland and Chicago was getting expensive and too built up for farming, so recent Dutch arrivals moved farther out of the city, crossed the Indiana state line, and bought the less expensive lowland acreage around the Little Calumet River that Mr. Hart had drained a few years earlier. His ditches moved the water from the Highland and Munster marshlands into the Little Calumet River. One of them is still called Hart's Ditch. So when the Dutch arrived, they could farm those "nether-lands" just as they had in the old country. They could even ice-skate on the ditches just as they had on the dikes in Holland.

Gary, Indiana, and the whole Illiana region were ideally located for industry. Gary was a port at the very southern tip of Lake Michigan and only about thirty miles southeast of Chicago. Iron ore could be shipped in from Duluth, Minnesota, or other ports on Lake Superior, and coal could be trained up from West Virginia and Pennsylvania. There were giant railroad terminals there, since Lake Michigan prohibited east-west passage any further north, so steel could be shipped by water to Detroit for cars but also by rail to anywhere in the U.S. When Bill went to work there in 1909 the Gary works was the largest steel mill in the world and U.S. Steel its largest company.

Wherever the Dutch go, we plant two things quickly: flowers and churches. The Dutch who moved to the Illiana region were no exception. Any Dutch family who owned a house dug holes about four inches deep for tulip bulbs in the fall and watched them sprout when the snow melted in the spring. Shortly after their first tulips came up in Munster, they planted a Christian Reformed Church not far from where Lena and Bill both lived. It was comforting to Ma and Pa that Lena and Bill had both family and church in their new town.

Soon Lena went to work on Ma and Pa, imploring them to move to Highland as well. She sent them plaintive but positive letters about the great opportunities in the Illiana area. There was plenty of work in nearby factories, Pa could play the organ in the Christian Reformed Church, a Christian School had started up nearby, so Dick, Tina, and Alice could attend, the Kortenhoven family and others would welcome them, etc.

Lena must have been persuasive. We all joined her in 1912. But first we had to auction off the Wisconsin farm. Auctions were a common way of selling property. People were always moving, usually west, and so were always selling and buying. We held our auction on March 12, 1912, and sold the land itself, a few cows, a couple of horses, plus some farm implements, including a sled and hay wagon. We hired the local auctioneer, who sent announcements out throughout the area. On the 12th maybe fifty people showed up in the yard to look over our stuff before the auctioneer started off:

"I've got a fine cow here, fine cow, gives four and a half gallons of milk, day in and day out. Had one calf, could have another. Now what do I hear for this beautiful animal? I'll start the bidding at $35.00."

Then in a high and high-speed voice he solicited the bids.

"35, 35, 35, who will give me 35?

"Yes! I've got 35. Who will give me 40 dollars?

"40, 40, 40, who will give me 40? Beautiful cow, three years old, good milker. Who says 40?

"Beautiful cow, fine cow, who gives me $38? Only 38 dollars for this fine animal.

"Yes, I've got 38! Who says 39? 39 dollars takes away this fine milk cow. 39? 39? 39?

"I've got 38, going once, going twice, sold!

"Congratulations to the gentleman in the back with the red hat."

The auction went on like this for a couple of hours till only our clothing and some furniture remained. It was sad to see what a little mark we left behind in Ringle.

We took the train to Indiana. It took a few hours to get to our connection in Chicago, but after that the ride to Highland was only about 45 minutes, and Lena, Bill, and other family members met us at the station. We bought a house near the railroad track that ran eastward out of Chicago, and Pa quickly found a job at the Libby, Libby, and McNeil sauerkraut factory. He really didn't want to farm the way they did in Indiana. They did "truck farming," which didn't mean they raised trucks. They grew a variety of vegetables and trucked them into the city markets, which meant bending over or kneeling in the muck, weeding, bunching radishes, onions, and carrots, etc. Pa was better suited to factory or construction work. Ma soon became part of the Dutch culture by attending the *Ladies Aid Society* and the *Women's Missionary Union* at church.

As I was finished with school at age thirteen, I went to work for the railroad station in Hammond, just north of Highland. I collected fares and sold tickets. It was interesting to see all the people who came through on that train. Every European ethnic group seemed represented, with Poles and Germans probably in the lead. We didn't see many Negros or Mexicans then because the Negroes still lived mainly in the south, and the Mexicans hadn't gotten that far north either. I worked for the South Shore Line that went from South Bend, Indiana, to Chicago. Some people rode the entire length to work in downtown Chicago. I once even saw former President Theodore Roosevelt on that train. We knew he was coming through, but word didn't get out on time, so just the people who happened to be waiting for the train or working there saw him. He tipped his hat and waved to all of us.

In Wisconsin Pa and Ma usually went to town once a week to get supplies, but now that we lived in town, we could make little trips whenever we needed something. Pa sometimes sent me or the smaller kids on errands.

"Tini, come here. I've got ten cents for you. Go to the store and pick me up a pack of pipe tobacco. Get the Amphora brand."

Like most men at that time, he enjoyed a pipe or cigar, even an occasional cigarette. Back then we had no idea smoking could cause cancer. In fact, some people thought it a healthy habit. But Ma didn't like it. To her, it was just a frivolous expense.

"Alrich, you should stop smoking. We need that money for other things."

"Ya, true, we need the money. Dick, get me a pen and paper."

"What do you need a pen and paper for?" Ma cut in. "We're talking about tobacco."

"You're right. We need the money. And since your brother owes us almost forty dollars, I thought I'd write a letter to him. When he pays us back, I'll have plenty for my tobacco."

Pa and Ma had sponsored Ma's brother to come over from the Netherlands, but he'd never paid them back for his expenses.

"Neh! You put that pen away. Buy your tobacco!"

Pa did. And he never wrote her brother, nor did he ever see a dime of that money.

Lena was sixteen and single when she moved to Highland, but she didn't remain single for long. Jake Kikkert, a blacksmith and a member of the Munster Christian Reformed Church, courted her, proposed, and married her in 1914 in the same church. Lena sewed her own wedding dress with material from the Minas' department store in Hammond, and we three younger sisters were her bridesmaids. I was the next oldest sister, so I got to be the Maid of Honor.

After the wedding was the "chivaree." This was usually put on by a male relative or friend of the groom right after the wedding and reception. In those days, the couple wouldn't immediately jet off to Hawaii or the Caribbean for a honeymoon like they do today. They wouldn't even go to a hotel. They'd just move into the house in which they were going to live, and the chivaree would begin shortly after they got there. Friends of the groom and some family would stand outside the house and bang pots and pans, sing foolish drinking songs, and try to embarrass the new couple. Some would offer unsolicited advice for the honeymoon.

"Say, Jake, did anyone ever tell you about the birds and the bees? It's not too late!"

Since Jake had been raised in Highland, he had quite enough friends and family to pull off a prodigious *chivaree*. Pa, however, was not amused, and Ma even less so. They thought the chivaree took away from the solemnity of holy matrimony. He just gave the *chivareers* a couple of dollars and asked them to go home.

I had my first date in Highland with a boy named Jake Van Til. We went to a church picnic together. He was a good-looking guy with dark hair and a large smile. He was witty too. When we walked along Ridge Road, a bird flew over and pooped right in front of us. Without missing a beat, Jake looked up and said, "Birdie, birdie, in the sky, I'm so glad that cows don't fly." I got my first kiss that evening. It was rather perfunctory. As he brought me home, Jake said, "Thank you for coming out with me Minnie. You are a lovely girl." Then he bent over and only gave me a little peck of a kiss, but at least it was on the lips. Without saying anything, I smiled, and went in the house.

Many years later Jake's brother Reinder would become my daughter Linda's father-in-law. Reinder was a stern Calvinist farmer who worked hard to support a large family. Reinder was the eldest brother and first to come from the old country, so he had to earn some money to pay for his siblings to follow. Later he had a large family of his own and never had the time or money to go to school. Nevertheless, he loved to read theology. He would go out to the barn in the morning to milk and feed the cows, then return to the house as quickly as possible to read his books. He'd sit in a squat, heavily cushioned chair, light a thick cigar, and open an even thicker theological tome. Meanwhile, his many sons would toil in the field, plowing, weeding, or harvesting. After lunch, he would go back outside to oversee their work but then quickly return to his study to smoke and read.

This intellectual diligence was typical of a lot of our men. Very few got beyond the 8th grade in school, but many went far ahead with their own self-education. Cornelius Van Til, who later taught at Westminster Seminary, was the same age as my brother Bill. Men their age would meet with others from the Christian Reformed Church in the imaginatively named "Young Men's Society." There they would show off their latest readings in theology and have lectures and debates on other subjects too, such as *A Christian Labor Union: Pros and Cons*, or *The Dutch versus American School Systems*, etc. The debaters would prepare their speeches well in advance taking pride in the range and depth of their reading.

Though stern, Reinder Van Til was a good man, who treated his wife and family well. But their hillbilly neighbor, Mr. Rokete, was not. He drank, beat his wife and children, and didn't feed them. One day Reinder, hoeing in the field nearby, heard Mr. Rokete making a racket beating his wife. She was screaming while he was yelling and hitting. Reinder stood about six feet tall and weighed perhaps 220 pounds. He had a barrel of a chest and arms that looked like oak logs had somehow sprouted hands. He had milked cows and worked the land his whole life, and his body showed it. That day, dressed in his usual work clothes—overalls and a sleeveless t-shirt, plenty of those muscles showed. He went to Roketes' door, still carrying, if not brandishing, his hoe. He knocked on the door loudly enough to be heard above the din, and Mrs. Rokete ran off to a bedroom to hide her bruises and her tears. When Mr. Rokete finally opened the door, a very angry Dutch Calvinist elder made his mission clear: "I know what's going on in your house, Rokete. It had better stop, now! You don't want me to come back here." Wisely, hillbilly Rokete took him seriously. Reinder never heard another peep.

I suppose Rokete might have just been quieter with his beatings, but we'll never know. I do know, however, that I never heard talk among our Dutch women about husbands who beat them. It just wasn't the way they were raised. We women were respected for who we were, children of God, just like the men. Sure, they didn't see us as equals in terms of working on the farm or serving in church, but we were equal before God.

In Highland we had a garden, as always, and brother Dick surprised Ma once when he offered to pick and sell some tomatoes. Ma smiling appreciatively, said, "There you go, Dick. How nice of you to help out like that." He picked the tomatoes, set them out on a bench along Ridge Road, and left a coffee can standing next to them with a note: "10 Cents per Half-Bushel." People were so honest that he didn't have to worry about leaving a can of coins sitting alongside the road. But Dick never had any repeat customers. It was many years later that I learned why—the bushels were only half full of tomatoes. The bottom halves were filled with horse manure! When buyers got home, they were in for a smelly surprise. Expecting to have a half bushel of tomatoes to can, they'd dig down to find manure instead. I'm sure Dick had some housewives swearing at him once they'd plucked down to the halfway point of their basket.

Around this time, land agents were constantly stopping by homes and farms in Highland. "Come out West," they'd say. "There is an abundance of fertile land! Good farmers like you can do very well." In the mid-1800s, the Northern Pacific Railroad Company built tracks across the vast northern U.S. territories all the way from Duluth, Minnesota to Tacoma, Washington. The U.S. government granted them millions of acres to do so. When the line was completed, the railroad kept the odd numbered sections adjacent to its rails while the U.S. government claimed the even ones. These were offered to the public in 360 acre sections under the Homestead Act. As most of Montana was grazing land, many ranchers claimed these parcels for their sheep, setting up one or two of their shepherds on each of the parcels as homesteaders. But when other homesteaders began to put up fences it was impossible for the ranchers to graze their sheep. So the ranchers formed enormous land holding companies to sell these lands. They sent land agents to sell the parcels to Midwestern farmers. Few of the agents had actually visited the land they were selling, but nonetheless saw themselves as saviors of the poor, dirt grubbing farmers of Indiana and Illinois. And not coincidentally, they would make a sizable commission on the transaction.

News of great harvests on inexpensive land tickled the ears of the men in our family, especially when the weather in Northwest Indiana was too wet, like it was in 1914. The land agents would always bring brochures and pictures with them.

"Look at this. Why that winter wheat is a good foot high. Look at how it stands next to that wagon wheel."

"I can remember seeing wheat crops like that back in Holland," Pa would note appreciatively.

"Out in Montana," the agents would point out, "you don't spend all day bent over in a field picking tomatoes or cabbage or onions. You ride your tractor or drive your team. They do the work. You just sit." It just so happened that Montana's wheat crop the year the brochure picture was taken had been excellent. Land that cost $10.00 an acre was yielding

40–45 bushels of wheat per acre. At roughly 95 cents per bushel in the Chicago market, you didn't need to be a math whiz to figure out how well-off you could become.

Pa wasn't convinced by these secular salesmen, but then he read an ad in our church magazine that convinced him. *The Banner* published articles on theology and church life and also included ads for almost anything else that did not "contradict the Word of God, or the Confessions." A 1914 issue contained this advertisement:

> *Now is the time to buy your ticket and travel to Columbus, Montana, land of good success and personal happiness. Here is an opportunity to gain possession of your own farm. An excursion is on the first and third Tuesday of each month. Travel expense is very low.*

The ad was placed by the Spoolstra Realty Company of Montana, real estate firm had contracted them to promote the western grain fields to Midwesterners. Columbus was the Stillwater County seat in southwestern Montana. Brothers Bill and Al, and even little brother Dick, were all in favor. "We can do it! We know how to farm. We did it in Wisconsin. We work hard, and we're young. If that land is anywhere near as good as they say it is, we'll have it made!"

Pa was rightfully cautious. "We've never actually seen those farms. We don't really know what it's like out there." To us, Montana was the Wild West, with cowboys and Indians, buffalo and wolves. But Pa was still a bit of an adventurer himself. Having come from the cramped cities of Amsterdam and Chicago, to him, going to the endless prairies and snow-covered mountains out west sounded like a dream. He gave the agent a down payment on 160 acres.

"Bill, I want you and Al to go out there as soon as possible. Take along some seed for winter wheat and a few cows, pigs, and horses. You see how it is, and get things started this year. When we get there next spring, we can harvest the wheat crop and plant another."

Westward ho!

Spies in the Land

(Bill's granddaughters Gayle and Nancy Recker wrote up the story about his trip to Montana with Al in her book *Spirit Trained Eyes: The Western Adventure,* so I can share it with you here.)

In 1915 my brothers Bill and Al packed things up in a boxcar that was waiting for them on a track in Hammond. When filled, it would make the short jog to Chicago where it would be hooked to an engine going west and north through Wisconsin and Minnesota, then switched to another engine headed west through North Dakota and finally across the wide state of Montana.

They loaded a few household goods to get them through one season: pots and pans, a mitt for the hot stove, and a few utensils. They had to have a couple of pairs of trousers and shirts that would keep them warm for what would be a very cold winter. For both warmth and cooking they brought along Ma's small laundry stove. She used it to heat her irons for Pa's shirts, but he could do without pressed shirts if the boys needed it. Otherwise, they nearly filled that boxcar with farm implements: a plow to break the sod, a harrow, and a seeder for the wheat. They also needed a small wagon to travel and work in and some basic tools like hammers and saws to build things, including a place to live in temporarily. Finally, they packed a few books, most importantly the Bible, but also some novels and histories to read when they were stuck inside during the harsh Montana winter.

They also wanted to take some livestock bought locally: four horses, two cows, and five little piglets. The cows were tested for hoof and mouth disease in Highland and found to be disease-free. But when they got to the stock yards in Chicago an inspector held them up anyway. "We need to test the horses for glanders and the cows for tuberculosis," he said. "And there is no way you can take those piglets. They carry more disease than all the others combined." So they waited for the inspector to do his tests, sitting in the train station for three days. The cows were found to have tuberculosis and so couldn't go. They had to be sold right there for beef. But brother Al was not willing to leave those little pigs behind. He said, "Let's put them on the car in the back, behind some freight. If the inspector finds them, we leave them, but if they stay quiet and he misses them, we take them."

They were nice, quiet, little piglets, so they ended up going along.

Meanwhile, a more difficult problem developed. Only one person was permitted to ride in each boxcar. If there was more than one, the second had to pay a passenger fee. Not realizing this, Pa had only paid for the boxcar, and they didn't have enough cash for another fare, so they came up with a plan. Since Al and Bill looked a lot alike, being brothers and only a couple of years apart, they decided one of them would hide in the boxcar, while the other went out. Since they never appeared together anyone who saw one of them wouldn't know there was another nearly identical brother also along for the ride. No, it wasn't honest, but they justified it by claiming they were too poor to pay for an additional ticket. And besides, the boxcar was already paid for. One more 'item' inside wouldn't cost the rail company any more.

Finally, the train set off from Chicago with one registered Recker boy, four horses, five piglets, a lot of equipment, and one stow-away Recker boy. They were on their way, first to St. Paul, Minnesota, and then on to the West. As planned, Al stayed hidden inside the car while Bill sat at the open door, watching the landscape change from prairie Illinois to hilly Wisconsin. But by about the time they reached Tomah, Wisconsin, they were both so bored that Bill said, "Al, why don't you come out? No one is going to see us from out in these fields."

But he was wrong. While chatting about all kinds of little things, they must not have noticed when the brake-man came walking along the top of their car. Unbeknownst to them at the time, he heard two voices talking and bent over the edge of the car, his body lying flat on the roof, then popped back up and walked off. That night when the train came to a slow, unscheduled stop, it dawned on the brothers that they had been spotted or heard.

"What shall we do?" asked Bill.

Al said, "I'll get off this car, run ahead, and climb on another car. Then when we stop next, I'll meet up with you again on this car."

The brakeman opened the boxcar door and shined his lantern inside, making a strange yellow glow against the horses and plow. He asked, "Where's your friend?"

"He jumped off when you stopped the train."

"Oh, really? I think I'll have a look."

He did, and a very thorough look it was. He found the piglets, but it was too late to do anything about them, and then he headed toward the horses. Bill knew that the mare didn't appreciate anyone coming at her from behind and warned, "Stop! She'll kick!"

"OK, then you take my lantern and go to the front of the car."

Bill shone the lantern into all the corners, and when the brakeman saw that no one was there he asked, "Who was that guy with you, and what did he want?"

Having lied once to get onboard the train, Bill had to lie again to make the story work, so he said, "Oh, just somebody else who wanted to go West. I'd never seen him before. He just hopped on while I was sitting there."

"Do you have any money with you?"

"Some."

"Well, you're lucky you have any now. Picking up bums and giving them a lift could cost you your wallet, if not your life. Those bums will slit your throat for less than half of what you've got, and then where would you be? Get out of this boxcar and come back to the caboose with me where you belong."

Bill got off, sneaking looks down the track for any sign of Al. The brakeman locked the boxcar door from the outside and gave the key to Bill. Now there was no way Al could get back in. The brakeman marched Bill back to the caboose where the conductor was seated at his desk, looking over the train's manifest. He gave Bill a sermon on the railroad's first commandment: "Thou shalt not pick up hobos." Though Bill was lying to them, these two strangers were caring for him, and his conscience was panging away at him like John Henry's hammer.

They gave Bill a bunk to sleep in, but sleep would not come. He lay awake, penitent about his lies and worried about his brother. They had barely begun their 1,000 plus mile journey and were already separated, and potentially in hot water. When daylight came, Bill jumped up and announced that he needed to feed the horses. But the conductor fired back, "Sit down, buddy. I'm not stopping the train for that. At the division point you'll have plenty of time to feed your horses. We'll be there in about seventy minutes."

What a long seventy minutes they were. If "the wages of sin is death," Bill must have died and come back to life a thousand times. Dire thoughts just kept running through his mind: "Why didn't we pay the fare? Al could have died while hanging on to a side rail. How am I going to explain to Ma and Pa that I let him do this? The conductor and the brakeman are trying to protect me, from my own brother!" At last the train stopped east of St. Paul. Bill ran to the boxcar with his key and quickly opened the door. Then he saw that the door on the other side stood open an inch or two, and he thought, "Aaahh, Al must have already gotten back in!"

But there was no Al. Bill whistled softly and whispered, "Al? Al, come on out. It's me, Bill."

Bill dutifully fed the horses and piglets, all the while keeping his eyes and ears open for his brother. Then he made a Dutch sandwich of bread and cheese for himself, wondering if Al had anything to eat. The little piglets even looked dispirited. Some hours later, on a bright spring afternoon, the train stopped at the rail yards west of St. Paul. Seeing hundreds of train cars on dozens of tracks and spurs, Bill wondered, "How on earth will Al even find me if he even gets out into these yards?"

Men began to work on the train, checking its brakes, and others went through the logs and manifests, seeing whether all was accounted for. Bill asked one where the office was and walked a good half mile through the trains and across tracks till he found it. He had his papers ready, showing that his car was to be transferred to another engine and pulled all the way to Montana. Then on the far side of the office Bill noticed a man limping. As he came closer, the man waved and with a smile said, "Hello, Bill. Did you miss me?" Bill grabbed and hugged Al, though at the same time he wanted to give him a good kick in the pants for scaring him so badly. But Bill saw that Al had a hole in his right leg that had grown swollen and blue and asked, "How did you hurt your leg?"

Al pulled Bill aside and told him his story.

> *When I jumped off the car last night while the train was stopped, I ran up ahead about ten cars. Then as the train was starting back up, I grabbed a handrail and was going to climb to the top, but there was a lantern light bobbing forward up there, so I just clung to the side. That brakeman walked all the way to the engine, and not finding me, he started back, leaning over and swinging his*

lantern below the roofs of the cars, first on one side, then on the other. When he came to my car, he swung the lantern right over my head. I thought he missed me, but he must have seen my white fingers clinging to the ladder on the side. The train was rolling along at a pretty good clip by now, and I was wondering what he would do. He said, 'Get off,' but I didn't feel like jumping into the dark, so I didn't say anything and hung on.

"He then said, 'Jump or I'll step on your fingers,' and started down toward me. So I heaved out and jumped. I landed on one of those cattle guards that they have near the road crossings and must have jabbed a piece of wood into my leg. I rolled into the ditch and laid there for a bit and watched the light of the caboose disappear into the night. I lay there for a few minutes and then figured I'd better find some place to sleep the rest of the night. My leg didn't pain me yet, so I had no difficulty walking up the road and crawled into an old straw stack for the night. The pain came on, and I didn't sleep much, so as soon as it was dawn, I looked for a house.

"There was a farmhouse not far from the tracks, and as my leg was now paining me badly, I hobbled down to it. Dogs began barking, and the farmer, who was just out of bed, came out to see what was up. I guess I didn't look like a bum to him, so he said, "What's the matter, stranger?" I tried to tell him, but he dismissed my explanations in a hurry after he saw I had hurt my leg. He said, "Go into the house. My wife will get you some breakfast."

"They fed me well and told me that it was six miles to the next depot where I could catch a train for St. Paul. After breakfast, I went out to their pump and bathed my leg in a tub of cold water. That helped some, and after thanking my good friends who would accept no pay for the breakfast, I started down the track to a little town. There I waited until the local train came in, and paying my fare to St. Paul, I soon caught up with your train. I passed you sometime around noon, knowing you would arrive this evening. So I hung around the yards looking at every train that came in."

Strangers had been showing kindness to Al while other strangers had been trying to protect Bill from him! Bill examined Al's leg. If he touched it, Al would jump.

"I'm afraid something is still in there."

"Well, go ahead and get it out. What are you waiting for?"

Bill sterilized a knife above a match and undertook his first surgery. Bill had made no more than one poke when Al jumped. "What are you doing, trying to amputate?"

"No, but I see something stuck in there."

Al pulled a button from his coat and stuck it between his teeth. Clenching, he said, "OK, get it out." Bill did, but had to do so on a moving train, with a jackknife, and with blood constantly filling in the wound. Bill probed and searched, and Al groaned and grimaced. Finally, Bill got out a piece of wood about the width of a pencil and ¾ of an inch long. They applied a poultice to the wound made with a little tobacco and soap and then wrapped the cut with some cloth ripped from one of their shirts. Al was hurting, but after a night's sleep he felt surprisingly better. Meanwhile, overnight, they had crossed from Minnesota into North Dakota.

The steel roof of the boxcar made it a furnace by day and a cold, misty cloud by night. Each day Bill had to get them water from the train's water tank, and every time they stopped in a little town, they loaded up on groceries. Since they had been delayed in Chicago, the trip was going to take two days longer than planned, and the horses ran out of hay. Fortunately, they could buy some in the last town they stopped in, in North Dakota. The eastern part of Montana was still high prairie, but the land gradually rose across the long stretch to the mountains. At last, they arrived—Columbus, Montana—and someone from the realty company met them there. They were exhausted but still had to unload the boxcar and go a good ten miles from the station to their parcel. They hooked two of the horses up to the wagon loaded with all the equipment and the piglets and tied the other two behind it. Within a couple of miles the two horses pulling the wagon were winded—they had never been in such thin air—so Bill and Al hooked up the other pair, who took another two-mile turn. It seemed like the entire trip was up-hill, and the rocky path could hardly be considered a road. It was more of a rutted trail that someone else had carved. Nevertheless, their own breath was taken away, and not just by the altitude. They were in awe of the amazing western scene opening before them: endless ridges with giant, snow-covered mountains off in the distance, and no sign of any other people.

Once on the plot Pa had put a deposit on, Bill and Al turned to building something to live in for themselves, their four horses, and five growing piglets. There was no native timber, so they had to go back and forth into town several miles away to buy lumber. Every trip they'd stay overnight in town and pay for a hotel and food. On trip number three, to save money, they packed lunches for their only daily meal and asked a local Dutch family if they could sleep in their hay mow. They managed to get a little barn built, since they had learned carpentry from Pa. One corner served as their quarters with a bed, some trunks lined up for a table, and a stove. They also managed to plow and plant about forty acres of winter wheat before the hard frost came.

One wintry trip into town they got lost, an easy thing to do when the snow-filled wind clouds your vision and the landscape around you all looks the same. Thankfully, they ended up at Mr. McIntyre's place. He wasn't home but had left the door open in case someone like Al and Bill needed to get in. Westerners took care of each other that way. They knew that anyone could get lost in the snow, or a storm, or the dark, and would need shelter to survive. Bill and Al went in to get warm and saw a few pieces of bread in the box. Since they hadn't eaten all day, they helped themselves. They were preparing to bed down for the night when old McIntyre returned home and surprised them: "Hello, boys! What brings you out to these parts?"

"We're passing through, homesteading a few miles out. But we couldn't make it all the way today, so we had to stop here. Sorry to bother you. We also had a few slices of your bread."

"Bother? That's no bother! What about the beans? Had any of them?"

They had looked longingly at the beans but felt that it would be taking advantage of his hospitality to eat them.

"Help yourselves, boys! I wouldn't have cooked those beans if I didn't mean for someone to eat 'em. Clean 'em up, and have a drink of my cider to wash 'em down with." This was typical western hospitality: everyone battling the elements and protecting one another from nature's harsh affronts. Bill and Al gratefully accepted his food and drink and bedded down for the evening.

Eventually, other young guys came from Illinois and Indiana too. Their Dutch fathers sent them ahead just as Pa had with Al and Bill. At one point they had five young men in that little barn and one double bed. To make room they built a separate barn for the animals, this one made from buffalo-grass sod peeled up by the plow and cut into eight by twelve-inch pieces. The tough roots made nice four—to six-inch bricks to stack up for walls. They made beams for the roof and piled sod over them as well. Those five young men had only the one double bed, so to make room for more they turned the bed sideways and rigged a few boxes and crates to make it roughly six feet wide by eight feet long. They had to sleep together since they had only two blankets. If one had to get up in the night, all five awoke, and if one needed to turn over, he'd say "Over!" and the other four would shift.

What a business. I'm glad I was able to stay in Indiana that winter.

Homesteading in Montana

BILL AND AL SENT back a good report of the land, so Pa went ahead to stake a claim on some more acreage. Together with his cousin Joe Kortenhoven, they bought 640 acres at $10.00 an acre. Pa was wise enough to choose a section that had a creek flowing through it. When he arrived, he and the boys quickly put up a real house. They made a wooden frame and then tacked tar-paper to it, which would have to do for the summer; later they would build proper walls. They hunted, skinned, cleaned, and cooked jackrabbits. That plus bread made from local wheat were their staples.

Ma and the rest of us arrived a month later. Alice was about to enter the eighth grade at the newly built Highland Christian School, so she stayed in Highland with sister Lena (now Kikkert) till she graduated. The rest of us again packed up furniture, clothing, pots and pans, etc., and having been warned by Bill and Al, extra blankets and winter coats. We loaded everything on another box-car for the 42-hour trip from Chicago, Illinois to Columbus, Montana, and took the same rail lines that Bill and Al had. By then we then knew about the pigs and the glanders, so we didn't get stuck in the yard at Chicago like they did. And since we had paid the fare for all four of us—Ma, me, Dick, and Tini—we didn't worry about getting thrown off the train.

When Ma and Pa sold the house in Indiana it was at least the sixth time they had moved: two or three times in the Netherlands, from the Netherlands to Roseland, from Roseland to Wisconsin, from Wisconsin to Indiana, and now to the far west, Montana. For me, the city of Roseland was a childhood memory, and I'm sure Amsterdam seemed like a dream to Ma and Pa. Amsterdam was one of the most civilized and densely populated places on earth, in well-established, traditional old Europe. Now they were headed to the frontier of a new nation. They had not only changed their identity from Europeans to Americans, but now to Westerners and settlers. The houses in Amsterdam and Chicago were built with little if any space between them, but in Montana they would have to squint to see a neighbor's house on the horizon. In Amsterdam the canals served as highways, but in Montana there was little water. In Amsterdam the streets were crowded during the day, and lit by night. In Montana there were no streets, only trails made by bison, or more recently by other pioneers.

Bill had warned us that our horses wouldn't be able to handle the altitude in Montana. Not even the best horses from the Midwest could handle it, and those that did survive sometimes "went loco." There is a grass out West called "loco weed." If the spring is wet, it's one of the first to come up, so the cattle are eager to eat it. But when they do, it affects their brain. Some horses jumped over imaginary fences or ditches and hurt themselves, or even ran crazily off into the mountains. Some refused to be led or to back up, and became useless to the farmers. Knowing this, we didn't bring any horses with us. We'd buy some western horses when we arrived.

When we got to the little train depot in Columbus, Bill, Al, and Pa were waiting for us, their big smiles easily spotted from the other side of the station. By then, more Dutch settlers had come, so they created something of a welcoming committee for us, with four wagons waiting to take everything out to our section. It was quite a long ride—18 miles from the train station to our land—but we rode on and on in amazement. It sure wasn't like the flat muck farms of Indiana. It was hill after hill, and by Midwestern standards the hills were more like mountains. And as there were no roads, the rocks and rills provided constant risk of tipping or getting stuck. Up we'd churn, with the horses bending their necks and straining, then down and down, with the driver constantly leaning back in his seat, pulling on the reins, trying to keep the horses from running down into a gulley and crashing at the bottom.

There were some fir and pine trees in the valleys and on the ridges, but further up the mountain, only bald tops with stone caps. But the flowers were wonderful! There were penstemons, with their beautiful purple buds climbing the stem and showing off a pair of white stamens within. There were coneflowers, a type of daisy with a large cone at the center from which the flower petals spread. And there was the bitter-root, a flower from which a Montana river and valley derive their names. Its pretty lavender blooms will grow just about anywhere.

Montana became a state in 1889, so it was still pretty wild when we arrived in 1916. The Indians were there on the reservations. There were wolves and coyotes, and in some places, you could still find grizzly bears. We never saw one, though we occasionally saw signs of their scratching. We were told of their amazing size, with heads like anvils that could chew through a man in one malicious bite. I looked around in amazement during the whole ride out to our section. I had never imagined I would see vistas like these, let alone live among them. And the sky seemed to go on forever once you got to the top of a hill. There were a number of mountain ranges nearby. The Absoroka, the Gallatin, and the Tobacco Root were all visible from our homestead. They peered in at us from the west and south.

Pa and the boys worked from early sunrise to the late, ten o'clock summer sunset to improve the place. They eventually built a horse barn, a cow shed, pig sties, and a chicken coop. They also dug a much-needed root and dairy cellar into the ground, covered the top with a wooden lid, and then covered the sides with sod. We could now keep food cool during the summer and moderately warm during the winter. Pa and Ma purchased some farm equipment on borrowed money—plows, binders, a harrow, a disk, etc., and went in on some things with the Kortenhovens, or other Dutch farmers, to disperse the debt. They also had to buy horses, cows, hogs, and chickens to get started. Farming is an expensive venture when you are just starting up.

The men boarded up the tar-papered cabin so we would have a solid home for the winter. Again, Pa's carpentry skills came in handy, but since we lived on the high prairie, the trees were far off in the distant valleys, so we had to bring lumber in on horse-drawn wagons. Like most high-plains houses, ours was not fancy, but serviceable. It had a kitchen that extended out a bit into a dining area, and two bedrooms. The ceiling was open, so we could lay boards over the rafters to create another bedroom upstairs. We had one dresser for all our clothes, and no need of closets since no one had but two or three skirts, shirts, or pairs of pants. We hung our coats over a hand-made rack by the door. The three windows for the whole house had no glass, only wooden shutters left open during much of the summer but closed to the bitter winds all winter. A coal stove served as both our heater and our oven. When it got extremely cold in the winter, we would sometimes hear a "ping, ping, ping" from outside. At first, we couldn't figure out what it was. It wasn't hail. It wasn't woodpeckers. What was it? It was nail heads popping off the outside walls like bullets when the freezing lumber contracted. Every spring we would have to go out and pound in more nails to keep the cabin standing and sturdy.

I needed to get work outside of the house to provide some income for the family, so I found some with a family in town. Every Monday morning Pa took me into Bozeman to work for the Duncan family. The American families loved us Dutch girls as maids. We were great cleaners! In their home I learned a lot about American ways and manners. These Americans didn't just put a pot on the table and let everyone scoop from it. They put the food into large bowls and then served each other. And the knife had to be on the right side, with the blade facing the plate. If there were salad spoons or forks, they went at the top of the plate.

I was also their family's tutor. They had little kids in school, so I helped them with their homework and read stories to them. I solved a few of their math problems for them, but only enough to teach them how to do it themselves. I liked the teaching far more than I did the cleaning. I also loved it when Pa picked me up on Saturdays with our horse and carriage.

Horses were the only means of transportation, and we rode them everywhere. When we went into town the horse knew the way, and when we arrived it knew to stay hooked to the hitching post. In fact, you really didn't even have to tie up the horse—when it saw a hitching post in front of it just stood there. A preacher once used this as an illustration for us: we are sometimes so tied up in our bad thoughts and feelings that we think we can't change them. But in fact we aren't tied up at all; we're just so used to those bad habits we don't recognize we're stuck in them.

The guys took care of the chores around the barn first thing in the morning. They fed the horses, and the cows, and did the morning milking. Then they cleaned out the stalls and put in fresh straw. They gave them water, and if it was frozen in the winter, they had to heat water to melt the ice in their tank. When they came in for breakfast we had oatmeal ready for them. Sometimes we had bacon, and we always had coffee with our own cream. Later, when Mr. Kellogg made some of his cereals, we occasionally bought a box of them, but compared to the oatmeal, cereal was too expensive. We always had fresh milk, and of course our own eggs.

Women out West did not have it easy either. We were expected to prepare three meals a day for the men, both family and workers. The house needed to be swept daily, since the dust constantly found its way through the cracks, and we made and repaired all the clothes for everyone. Feeding the chickens and collecting the eggs was our job too, as was nursing anyone who got sick and taking care of the younger children. On top of all that Pa often sent us on errands:

"Tini, could you bring the hay wagon out to us around mid-day? By then we should be ready to put some hay up."

"Minnie, would you go to town and get some oats for the horses. We're running low."

"Ma, Dick stepped on something and cut a hole through the sole of his shoe. Could you find some way of patching it?"

Montana was beautiful, but hard. The year Bill and Al got there was exceptionally wet, and the farmers got a good crop. But that soon changed. Year after year the rains diminished, even going below the annual average of sixteen inches. Not much grew in that climate, which is why it was called "dry-land farming." And the temperatures were extreme too. The summers could get as hot as 100 degrees, while winter nights could drop to thirty or even forty below zero.

We had to reuse pretty much everything. We'd first use bolts of cloth from Indiana to make new clothing for church or work, but when those pants and shirts wore out or got holes in them, we would use other cloth to patch them. When most of the clothes we were wearing were worn and holey we would make "curtains" or rugs out of the remainders. We'd use water two or three times too. A small creek ran through our property, but in summertime it usually ran dry, so the men drilled a well that struck water some thirty feet down. We women, like Rachel of the Old Testament, would bring the water up from the well. We used some for cooking and some for cleaning. The cooking water would then become the dishwashing water. That water would finally get carried out to the garden to water the vegetables, over which the women were also given charge. We raised potatoes, carrots, and beets, all root vegetables. We tried to raise tomatoes, beans, peppers, and cucumbers, but that usually didn't work. Not enough rain. We planted, then weeded, then watered, then hoed, then harvested. Those vegetables added lots of good vitamins to our menu. We re-used the grease from bacon or ham to make other foods.

For Sundays we would make a cake, using our own flour, plus baking soda, salt and sugar we got from the store. Everything for Sunday was made on Saturday, so we wouldn't have to labor on the Sabbath. Since there was so little water, we could only bathe once a week, Saturday. During the week we would rinse off with a wet rag or a sponge. Toward Thursday or Friday, the smell inside that little house could get a bit ripe.

Brother Al rode to town one morning to get supplies. He took his usual zig-zag route down a rocky ravine. He saw something at the bottom. It was a horse, dead, with legs up. Al carefully rode down the gorge to see whose horse it was. He then noticed that there was something under the horse. He got off his own horse and pulled away the baggage. It was dear old McIntyre. The horse had apparently fallen and landed on him, the pommel penetrating his chest. That good man and his good horse lay dead. Al came back home and told us. The guys went out with a wagon, pulled his body out from under the horse and dragged it up to the ledge atop the ravine. The horses' body remained there, no doubt providing a rich feast for the coyotes. They took off the saddle, reins, bit, etc. and brought them back to his cabin.

They took McIntyre's body back to his house and drained any remaining fluids from it. He was an old bachelor, so he didn't have anyone to look after him. Dick and Tini were dispatched to town as messengers to see whether anyone who knew him could come for a brief western funeral. Pa quickly assembled a make-shift coffin that would have to do, and my brothers dug a hole. Pa also took the role of preacher: "Dust to dust, ashes to ashes, we commend to Thee the soul of our friend, McIntyre." All present knew it could have been one of them.

Summer work versus winter work on the ranch was like night and day. In the spring and summer we had so much work to do in the fields and garden that we could hardly find time for a spare breath, let alone a nap. The fields needed plowing, then cultivating, then weeding, then cutting, then sheaving, then loading. The animals gave birth in the spring. We had calves, chicks, foals, and piglets. All had their own diet, and all had to be fenced in and protected from the wolves and coyotes. During summer and on into October or even November we just worked. For six days each week there was no time for anything else. But after six days of hard labor, did we ever rest on the seventh! We slept in late and rode to church, met the other Christian Reformed families there, and sang hymns and Psalms to God.

Once the crops were in and the frost and the snow came along, however, life changed. What could you do? The men couldn't work in the fields, so they fixed the equipment. A wagon wheel always needed a new spoke. Something needed greasing. The barn or the chicken coop had a hole where the mice had bitten through, and the roof on the house had been battered by the wind and the rains, so shingles needed replacing, etc. There was always more building and fixing to be done. But you can't do all those outdoor things very long in the winter, especially when it's zero degrees. You can only work for a little while before you need to come in and warm up. Winter became our social season. We would play card games like Whist or Rook or Hearts. Pretty soon we got to know each other's talents and techniques at those games. Then we made music. Pa couldn't bring along an organ of course, but we had a trumpet and a baritone horn that Bill and Dick played, and we all could sing. So in addition to the hymns and Psalms of Sunday, we would play tunes like *Arkansas Traveler*, or *Turkey in the Straw* or *Buffalo Gal*.

Then we would go visiting. The nearest neighbor was half a mile away, and further ones each roughly another half-mile distant. So, we would pack up the family and ride off in the wagon or sleigh to see them. We had no phones, so we made plans for visiting when we all met at church on Sunday. The other families were in the same boat, bored and isolated, so they welcomed us, and we welcomed them. The music was pretty good. We brought our instruments, they had theirs, and during the winter there wasn't much to do except practice. Brother Bill got to be pretty good on his horn. After a couple of years, he even organized and directed a band. They had to scramble to get music sent from the East. Once they got it, they rehearsed in the church, since it was the only building big enough to hold them and their sound. They were asked to play at many events.

At home, family members would often break out in song, popular or religious. There was no radio then, so we were our own entertainers. One of the foreign songs from that time went, "Papa drinken papan wijn, Papa zingen frolic zijn," which was probably meant as an insult to the Pope. In English it means something like, "The pope drinks papal wine, the pope is singing happily." And there was this little ditty in French: "Vive l'amour, vive l'a amour, vive la compagnie." If one would break out in song, the others joined in. In this way, we learned a lot of songs. And if we couldn't remember the words, we made them up, sometimes with our own "frolic."

The church was largely run by the laity, since we couldn't afford to pay a preacher. Elders read messages on Sundays from the file of sermons provided by Synod. Once in a while a visiting preacher would offer the Lord's Supper or baptize new babies. Elders did the family visiting, performed the funerals, and taught catechism. Deacons saw to it that all had enough to eat and that the widows were cared for. Since our whole congregation consisted of young settlers, many of these leaders were young men. My brother Bill for instance, was an elder while still in his twenties.

Columbus was about half-way between Billings and Bozeman, so we were not far from the Wyoming border, with the Grand Tetons to the southwest. We were also pretty close to both Cheyenne and Crow Indian Reservations. The last battles between the whites and the Indians had occurred in the 1870s, so fifty years later, when we were in Montana, there were still some people, both Indian and white, who remembered those days. I guess we treated the Indians pretty badly. I say "we" meaning the whites. This had all been Indian land at one time, and we'd pushed them into little corners of it. Our family was not actually a part of that—we were still back in Europe when it was going on—but I know the push of European settlers is what drove the Indians westward, eventually onto the reservations. The famous battle of the Little Big Horn, in which the Indians decimated George Custer and his troops, was not that far from the nearby Crow reservation.

I made a friend from the Crow nation, Peggy Yellowtail. We were both in our late teens. I guess to call her a friend would be a stretch, but we would run into each other now and then. Once I was riding into Columbus on my horse and saw her, and we chatted a bit. She spoke English, but I knew none of her native language. At one point she pointed to a tree in the distance and said, "Let's race," and went galloping off. Well, I wasn't going to just watch. I gave my horse a good kick and we were off. The land was not smooth, so I had a bouncy ride to that tree about a half mile ahead. I could ride horseback pretty well, since I had been doing so even before we moved to Montana, but her Indian pony was faster than my horse, which usually pulled a wagon or a plow and wasn't really built for speed. Her pony, on the other hand, was no doubt a descendent of the horses the Indians hunted buffalo on. She won.

The Crow Indians had a fair not far from Billings. It had started in about 1904 and so was well established by the time we arrived. It was part rodeo and part county fair. The Indians brought some of their pretty blankets and beads to sell, and we took some vegetables to display and sell. The Indians would get on their ponies and rope cattle and ride bareback on the broncos. It was quite a show. They would be dressed in their native costumes, such as nice pants that were over-stitched and shirts that had paintings on them. The women usually wore some sort of shawl, and for some reason a lot of them wore round bowler hats.

When an Indian was about to mount a steer or a bronco, he would give lots of shouts and yelps. We'd be so close we could see the animal quivering and stamping in anticipation of his rough ride. Quite a few bets were placed, one time including one by brother Al. I saw him do it. But as gambling was strictly forbidden in our Christian Reformed household, he swore me to secrecy. We'd go into some of the exhibition tents and see the best sheep and cattle raised in the area and the beautiful clothing that the Crow women had made. They had a special way of stitching and piercing that I learned.

As I recall it now, winters were times of physical, emotional, and spiritual growth or healing. It really took a month or two of cold weather to get us back into wholeness. Our bodies would put some weight back on, and I think our spirits would amplify too. We could talk to each other about things besides which horse needed shoeing or what food needed preparation. We could read, we'd tease each other a bit, we'd chat.

We were in Montana toward the end of the First World War, and we Dutch were suspected of being German sympathizers. It was guilt by association: we were Dutch, and they spoke Deutsch. Or, perhaps since our country was so close to Germany, they thought we must be friends of the Germans. It got to be so bad that one Dutch Reformed Church in Iowa was burned to the ground! But trust me, we were not German sympathizers! The Dutch and the Germans have always had an uneasy relationship. The Germans seem to think of the Dutch as their "little cousins" who should march to their loud, impatient drumbeat. But we Dutch are a people in our own right and don't appreciate the instructions of an imperious "older cousin."

We were now Americans. Half our family had been born here, and half had taken a vigorous oath of allegiance to the United States of America. Why would anyone think we would be loyal to some other nation?

More Dutch Immigrants
The Zwiers

The Zwier family came from Opperdoes, a little village in the Dutch Province of North Holland, northwest of Amsterdam, up the little claw of land that sticks out into the North Sea. It was once called just Doess, which means "low woods," and like many parts of the lowlands, it has a history of flooding as it is so close to the ocean. The Zwiers were a relatively wealthy family, having been in the seed business for generations. In Holland that meant shipping vegetable seed and tulip bulbs all over the world. It also meant working the soil every day, on your hands and knees. As a result of this, many family members developed "consumption," also known as tuberculosis. While there was no known cure for tuberculosis, most believed that a dry, hot climate would prevent it, or at least hinder its progress.

Opperdoes is recognized for its special variety of potatoes, *Opperdoezer Ronde*, a nice tasting potato baked or fried. Opperdoes is also known as a birthplace for mathematicians. One early 20th-century man from that village, Pieter Wijdenes, wrote the basic math textbook used in all the Dutch schools. That genetic disposition seems to have been prevalent throughout Opperdoes, because the Zwiers were good in math too.

While North Holland was a liberal area of the Netherlands, Opperdoes was an exception both religiously and politically. This was likely due to a man named Jan Mazereeuw, the so-called *Profete* of Opperdoes. A local farmer and the former mayor of the village, around 1822 he felt God's calling and began to preach. He called the Reformed Church of the Netherlands a "godless temple" and urged true believers to leave it and take on a sober, pious lifestyle.

More Dutch Immigrants

The early decades of the 19th century were a time of ferment and renewal in the Dutch churches. In 1814, after the Napoleonic Wars, King William I of the Netherlands subjugated the Dutch Reformed Church to the state under the Department of Religion, making it just one more part of the federal bureaucracy. When that happened, the Reformed Confessions, especially the church order adopted by the Synod of Dordt, were sidelined in church life. Ultimately, the king and his appointees, rather than the synod, ran the church, and allowed it to go soft in both theology and piety. It got to the point where some of its preachers were not even Christians.

In reaction, many poorer people of the Netherlands formed "conventicles," small groups dedicated to piety and old-school orthodoxy, many of which seceded from the state church in 1834 to form the *Gereformeerde Kerk*. At first the government used Napoleonic-era laws to ban these unofficial church meetings, even quartering soldiers in believers' homes. But this got to be too costly, both politically and financially, so traditional Dutch tolerance won out, and the seceding churches were accepted. The Zwier family joined this pietistic church movement, and a large percentage of these seceders, including the Zwiers, immigrated to America.

In the late 1880s two large-scale farmers from Utrecht, Zoutman and Vander Hoogt, founded the Dutch American Land Corporation. They bought land on speculation in the United States to get their fellow Dutchmen to migrate and buy the land. In the press they promoted the fresh, unbroken land of a new state called Colorado, claiming its climate was like Venice and its soil like the rich loam of the Dutch polder.

As seceders, the Zwier family had endured government opposition for decades, and the early-1890's economic conditions in the Netherlands were tough. So brothers Jan and Peter Zwier, both in their fifties, with children who suffered from consumption, bought some of that fertile, Colorado land. They, along with their wives, children, and fellow church members—all in all a group of about 200 Hollanders—sailed aboard the *SS Dubbeldam* for America on November 26, 1892, and after a rough, two-week journey arrived at Ellis Island. The group headed west by train to St. Louis. Crossing the Appalachians, they saw mountains for the first time, the coal-fed train exerting itself to its limits to make the summits.

"We're not only still in the same country," remarked Pete at one point, "we're still in the same state!"

"Ya, it seems like every state we go through is bigger than the Netherlands."

From St. Louis they journeyed by wagon to Colorado, the promised land, flowing with milk and honey. When they reached Alamosa, Colorado, at the end of November, however, they found not fertile loam, but desert sands mixed with stones, and the temperature soon dropped to a very un-Venice-like 17 degrees Fahrenheit. Stuck in Colorado, the Zwiers and other Dutch families only had two large un-heated sheds for housing. They huddled together, hiding under the few blankets they had brought along from the old country. They didn't have enough to eat and began to suffer from diphtheria, diarrhea, and other ailments. They also had no money, since they'd placed the funds they'd planned to use in Colorado on deposit with the very same Dutch American Land Corporation that had sold them the land. But instead of depositing that money in escrow, Zoutman and Vander Hoogt deposited it in their personal bank accounts. Four large families, including the Zwiers, had to file a lawsuit to recover their life savings.

There was even more bad news. It turned out that the Dutch American Land Corporation really owned no land in Colorado at all. They had only purchased an option to buy on some of it. Nor had Zoutman and Vander Hoogt ever seen the land themselves. They'd made a $12,000 deposit on a large parcel, using the immigrants' money, expecting the new settlers to exercise the option to purchase once they arrived. The immigrants later learned that the land Zoutman and Vander Hoogt had sold them at $26 an acre in the Netherlands could be purchased for $11.25 an acre in Colorado itself. The two swindlers stood to make a profit of $14.75 per acre from their fellow Hollanders, plus a $23 profit, per person on the transportation costs from New Jersey to Colorado.

The story made the headlines of the *Denver Republican*, which on December 18, 1892, carried it on page one under the title, "Boldest of Swindles!" That news sailed all the way back to the Netherlands, where the Dutch government got involved. The Dutch ambassador to the United States asked the governor of Colorado to intervene. The State of Colorado opened an investigation and learned that The Dutch American Land Corporation was not legally incorporated in the state, did not own the property they had put up as collateral, and had not exercised a proper purchase option. In short, it was a complete scam. They had swindled their own countrymen.

Since the corporation was illegal, the settlers did eventually get their money back and dealt directly with the Empire Land and Canal Company of Colorado. That company found them better, less expensive land south of Alamosa, and gave them cattle, chickens, and farm implements on easy credit terms with no money down. The settlers also paid ten cents an acre for the all-important water rights, which was exactly one fifth of what the two dirty Dutchmen would have charged them. Some, including the Zwiers, still weren't impressed with the sandy, rocky soil around Alamosa and began to look elsewhere. A Dutch doctor from New Jersey had advised his tubercular patients to go to New Mexico for its curative climate, and since some Dutch in the east suffered from tuberculosis, a little Dutch colony sprang up in northern New Mexico. This appealed to Jan and Pete Zwier, as their own daughters were tubercular.

They journeyed yet again to the northern New Mexican town of Maxwell. To get there they traveled southeast by wagon, crossing the southernmost part of the Rockies, the Sangre de Cristo Range, which was some exceedingly dry, hot, and mountainous terrain. They were hoping to find, if not "Venice," then at least a place where they could make a living. They'd been told they could easily buy a house once they got there, but when they finally arrived, there were no houses. Instead, the few settlers were living in old box cars. What's more, the land there was essentially a desert, even worse than Alamosa, and of little use for farming. Nonetheless, given their daughters' health, and perhaps exhaustion from their difficult sojourn in Colorado, they stayed in Maxwell.

Jan Zwier built a house of adobe bricks, which is basically dried mud, but just the right material for that climate. The Pueblo Indians had used it for ages, since it stays cool in the hot, summer sun. In tiny Maxwell everything was primitive, and the Zwiers' home was no exception. It included neither curtains nor carpets, nor electricity, nor running water. The furniture was plain, as was the food. Even so, the Zwiers were virtual royalty, since once they got their money back from the Colorado scammers, they could afford to buy land, whereas the other immigrants had to rent. The Zwiers bought up some cheap land, as well as a few horses and some rudimentary farming equipment. Hay was the main crop, but if the rains were sparse not much of anything would grow.

Jan Zwier had been an elder in the church of Opperdoes and became the leader in the church of Maxwell. His family's living room functioned not only as a dining room but also as a sanctuary. The little congregation faithfully gathered Sunday after Sunday in that adobe house, using Mrs.

Zwier's sewing machine case as a pulpit. The singing was vibrant, but necessarily a-capella. Jan Zwier even conducted catechism classes in that little house for his own children, as well as those of others. Since most of the families had young children, worship was a noisy, crowded event.

"Piet" Zwier constructed his own adobe house just south of his brother Jan's farm. Later he, a carpenter, also built a true church building for the settlers. Pete and his wife Neeltje, or Nellie, had had a son Simon born to them in the Netherlands in 1869, so when they crossed the Atlantic, he was a young man of twenty-two. Simon wanted to marry, but in this little desert colony there were no eligible Dutch girls available. He put a notice in the Christian Reformed Church newspaper *de Wachter* (*The Watchman*) advertising for a wife, and a young woman from Roseland, Illinois, Rena B. responded. Perhaps she loved adventure, or perhaps she thought Simon's picture in the ad was quite attractive, but for whatever reason, she came.

Simon couldn't believe his luck. She was beautiful, had gone to High School, and spoke both Dutch and English fluently. She came out west, never having met Simon or traveled west of Illinois. They were married by a circuit-riding Christian Reformed minister and settled down to a dry, hard life in New Mexico. Very soon, in fact only nine months after the wedding, they had a little boy whom they named Peter, after his grandfather. Not long after, Rena took ill. Perhaps she had an infection after the birth that never went away. She also took ill emotionally. Her family members had long been subject to depression, and on top of the familial malady, she suffered from the baby blues on top of it. She endured in Maxwell, but at considerable, personal cost. Leaving her family and being all alone in a strange place caused her melancholy to deepen. She felt hopeless.

Since there was no such thing as birth-control in those days, along came another little boy less than two years later. They named him Mento. He lived for only a few short weeks. A third child, a girl this time, Anne, was born just a year after Mento died.

Simon tried to soldier on. But by now Rena was so distraught that she grabbed a gun, pointed it at Simon, and threatened to kill him for bringing her out to that god-forsaken land. She broke down completely. She was unable to take care of herself, let alone her home and children.

After conferring with the elders and Rev. Van Dellen, the family decided she should be committed to an asylum some 100 miles away in Las Vegas, New Mexico. There she was declared insane. This left the thirty-four-year-old Simon as effectively a widower with two young children. Thankfully his parents, Peter and Nellie, as well as other family members were there to help. Simon struggled on for a couple of years without a wife, while his children were largely cared for by his parents. But for unfathomable reasons, God allowed Simon to contract tuberculosis. He died a young man, at the age of 34, on June 15, 1903, and was buried in the Maxwell Cemetery, leaving his four-year-old son Peter and two-year-old daughter Anne as orphans, though in fact, their mother was still alive. She lived on in the asylum till July 8, 1906, almost exactly three years longer than her husband. But she was no longer able to recognize her children, let alone take care of them.

The two little ones moved in with their grandparents, Peter and Neeltje, who in 1904 purchased the Bethesda Consumptive Relief Sanitarium for $300. People from the East, especially Dutch Reformed people, who sought relief from tuberculosis migrated to the clinic. Peter and Neeltje managed that hospital for a period of time, but again death struck. Pieter Zwier Sr. died on May 19, 1908, only a few months after his older brother Jan had also died. The loss of these two pillars of the church caused the whole Dutch community to fall apart. Farming in the desert was nearly impossible, and the deaths of those two men sucked all hope from the little colony. The church was dissolved, and the last remaining Dutch families left Maxwell late in 1908, including Nellie Zwier and her two orphaned grandchildren.

Grandma Nellie took the two little ones to Montana, where her daughter Hettie had moved some years earlier and met her husband Joe Smit. Nellie and Joe had two boys, one named after his father, Joe, and another named Alfred. They lived in the foothills of the Rockies, near Bozeman. But death struck yet again, this time the young Mr. Smit. So many early deaths were sadly common. In those days there were no antibiotics, so any infection could kill you. Men worked around dangerous machinery and often had accidents. General sicknesses would also spread freely, since there were few if any vaccines. Diseases easily killed off the weak and the old. After the death of her husband Joe, the young widow Hettie married another man from that area named Herm Boxum. Little Pete and Anne also moved in with their Aunt Hettie, who by then had three daughters with Mr. Boxum, one named for herself, plus Martha and Nellie. So Pete and Anne had two boy cousins and three girl cousins to grow up with. To Pete, Mrs. Boxum was always "Tante," or Aunt Boxum.

Pete and Anne went to school in a one-room school-house in Conrad, Montana, though not for long. When Pete was just a fourth grader his step-uncle asked him, "Are you going to preach or teach?"

"No, I don't think so."

"Then why do you need to keep going to school? You can already read, write, and figure."

For an active boy of ten who loved the outdoors and animals, the answer was simple: quit school, stay outside, and work, which is exactly what he did. Pete worked for Herm for many years, but since he was "supporting the family," he never got paid. When he got a little older and went to work for someone else, Herm insisted Pete give him that money too, since Pete was "under his roof." Thankfully Pete's grandma Nellie was still around to stand up for him and help him out now and then. In fact, Grandma Nellie bought him his first horse when he was fifteen. He learned to ride bareback and enjoyed roaming the nearby Rocky foothills.

This was the time of The World War, later, unfortunately, known as World War One. There were posters all over town, from which a stern, white-bearded man glared and pointed his finger at all who passed by, saying, "Uncle Sam Wants You!" Pete registered for the service on September 12, 1918. His registration card records:

> Residence: Columbus, MT, in Stillwater County
> Date of Birth: September 13, 1898
> Age at the time of registration: 19
> Height: Medium
> Build: Medium
> Hair: Brown
> Eyes: Blue
> Next of Kin: Nellie Zwier, grandmother
> Occupation: Farm Laborer

Pete got as far as Chicago for military training, but they sent him back home. It looked as if the war would soon be over and they were losing more men to the Spanish Influenza in the training camps than they were to the Germans in Europe.

The Spanish Influenza was indeed killing as many people as was the war. People suffered from fever, muscle and joint pain, nausea, vomiting, diarrhea, seizures, headache, and even delirium. It is estimated that the flu killed at least fifty million people throughout the world, about the same number as were killed in the war, overall between three and five percent of the global population. Healthy young people, whose immune systems over-reacted to the bug, as well as pregnant women, were especially vulnerable to the disease. The flu spread quickly. In Europe the soldiers were living outside in trenches, and the wounded were taken to field hospitals where viruses and bacteria could spread. Add to all that the cattle and poultry needed to feed them, and you had an incubator for the virus. Since the soldiers came from all over, they spread the flu when they returned home. The fact that Pete didn't have to serve in Europe might well have saved his life. Instead of going to Europe, he took the long train ride back to Montana.

Pete was a true westerner, born in New Mexico and raised in Montana. For him, the Netherlands was alive only in his grandmother's memory, though thanks to her he could speak Dutch. He had a step-uncle who used him as a forced laborer, but nonetheless he loved the land and animals. He was also a professing member of the Christian Reformed Church. I would meet him, when our family moved to Montana, and become his bride.

Love in the West

IN 1920 WE, TOGETHER with a number of other Dutch families, organized a church in Manhattan, MT. It soon grew to sixty families. The morning service was conducted in Dutch, but catechism classes for us young people were in English. Harm Boxum donated land for the building in the center of town. Pa, the boys, and all the men from the church put the building up. It held some 200 people; had a bell tower and was the only painted building in town. The church's barn held up to 20 teams of horses, and on Sundays it was full. We were rightly proud. Our community now had a spiritual center. Pa was elected as an elder, and brother-in-law Jake Kikkert, who had moved once Alice graduated, was named a deacon.

If we got to church early on Sundays we were treated to a beautiful spectacle: wagon after wagon came rolling up across the plains, then down unseen into the crevasses, only to come up again nearer and nearer the church. There were no roads till you got to the center of town itself, so we could see wagons coming from all directions, depending on where the homesteads were. That church, the Manhattan Christian Reformed Church became the center of our lives. We met there not only for two services on Sunday, but for catechism on Monday, Ladies Society on Tuesday, and Men's Society on Wednesday. I was part of a Young People's Group. We would have Bible Studies, but also picnics, and games. I spoke up at Bible Study, since I had been reading the Bible since I was first able to read and knew it inside and out. We Recker kids learned Bible stories like David and Goliath, the Birth of Jesus, Adam and Eve, etc. when we could barely walk. By the time we were in our twenties we'd been drenched in the Bible.

That church turned out to be a great match-maker. Most of the families who came to Montana were big and had marriageable young people in them. The families were typically middle-aged couples with grown children who thought they could make it out west. Each child was not a liability, but a valuable worker whose labor increased their family's chance of success. The Staal family was one of these. They had two daughters a bit older than I, Jessie and Rica. Brother Bill was smitten by Jessie, courted and married her. Brother Al fell in love with Rica and did the same. Both couples were married in that new little church. Two brothers marrying two sisters was fairly common then, since there were only so many eligible partners around. And when I say eligible, I mean that they were good Christians—Dutch, and Reformed. We didn't even think of marrying outside of our religion. Since Lena had married in Highland, and Bill and Al married sisters in Montana, I was next in line.

I met Pete at church. I don't remember the first time we met, but he had been raised in Montana, and was there when we arrived. He was an attractive young man, about a year older than me. He had fine features, with no rough edges; his lips were thin, his nose modest and straight; but it was his eyes got me; blue and thoughtful, with a note of tenderness. He had light brown hair that he combed back, leaving his nicely sloped forehead in full view. There was not a flaw in him. He had a strong jaw, and ears that stayed put. I felt lucky that he liked me. Pete was as kind and as gentle a man as I had ever met. He was truly a "gentleman," not in the sense that he had fancy manners or expensive clothes, but a genuinely gentle man. Never a rough or coarse word came from his mouth. There was no hint of violence or anger in him. Instead, he nearly always wore a pleasant, contented smile. I loved him so. He was so sensitive I sometimes worried that I might disappoint him, or even hurt him unwittingly. He was tender, and thoughtful, and he loved me as much as I did him.

By now I was twenty-one. My own looks were OK, but certainly nothing that stopped men in their tracks. I got the black hair of our French grandmother, and dark eyebrows to go with it, neither of which really matched my light skin. My eyes were fairly large, but hardly dreamy. My nose was a little big, my lips average, and my jaw somehow seemed a bit out of proportion to my face. On the other hand, Pete's little sister Anne, was a show-stopper. She had Pete's features, and maybe even more deeply accented eyes. Her hair was brown, and she had a nice figure. I was a little jealous of her: why couldn't I have gotten looks like that? Much later she had a grand-daughter with the same features plus nice Dutch, blond hair. Boy did she turn heads.

One evening in the fall, when the crops were all in, but the coldest winds of winter had yet to arrive, Pete asked me to go for a ride. Of course

I would! We saddled our horses and rode side by side, cantering down and walking up the ridges. We looked out at the mountains.

"Isn't God a creative builder?" He asked.

"Oh, yes."

"And those millions of stars in the Milky Way, can you imagine that this is just one galaxy among millions?"

"Yes, yet He looks down upon us, and knows our names, and has even counted the hairs on our heads."

"He has given us so many blessings. You know which one I appreciate the most?'

"Well, Christ."

"Yes, yes, of course," he said with a smile, "but then which one?"

"The mountains," I ventured.

He gave me another smile. He shifted his horse as close to me as possible, till they were side to side. He reached out and held my face in his left hand.

"It's you, silly. I think God sent Minnie Recker here to Montana as my greatest blessing."

I finally caught on. He looked at me with those sharp, yet tender blue eyes, and asked:

"Will you be mine forever?"

"Oh Pete, I can't imagine life without you. Yes, of course, yes."

I leaned over from my horse, and he from his. We kissed. We would be wed.

Pete always had the job of driver. He drove the wagons, the carriages, the mules, etc. Shortly before our wedding he drove a load of grain to the mill but stopped first to talk with his aunt.

"Tante, this last load is for Minnie and me. We're going to need it."

Tante Boxum nodded and smiled at him. "And I hope your life with her is blessed in every way." He kept the proceeds from that one load, so with it, a few wedding gifts, and some basics our families gave us, we could start on our own.

We were married in the little Christian Reformed Church our families had built. Our formal announcement says that Peter Zwier and Hermina Recker were to be married on January 25, 1922. I was the third one in my family to get married in that church. Like my sister Lena, I made my own wedding dress. Pete asked his step-brother Joe Smit to be his best man. My two older brothers served as groomsmen. Lena was my maid of honor, and sisters Alice and Tini were bridesmaids.

Our wedding was really a full church service. The entire congregation was invited, so it was a church wedding in more than one way. The consistory met before the service and gave its blessing on the marriage. Reverend Vander Ark performed our wedding ceremony, placing the wedding within the usual liturgy. We sat in the front row while he spoke, like a good Reformed pastor, for a full 45 minutes, adjuring us to love, self-sacrifice and sanctity. I can't remember much of what he said, since I only had eyes for Pete. I'm sure he told us that the man is the head of the woman as Christ is the head of the church, and that I should serve in humility. That was normal. I gladly agreed to have and to hold him till death would part us.

It's always interesting that at a wedding there is a mix of solemnity and humor. It is a very serious occasion—two people are committing themselves to one another for life, before God and many witnesses. Yet, it seems that everyone is on the verge of laughter as well. I remember when my daughter got married years later. As she walked down the aisle, thunder clapped deafeningly, as if it were exploding in the church building itself. The whole church burst into laughter.

We were both virgins till that night. We assumed it had to be that way. The Bible said not to commit fornication, and our families honored the marriage bed. We knew this was what God had in mind. You get married; you have children; you live together in faithfulness. Not like today—I know even some Christian young people live together first, and then get married afterward.

For our honeymoon we traveled across the panhandle of Idaho, and on to Zillah, in south central Washington. Some Dutch settlers had gone there before us, and Pete heard there was good work in the orchards, so we stayed to work, long after the honeymoon came to an end. The soil was far better than that of Montana. The early settlers had dug an expansive irrigation ditch from the Yakima River, so the land was fertile and well irrigated. Pete and I found work in the apple orchards as laborers and lived in a little cabin they set up for the workers. The work was seasonal; nothing much to do during the winter, but the summer and fall kept us busy pruning, picking and packing. Most of the other workers were young single guys who had come from out East, and a few Mexicans who had made a long journey north. One thing we all had in common was a lack of money. That's why we took whatever hard work we could find to keep body and soul together. There was just one other married woman in the camp, Betsy Spahn, whom I got to know pretty well. We would work in the orchard for most of the day, and then go back to the cabins before the men so we could make some supper. I thought we might settle in Washington, but when Pete developed some bad allergies to the pollen from the fruit trees we had to move back to Montana.

Farming in Montana required both manpower and horse-power. Land needed to be plowed, then disked, and then, perhaps harrowed. Pete did all of that. First, he plowed that native land that was buffalo grass, or other native plants. A plow is shaped like a slightly concave triangle. One point of the triangle slices into the ground. It peels into the sod and sends a swirl of earth curling alongside the blade. One man and one horse can only plow about an acre and a half per day. It's just hard work since that blade has to dig in deep. Then it's time to disk. A disk is quite different from a plow. It is basically a bar, six or eight feet long, with a series of plates or discs perpendicularly attached to it. Discs are the size of large dinner plates and are hooked to the bar about six inches apart, at a slight angle. Once the land is plowed, the disks spin through the great rows of curved soil and level them out enough for the seeder to get in. Since the land has already been plowed and the disk is six to eight feet wide, a man and one horse can get about seven acres disked per day. If you need the land to be especially level for seed like wheat, you also need to run a harrow. The harrow is a metal bar too. Attached to it are curved metal prongs, or half-circles, about a foot long. The prongs scrape along the top of the soil and knock apart the clods or small ridges left by the plow and disk. Pete could get about ten acres a day harrowed.

We kept a wide variety of draft horses around. They were never pedigreed Belgians, or Clydesdales or anything, but rather equine mutts. Since they were meant to pull, they were usually big, but as far as color and genealogy were anywhere on the rainbow: roan, bay, sorrel, or black, with ancestors who were wild ponies from the Rockies or purebred draft horses from Europe. We bought them when we needed them. Almost no one kept a stallion on their farm to breed their own horses with, it was too much trouble. The stallion would be tough to control and would want to breed with every mare from miles around. A foal might be born rear first, or still-born, and the mare wouldn't be able to work while nursing the foal, so it was much simpler to buy a young horse from a breeder.

Pete could harness a couple of horses to a plow, or disk or harrow in about ten minutes. After he fed and watered them, the horses bedded down in the straw overnight. Early in the morning, Pete would go out to the stable to hook up the horses. He could probably have done it blindfolded, but it's really a complex process, hardly as simple as turning the key on a tractor. The first thing to go on and the last thing to take off is the bridle. The bridle has a lead line on it that hooks to a band around the horses' nose, and a bit that goes over the horses' tongue, which lets you control the horse. So, unless the horse is in the stable, you want that on. The next thing to go on is the collar. The collar is a big, round leather piece that fits around the neck of the horse, ahead of the shoulder. Some collars are complete circles and have to be put over the nose, but most have a buckle on top that lets you slide it around the neck. Further back, behind the front leg, is the girth. The top of the girth sits on a little saddle, which provides padding and stability. The girth runs all around the horse with a belly-band, and has to be tightened up snug. Toward the rear of the horse is the loin strap, which does not go all the way around the horse. From the loin strap you attach the breeching, which wraps around the horses' rear, and also has to be tightened down. All of the straps are made of leather, so they hold and wear well. "Traces" run from front to back along the side of the horse. They are big braided leather straps that go all the way back to the implement. The ends of the traces are hooked to chain links that connect to the implement. If the horse is short, you might need more chain lengths than you would for a long-bodied animal to get the distance from horse to implement right.

The shaft from the implement would go into the trace at the loin strap, and then hook up into the girth. If you were running a pair of horses, each horse would have one shaft attached. After each horse has all the lines on, you put the neck yoke between the two horses, which is a cylinder of wood, with hooks on each end to snap the lines on. The teamster, the man who drives the team, holds two reins, the right and the left. The right rein would run to the right side of the horse on the right, but before getting to the bit, would split in two over the back of the right horses' head and run to the right side of the left horses' bit. So too, in opposite directions, with the left rein. With those two reins the teamster could turn the horses directly by their bits. "Gee" is right, and "Haw" is left. "Whoa" is stop, of course.

The driver had to hang on to the handles of the plow, disk, or harrow, and at the same time direct the horses. Pete had to lean back hard against the horses in order to pull the implements into the ground.

We had one horse, Prince, who was a bit of trouble. He was a big strong gelding, a roan. He would fight Pete every day. He wouldn't take the bit. He tried to pin Pete up against the stable door. He tried to bite.

He shied away from the halter. So Pete thought he'd teach him a lesson, and work him till he dropped. One day he hooked him to the heavy plow. Then he put a good-sized stone on top of the plow for more weight. He was in the field by 7 AM and worked that horse in the hard ground all morning. After an abbreviated lunch-break Pete watered him and took him back to the field. He worked Prince behind that heavy plow all afternoon in the hot sun without rest. At the end of the day, Pete came back to the pasture, and unhooked Prince, eagerly watching for him to fall down on all fours, in penitence. Instead, Prince merrily galloped off at full speed. Note: a young man will never out-work a young horse.

The men's work was so closely tied to the animals that I sometimes wondered who was taking care of whom, the men caring for the animals, or the animals caring for the men. I think taking care of a man can sometimes be a bit like taking care of a horse. Feed and water them daily, give them comfortable bedding, and go easy on the reins. It went fine that way with Pete.

All this work was in preparation for planting. Ideally, corn should be planted in moist soil during a waxing moon. The waxing moon has an increasing gravitational pull on the earth, and that gravity pulls the water up to the surface of the soil where it helps to germinate the new seeds. But sometimes the weather ruins such plans. If it was too wet, we couldn't get the seeder out in the field. If it was to dry, the seed would not germinate once it was sown. I think farming is the riskiest business there is. You can't control much of anything.

Pete and the guys worked out in the fields in spring and summer. During the winter, they went looking for jobs in town. Bill and Al left their wives, and later their children in the cabins, while they got lodging in town. Bill got a taxidermy license and worked for a fur dealer. Al worked for the railroad. Brother-in-law Jake Kikkert became the town blacksmith. Brother Bill was frustrated with both the farming and the taxidermy. What he really wanted to do was go into the ministry. He went to Classis Pacific Northwest and asked for support so that he could attend seminary. They looked at him and shook their heads. "Bill, you are married, you have two children, and have not finished High School; you better stick to farming."

Pete's step-brother, Joe Smit, was probably as close to Pete as any natural brother could be. They were pretty much the same age and had grown up in the same house. Like all the Montana kids, he looked forward to the day each year when the ranchers would move their large herds of cattle through town to send them on east to the slaughterhouses. It was quite an event; everyone came to watch. The streets that earlier had light traffic of a few horses, people, and wagons, were now jam-packed with speckled roan steers; horned, and half wild. Joe knew there would be lots of noise from all the cattle bellowing and cowboys hooting. So just for kicks, he got out his rifle and shot a steer right in the middle of town. As there were hundreds of steers, no one noticed that one was down till far later. Joe didn't even dress and butcher the steer; he shot it just for fun.

Two years after we married, my brother Bill and his wife Jessie decided they had had enough. Montana was just not a fruitful place to farm and raise a family. The first year that Bill and Al came was the exception—there was rain. Ever since, we had just been scratching and pushing, compelling the arid land to yield. But without rain, nothing went right. The seed didn't sprout; the horses and cattle went hungry or even starved; and the harvest was so minimal there was barely seed enough for the following year. One year when we did have enough rain the locusts ate the wheat. Another year hail destroyed what looked to be a good crop. We looked over our shoulders, fearful that Pharaoh had come to town.

Bill went back to Indiana, knowing that he could get a job at the Standard Steel Company of Gary. They left Columbus, Montana, and held an auction for their goods on October 15, 1924. But the west had gotten into Bill's soul. Before leaving he wrote this poem.

Ode to Montana.

The impression made on me, when first I saw
The Rockies filled my heart with awe,
As I gazed on those snow-capped peaks sublime
Those rugged pinnacles that withstood time
It made me think of the Master Mind,
For where on earth could we better find,
Examples of the Creator's skill
Who created it all, both valley and hill.
We lived on a homestead, high up in the hills,
In a two by four shanty without any frills,
From there we could gaze at the foothills blue
Where jack pine, fir and junipers grew.
When upward our eyes would follow and see
That the timberline grew not a tree.
And in the evening the sunsets glow

Would turn to red, the everlasting snow.
Then it would become so terribly still,
That you would be of stone, if you didn't feel the thrill.
Then at night we would hear the coyote howl
In the creek bottoms where also lived the Horned Owl.
Then somehow you came to conclude after all
That man surely is but very small.

When Ma and Pa learned that Bill and Jessie were leaving, they decided to go as well. By that time Pa was 59 years old, hardly a young frontiersman anymore. Upon their return to Illinois he picked up his tools, built his own house, and began working again as a carpenter. They took the precious little money they had left from Montana and deposited it in the Bank of Lansing. It sat there gaining pennies of interest for a couple of years until the Great Crash of 1929 when they, along with everyone else, lost everything. We took over the land that Bill and Jess had farmed. We didn't have to buy it, we just kept farming it. Since they had stayed there for five years, they were able to take title to the land and gift it to us.

"Good luck with the ranch, Minnie. Hope it goes better for you and Pete than it did for Jessie and me."

"Thanks Bill, we'll give it all we've got. Maybe my westerner of a husband can make something work."

Pete sure did work. He was out in the field every day of the spring, summer, and fall, and fixed one thing after the next in the winter. Yet at night he always seemed to have enough energy for amorous congress. I'd ask him, "Aren't you tired?"

"Oh no, I save just enough energy for you."

"Thanks."

He must have had enough energy all right, since I was pregnant with our first after a year of marriage. The pregnancy was normal, which is to say, I had swelling in my legs, vomiting in the morning, abdominal pains, found sleeping uncomfortable, was weepy, tired, and felt like I was carrying a mule instead of a child.

All of my children would be born at home. Hospitals were expensive and far away. When I went into labor Pete called his sister over, along with his grandmother. They came and tried to get me comfortable and encourage me, putting cool towels on my face, and holding my hands. But frankly there is not much anyone else can do to deliver a baby; it was my job. It felt like someone was trying to pull a large ball out from between my hips. I wanted to tear open my abdomen and pull the baby out of my middle directly, with my clenched, claw-shaped hand. So all in all, it was a normal delivery.

We decided to name him Stanley. We really had no family members with that name, but it seemed like a good American name that would get him through life without trouble. Unlike my name, we could accurately predict that the shortened American version would be simply, "Stan." I suppose we could have given him a real Dutch name like "Hendrikus," or "Remkes," or something, but why? We were Americans. Our kids would have American names.

Little Stanley was perfect. I remember lying on top of the long prairie grasses, finding a smooth spot with no stones. Little Stanley fell asleep on my chest. I could feel and smell his breath; it returned the scent of my own breast milk to me. I saw his little hands curled up in a fist, the bones still soft, each little digit a work of artistry. I could hear the grouse and the doves and the meadowlarks calling, the crickets, flies, and bees buzzing. I could smell the sweet wild flowers and the good, dry soil. I looked off in the distance and saw the mountains rise, stretching up to touch the heavens. I watched as a small cloud gamboled across the sky, dropping a spot of shade wherever its path crossed the suns'. I fell asleep. When I awoke, I was drenched in sweat, and little Stanley was still peacefully breathing, looking contentedly at me with his honest baby smile. His chest rose and fell. He was almost one now, and his new life was precious to me, to Pete, and no doubt to God.

Once, a visiting pastor came to Columbus with his wife and child. We had just bought a new mattress, so the church asked us to host them. Since the pastor and his wife were guests, we insisted they sleep on it. Well, wouldn't you know it; their little boy peed on the new mattress. They felt terrible about it but could hardly do anything to change it. When they left, we washed it as best we could with soda and set it outside, upright, against the side of the house. In the dry Montana summer it didn't take long to air out, but a hint of the ammonia-like smell always remained.

A year later I was pregnant again. We had another boy. This one I named after my dad—Al. But since we were in America I didn't make him a Germanic Ahlrich, but an Alton—Alton Peter Zwier. Thank God, he too was a beautiful, healthy little baby.

We soldiered on in Montana, but like Bill and Jess, we really couldn't make a go of it either. We had to give up on Montana. The dry, rocky, mountainous land would just not support us. It was beautiful; but beauty isn't a cash crop. The farms were too small, and we were trying to raise grains that demanded too much water. Years later they raised cattle there on ranches that spanned thousands of acres. That succeeded since the cattle could eat the native grasses. But farming a few hundred acres with a horse and plow just wouldn't work.

We had an auction of our own. We sold the horses, the cattle, and the equipment. I still have a poster for the auction, with Pete standing astride one of the horses. We couldn't sell the house and the land though; there were no buyers. By then everyone knew that you couldn't make a living. We moved back to the Illiana area, close to my family. That would be a good place to raise our own family.

Family and Gangsters in Chicago

Moving back to Illinois in 1926 after a decade in Montana was discouraging. It seemed as if we had failed. Of course we weren't the only ones. Thousands learned what we did, that raising Midwestern crops in the dry foothills of the American West just won't work. Though we worked about as hard as anyone could, the land and the climate just wouldn't produce. We came back to Illinois in a train's passenger car, not a box car.

We hadn't been back from Montana for more than a few months when Pete learned that his grandma Zwier had died back in Montana. He was heartsick. She was really the one who had raised him. Oh, he'd lived in his aunt and uncle's house, but his grandmother was the one who showed him the love and care that he'd needed as a tender young boy. We didn't have the money for Pete to take another train ride back, and by the time we heard about her death, it was too late to attend the funeral. He later learned his grandma had left him and Anne a bit of an inheritance, but Herm Boxum had taken it. Knowing him, he probably figured, "We paid to feed and house those kids all those years. It's the least she could do!"

We moved into a small house in Lansing, Illinois, not far from Ma and Pa and quite close to the Lansing Christian Reformed Church. Our house had just two bedrooms and one bath. The little boys, Stan and Al, shared one bedroom and Pete and I the other. Before long that house got to be a bit small, since I was pregnant for the third time. The baby turned out to be a girl, whom we named Irene. I chose that name since it was popular in America at the time. She too went full term and was born at home. It's quite a blessing to have healthy children.

About that time, little Al got terribly sick with the whooping cough. The poor little guy had what seemed like a bad cold for a week or so, plus a fever of over 100 degrees the whole time. He had terrible coughing spells that wouldn't stop. He threw up and couldn't sleep due to the coughing. We were afraid we might lose him. We took him to a doctor, but there wasn't much he could do. Pa came over and held little Al in his arms, crying out, "Whoop it up boy; whoop it up!" We prayed and let it run its course till he was restored.

Pete got a job at the Lansing Lumber Yard, which not only had lumber and hardware but also coal. All the houses in town were heated with coal stoves and needed a regular supply, so Pete's job was to deliver it by team and wagon. Driving that team made him a "teamster." He'd get a load in the morning at the lumber yard, drive through town, and unload it with a wide shovel into the coal bins on the outside of each house down into the basement where the heater was. After eating the lunch I'd packed him he would usually deliver another load in the afternoon. He was pretty content with that job, since he was such a good driver, but it sure didn't make us rich. He made $100 a month, all the income that came into our house. I told Pete we should buy a house instead of renting:

"If we keep renting, we'll never build up any money."

But he said, "Look how that would tie us down. What if we want to move back out west? Then we'll have a house here holding us back."

I wanted to tell him what I really thought: *I doubt we'll ever move back west. We already learned that we can't make a living there, and our families are here now. Stan, Al, and Irene can all go to good Christian Schools around here, and we have a Christian Reformed Church right across the street.*

But how could I say that? It would have broken his heart; he was such a westerner. He woke up every morning and looked out the window, sad to see another house in front of him rather than the mountains. I knew we weren't moving back but couldn't bring myself to tell him, so I acquiesced: "OK, Pete. We don't need to own a house. As long as we're together, that's the important thing."

Our little house was some twenty miles south of Chicago, so our lives were caught up in that great metropolis, now the second largest in the United States. We got the daily paper, the *Chicago Tribune*, and read it from cover to cover. When I'd finished, I'd pass it on to Pete, and as the kids grew older, they did their best to get through it too. On the first page would be a "Poem You Ought to Know." Since we wanted to be good Americans, we often tried to memorize these poems, like this one called "The Penitent," by Edna St. Vincent Millay:

I had a little Sorrow,
Born of a little Sin,
I found a room all damp with gloom
And shut us all within;
And, "Little Sorrow, weep," said I,
"And, Little Sin, pray God to die,
And I upon the floor will lie
And think how bad I've been!"

Alas for pious planning—
It mattered not a whit!
As far as gloom went in that room,
The lamp might have been lit!
My Little Sorrow would not weep,
My Little Sin would go to sleep—
To save my soul I could not keep
My graceless mind on it!
So up I got in anger,
And took a book I had,
And put a ribbon on my hair
To please a passing lad.
And, "One thing there's no getting by—
I've been a wicked girl," said I;
"But if I can't be sorry, why,
I might as well be glad!

Her poem reflected the times. By the 1920's people out East like her were starting to feel that their "little sins" weren't such a big deal. Rather, they were just a normal part of life, nothing to be sorry for.

That sure was different than what I'd been taught. In our church we learned that we were "born in sin, and subject to the wrath of God." I didn't exactly love to hear that when it was read during the baptismal service, but it seemed true. Who wasn't born into sin? Who could argue that God didn't hate sin? I suppose Mrs. Millay's plan might work for a while, for a few of our smaller indiscretions, but what about the long-term? What if you realized that you just weren't right because sin was deeply buried within your soul? I sure couldn't be "glad" about that. I think it's better to feel a little guilt now and then, confess the sin that caused it, and go on. I'll stick with the system of Guilt, Grace, and Gratitude that was drilled into us in catechism class.

Women like Mrs. Millay were changing attitudes, though. In 1919 women got the vote in the U.S. I wasn't a suffragist, but I'm glad they did. Pete and I shared more or less the same political views, so our votes were likely to be the same. But why not vote myself? I was an adult, had a little more education than my husband, and cared deeply about what was going on in this country. I'm glad those women out East went on strike.

The twenties were later called the "Roaring Twenties," but around us the only things roaring were the cattle and an occasional big truck. We worked, went to church, and took care of family. I guess out East they had some rip-roaring parties while the stock market climbed higher and higher. But the rising stock market sure didn't affect us. The idea that we could have money left-over from Pete's salary, or from the sale of a few eggs, to buy corporate stock was laughable. If we had enough money for rent, food, and clothing, plus church offerings, we were content. Then in 1929 the stock market crashed, and their party ended. We read about men in New York who jumped out of skyscraper windows when their thousands turned into hundreds. Pretty sad. Couldn't they have lived with hundreds, or less, as we did? It's hard to imagine people would kill themselves because they'd lost money.

In 1920, the 18th Amendment brought in Prohibition. That didn't affect us much since we didn't drink anyway. Oh, we might have a celebratory glass of wine at Christmas or New Year's, but that was about it. Prohibition sure did change things in Chicago, though, and for the worse. Most adults do like to drink alcohol. I guess that's okay, as long as they don't get drunk, which is what the Bible seems to say. But the Women's Christian Temperance Union saw so much evil coming from drinking, they felt they had to put a stop to it. Men came home drunk and beat their wives. They got in the new cars that were being built in Detroit and caused accidents. They got addicted to alcohol and couldn't hold a job or pay their rent. Plenty of other bad things happened in and around the taverns too. All in all, the W.C.T.U. had good reasons to stop the drinking. But drinking is apparently going to happen no matter what the law says. It's sort of like telling people "No sex!" Good luck with that.

In Chicago the drinking went underground. There were "Speakeasies" and "Blind Pigs" where people could buy liquor by the drink or the bottle. But in order to make that work, the bar owner had to bribe some cops, and in order to get the booze he had to buy it from a hoodlum. So moving drinking underground begat bribery and gangsterism.

Al Capone was the worst gangster of the bunch. He smuggled in the booze, charged exorbitantly for it, and then charged money to "protect" the businesses that sold it. If you didn't want his "protection" he put you out of business or killed you. He was a horrible man. Who knows how many he killed, all for the love of money? Or perhaps it was power that he loved, raw power to decide who should live and who should die. Money and power usually go together, and he had plenty of both. The sad thing was that, while most people in Chicago were like us—working hard and raising a family—Al Capone's name became synonymous with Chicago. Even much later, in the 1960's, when some friends traveled to Europe and told the French or the Germans they were from Chicago, people would respond, "Ah! Chicago—Al Capone! Dadadadadada" and point their fingers as if they were firing machine guns.

All of this seemed remote to me until Irene came home from school one day and said, "My friend (the name of an Italian girl) says her family is friends of the Capone family." And that certainly could have been true. Capone was known to have a residence in Chicago Heights, and there were lots of Italians who went to school with Irene. Capone was a human being, just as we were, with a home and a family, but that's about where the similarities stopped.

I think one of our Christian Reformed guys might have gotten caught up in the moonshining business too—Ralph P. Ralph had a little airplane and was a pilot. At the beginning of Prohibition, he had some money but wasn't all that rich. By the end of the Prohibition, though, he was a very rich man, and none of us could see how he'd gotten his wealth. His regular job was nothing special, and he had no other businesses. We suspect he flew from Chicago to Canada, or perhaps some other place where there was a distillery, and then back to our area with the booze. There was a little airport nearby in Lansing, and I'll bet the guys who worked there were paid to look the other way when his plane landed

Ralph regularly came to church and put his money in the collection plate, and since the profits from rum-running were sky high, his offerings were substantial too. What do you do with a guy like that? Dutch Reformed people don't object to alcohol. We have always enjoyed a good drink, and we use real wine for communion. But during Prohibition, selling alcohol was illegal. Should I have reported Ralph to the Feds? Should the elders have put him under church discipline?

The church didn't put him under discipline. In fact, it looked the other way and thanked him for his generous offerings. We could say that we never really *knew* he was a bootlegger, but it has always made me wonder: should the church get involved in enforcing civil law? Back in those days we made young couples who got pregnant before marriage stand in front of church and confess, and, boy, was that an ugly business. So why not have someone like Ralph stand up front and confess his sin? The church is the communion of the saints but also the home of sinners. Which sinners of which sins should publicly repent? Which should face church discipline or civil penalties? I guess our preachers and theologians had worked that all out, but I was never clear.

The house we had in Lansing got to be too small once I was pregnant for the fourth time in 1930. We didn't have birth control back then, so nature took its course. Nevertheless, though it was the Depression, this baby, like all the others, was a blessing. He was a fine little boy, and we again chose a very American name: Donald. We found yet another home, now with three bedrooms, just a few blocks away and rented that too.

By now all my brothers and sisters were married and had homes of their own nearby. My brother Dick had married Pete's step-sister Nellie and moved back from Montana about the time we did. Pete's sister Anne was married to Herb P., the Lansing postmaster. Being Postmaster was a pretty good job at the time and must have paid pretty well. I remember one Christmastime when Stan was a little guy, Herb and Anne came over with a nicely wrapped gift for him and made quite a show of giving it to him. He opened it, a toy truck, and was pleased.

Herb said,

"Merry Christmas, Stan. But now don't think we can give you something like this every Christmas. It cost a lot of money."

Really? Did a toy truck cost so much that they couldn't get him something like it next year? And did he have to tell his little nephew how much it cost? The truth is that he was just a penny-pincher. That old English saying is true:

> *In questions of business, the problem with the Dutch*
> *Is they pay too little, and they ask too much!*

But Stan, together with Pete and me, thanked Ann and Herb politely.

In 1928 brother Bill was a foreman at U.S. Steel in Gary, Indiana. He and his family lived a short commute away in Highland. But one Sunday at coffee he humbly told us that he'd had a dream. God had come to him and said, "Get out of that job. Go farm." It was quite puzzling to Bill, and to all of us. Having a vision wasn't something any of us had ever experienced. Strange as it was, Bill heeded the vision. He went south a way to DeMotte, Indiana, and put money down on a small farm. It was lowland, and fertile, and still fairly cheap, since it was still well beyond the reach of ever-expanding Chicago. He was so beloved by his workers at the mill that they all volunteered to help him paint the new house.

A year or two later he was relieved to have heeded the dream. The stock market crashed in October of 1929, and men everywhere lost their jobs. The mill he'd worked in shut down, so he would have been in the breadlines. Instead, he had a little farm that could produce enough for their family.

About half the family were Hoosiers, living in Highland, Munster, or now DeMotte. The most famous, or infamous, Hoosier of the time was John Dillinger. He was kind of hero to kids during the Depression and had his name in the headlines for months at a time. He'd been raised near Indianapolis and was apparently a naughty, but not rotten kid. Like many, he dropped out of school. He robbed a store in his home-town, but left empty-handed, since there was no money in the till. His gun accidentally went off while the robbery was underway, but it harmed no one. Nonetheless, since someone saw him leaving the store with a gun, his father insisted that he confess his crime before he could be apprehended for it. Though he pled guilty, he was sentenced to ten full years in the Indiana penitentiary in Michigan City. Embittered by his harsh sentence, he used the time to learn the tools of the trade of robbery. While in prison he somehow got an up-to-date map of where the banks in Indiana, Illinois, and Ohio were. Dillinger went on to rob many of them.

During his bank robberies he would smile at the ladies and tell them not to worry. He even gave coins to any kids who might be in the bank with their parents. He was quite a charmer. He was handsome and athletic, and once scaled a six-foot wall in a bank. He was almost an entertainer. His name was mentioned on the radio news all the time. He was known as the "Hoosier Hoodlum."

The thing was that during the Depression, the banks were thought of as the real thieves. They closed without warning, leaving people without their deposits. Or, if they stayed open, they went prowling around looking for homes and businesses to re-possess. Dillinger was no Robin Hood, but he did have some sympathy for the common people. He eventually killed a police officer in East Chicago, Indiana, which led him to be charged with murder.

While on the lam, Dillinger sent Matt Leach, the chief of the Indiana State Police, friendly post cards and phone calls, generating quite a bit of publicity for himself, and embarrassment for the police. He got his pals who remained in the Michigan City penitentiary out by sending arms into the jail, hidden under clothing. The freed gang soon broke into a police station and collected a machine gun, rifles, pistols, and bullet-proof vests. Then they went to another police station and did the same. Dillinger was considered "Public Enemy Number One" by J. Edgar Hoover, chief of the FBI. President F.D. Roosevelt even signed bills that would give federal agents more power to catch him. The F.B.I. set up a forty-man team solely devoted to Dillinger. When they were closing in, Dillinger fled to Mexico, but was captured while yet in Arizona.

He was flown from Arizona to Chicago, the first time an airplane had ever been used to transport a prisoner. Since he faced the murder charge in Indiana, he was brought to Chicago by plane, and then transferred to Indiana by car. In Chicago there were 85 police vehicles waiting at the airport to transport him to Indiana. He was taken to the Crown Point, Indiana, jail where the sheriff, Lilian Harvey, boasted that he'd never get out, since there were eight doors between Dillinger and freedom. In the jailhouse, the prosecutor put his arm around him, and the sheriff had a picture taken with him, both wanting to be photographed with the great celebrity. After a few weeks, the security around Dillinger relaxed. Dillinger made a gun of wood, stuck it in the jailer's back and forced him to let him out through the kitchen, and then out the back. He then stole the sheriff's own car and headed to Chicago.

Dillinger was caught and killed in Chicago some time later. He had changed his appearance by means of surgery, but someone tipped off the cops. A "Woman in Red" set him up when they went out to the movies.

We read all about Dillinger, just as we had about Capone. Our house in Lansing was about equidistant from the Crown Point County jail and the theater where he was shot. But we might as well have been on another planet. Gunfights, bank robberies, film stars were all as foreign to us as Martians.

But then a member of the Dillinger gang struck quite close to home.

Millie DeYoung was a Christian Reformed woman whom I had met at one of the Women's Missionary Union meetings for classis Illiana. Jacob DeYoung, her husband, was a guard at the South Holland Trust and Savings Bank. Before taking a trip to Grand Rapids to visit some family members on February 10, 1934, he assigned his son Pete to do a bit of custodial and guard work at the bank in his stead. Some of Dillinger's gang, though not Dillinger himself, came in and robbed the bank before it opened. They didn't find any money since the deposits hadn't come in yet, but they killed the innocent young man. Jake and Millie were devastated, and Jake plotted revenge.

The South Holland bank was one of the few in the country to stay open through the Great Depression, so Jake was sure they'd be back. The bank's survival was thanks to its conservative management, and to onions. At that time South Holland was the onion-set capital of the world. To grow onions takes two seasons. The first season you plant the seeds, which grow into slender plants that produce scallion leaves. The bottom of that onion is called a green onion, which can be eaten. But if you let the green onion grow for another season it will produce a bulb, which can be dug up and then stored over the winter, if temperatures don't get crazy cold. All the thrifty Dutch onion farmers of South Holland put their money in the South Holland Trust and Saving Bank. Anticipating that the gang would come back again when there was money in the safe, the bereft father guarded the bank each day, sitting on a perch on the bank's balcony, his rifle on his lap.

Meanwhile, fellow church member and Police Chief Leonard Lagastee kept a sharp eye out for anything unusual. On May 25 of the same year, Lagastee noticed a suspicious looking Ford V8 with smoked windows going down 159th St. When the car pulled up in front of the bank, three masked men leapt out, entered the bank, and shouted, "Stick-em up!" Jake was ready and waiting. He shot and killed one bandit before he could climb the partition between the vestibule and the cash drawers. The two remaining bandits ran for the door, but Jake dropped the second before he could get out of the building. The third fared no better, and not much longer. He did make it out the door, but was met with a deadly fusillade from Lagastee and officer Neal Van Kanegan. Three remaining hoodlums sped off in the getaway car with bullets from the two officers stimulating their flight.

Don't mess with the Dutch. We are not pacifists.

Now Everyone is Poor

PETE MOVED FROM THE Lumber Yard to the Ford factory on the south side of Chicago in 1928. He was lucky to get that job, since it paid $5.00 a day, almost double what other jobs were offering at the time. Pete had to take a long bus ride into Chicago in order to get to work, then put in his shift, and take another bus home. When he came home, he was both exhausted and anxious. He never told me what he was so worried about. Maybe the machines he was working with were dangerous. Maybe some of the guys he was working with were hiring prostitutes. I really don't know. I do know that on some nights I would have to wake him out of a nightmare. He was kicking me in his sleep!

"Pete, Pete, wake up! What's the matter?"

"I was dreaming."

"You were kicking me. What's the problem?"

"I don't know; I dreamt I was kicking away the foxes."

Foxes?? Strange, as are many dreams.

At that time the workers were trying to start a union at Ford. Pete saw some things that weren't going well in the factory and wanted to make them better. Laborers in Chicago and all through the United States at that time were treated terribly. Upton Sinclair wrote about the nearby Chicago Stock Yards in *The Jungle*, showing how bad they were. People fell in vats and came out in the sausage. Kids were working twelve-hour days, and if they got hurt, they were just sent home. It was tough to make a living in those days, and tough to change the working conditions too.

Pete got involved. He wanted to do something about whatever was keeping him up with the foxes. He stood up in a meeting and praised the union leaders for what they were doing, and said he'd join.

"We need a union here. If we don't get one, Mr. Ford will do whatever he wants to us. "

The next day he was fired.

"Pete, we've got a hundred guys who would be happy to have your job without becoming communist agitators. Get out!"

Pete was a communist agitator like our plow-horse Barney was a peregrine falcon—nothing doing

After the Ford job, Pete got another in a smaller factory that made buses. He operated a crane. Back then you didn't need a degree or a certification or anything; you just went in and showed them you knew what you were doing. And like all things mechanical, Pete knew how to run a crane. He showed up to work early every day, by at least ten minutes. He believed that if you were supposed to start at 8:00 you had better be working by 8:00, not just coming in, or getting ready to work. Coming in late, would have been theft, stealing time from your boss. But Pete's good habits didn't matter, not long into the Depression he got laid off that job too.

President Roosevelt put him and thousands of others like him to work at the W.P.A. (the Works Progress Administration.) Thankfully, he didn't have to move all over the country in order to do it. Around our area their job was mostly building roads. Elsewhere they built schools and hospitals, put in sewer lines, or planted trees. It was hard and dirty work; but it was work. My Pa, now in his sixties even had to work for the W.P.A.

Pete then heard about a farm he could work on. We wouldn't own the land, just work it; they called that being a "tenant farmer." We moved into the farmhouse and took care of the farm, but someone else owned the land and the cattle. So we never got paid for a harvest; or for the sale of the beef cattle, but we never worried about the price for a bushel of corn, or side of beef either.

Since we lived on a farm we always had enough to eat, but not much more than that. I had a second baby girl in February of 1936. We gave her another nice American name: Linda. We always dropped the "da" and just called her "Lin." Only when she was an adult did anyone return the more formal "da" to her name. I learned later that in Spanish "linda" means "pretty," and she was. She was also a sweetie.

Pete loved animals, and did a fine job with the horses, cows, and pigs. He had been driving wagons and machinery since he was eight years old, so that part of the work was good for him too. He was especially good with horses. Were that not enough, he could fix anything. So all in all he was an ideal tenant farmer. By this time Stan was a young teenager. He, like Pete, was quite handy, and was an asset around the farm too.

The owners, the Roneys, lived in the other house on the property. Mr. Roney worked in town, so was away all day, leaving us to do the farm-work. The Roneys had a housekeeper, Miss Liekel, so I had two other women next door whom I could talk with daily. We had a lot in common but went to different churches; they were Lutheran and Methodist, and we were Christian Reformed. That sometimes made for interesting conversations.

In 1928 our church had come out with a synodical decision against "worldly amusements." These included dancing, movies, and most card games. They said that these amusements would lead the young people away from the faith. The movies showed nothing but violence or romance; dancing put two single young people in close physical contact where temptation was sure to arise; and card playing emphasized chance, not providence. So I had never gone to a movie, or danced, or played poker.

But Mrs. Roney and Miss Liekel had seen a few movies, since their churches had no such ban. As friendly neighbors they once invited me along, not knowing of our church's position. Oh boy. Now what? I said I'd get back to them before the matinee on Friday afternoon.

So should I go to a movie even if my church said not to?

Movies certainly weren't forbidden in the Bible, but then that was no excuse, since there was nothing like movies in Bible times.

Or were movies like graven images?

No, I wasn't going to worship in the theater, just to enjoy a story with moving pictures.

Yes, that's it! Movies were like novels. I had read novel after novel, so going to a movie was like seeing the pictures of the novel! Looking at pictures was not a bad thing, as long as the pictures themselves didn't show something sinful. So if the novel was a good one, a movie made from a good novel should be the same.

Yet, our church was pretty clear on this. All the preachers at Synod had come up with this statement and voted on it. Who was I to contradict them? In fact, when the elders came around for "huisbezoek" (house visitation) they would check on movie attendance. With great gravity, an elder would ask,

"Has anyone in the household been going to the movies?"

"Why no, we don't do that," replied Pete.

I decided not to bother Pete or the elders with my questions.

Mrs. Roney and Miss Liekel were not trying to lead me into temptation, they were just being friendly neighbors. We women worked hard and needed an occasional break from our labor. Was entertainment itself bad? No, we played music and read novels, and our kids were in plays in school and church. So why were movies bad? I suppose that some movies, cards or dancing *could* be bad, but it depended on which ones you were talking about. A movie about Jesus, for example, could hardly be bad, so movies in themselves must not be the issue. Holding your husband close in a dance couldn't be bad, so dancing in general couldn't be either. And card games? Some, like Rook, were good family entertainment, whereas the other kinds they played in the casinos in Calumet City were no doubt evil.

I thought I'd try it. I would find out for myself whether movies were bad. The fact that I was nearly forty and hadn't much of a record in mortal sins gave me confidence that going to one movie would not propel me down the road to perdition. But now. Do I tell Pete? The boys? The girls? Oh, why drag them into it? If I came back convinced that movies were sinful, I could share my opinions with them, and try to keep them away from the theaters. If I came back convinced that they were OK, I could passively help them to see things the same way. We went. I put on a nice dress, and we all left together. Irene saw me leave.

"Where you going, Ma?"

"Oh, just a little shopping with Mrs. Roney and Miss Liekel."

"Can I come?"

"No, not this time."

"Aw."

Years later she told me that she worked it out. She saw we were all dressed nicely, and that we came back only two and a half hours later, and none of us was carrying any packages from the store. She also saw a newspaper I had left open to the page of announcements for movie showings. Rather careless of me.

The movie was: *How Green is My Mountain*. I saw it in 1941, toward the end of the Depression, but before America entered the war. It showed the coal miner's strike in Great Britain during the Industrial Revolution. It sure reminded me of what Pete and our guys had gone through in Chicago. The movement from man to machine seems to have been tough all over.

In 1938 I had yet another child. I was 39 years old. We named him Kenneth. He lived for only a couple of days. We had again prepared the crib, and the clothes, and all his big brothers and sisters looked forward to having a baby in the house again. But that little guy just didn't have a good body; probably because my own body was getting too old for childbearing. We didn't have money to bury him. Thankfully, our church put up the money for the casket and funeral, almost $100. That was a big gift in the Depression. The preacher prayed for his little soul, and I have every hope that I will see him again someday.

About that time Mr. Roney thought we needed more help around the farm. He didn't ask us about it. He just brought in another family to help—the McConnells. They were to live in one part of the house, while we stayed in the other. They were from somewhere down south, maybe Tennessee. It was like an invasion of the infidel hordes. I kept them in their part of the house, sometime chasing the kids with my broom. They weren't going to take over my house!

Pete had to work with Mr. McConnell and show him what to do. Pete let him have an easy job—feed the animals. You'd think anybody could do that. But not McConnell. He fed them, but not enough, and not often enough, so the horses started getting skinny.

"Aren't you feeding the horses?" Pete asked.

"Waaa sure am, Mistah Zweeah."

"How much are you feeding them?"

"Don' zactly know, I jes put down some hay till it looks bout 'nough."

Pete took over the horse feeding again.

Then there was the music. They had a guitar. I don't know how anyone could mis-tune a guitar so thoroughly. Each string was perfectly set to make a noise that contradicted and clashed with its neighbor. Yow! Then there was the singing, or was it howling?

> *In scarlet town, where I was born*
> *There lived a fair maid dwelling*
> *Made every youth cry 'well a day.'*
> *Her name was Barbara Ellen.*

I later heard the song on the radio. I barely recognized it: it was pretty. But when that little neighbor girl came over to teach it to us, it was awful. It was cute the first time she sang it, but that feeling did not last long. Maybe she was singing it in Irish or some other language. She sang every note from the bottom up; sluuuruup, sluuuruup. With that finely un-tuned guitar, the accent, and a sense of pitch that was relative to no known scale, it was painful.

We lived well out of town, so we had to go to town for supplies every week or two. We had our own eggs, and milk and pork, but needed many other things. We would bring in our own baskets, buckets or barrels to fill with oats for the horses. We got oatmeal for us, plus sugar, salt, vinegar, navy beans molasses, and apple cider, etc. We usually had the wagon pretty well loaded up.

We bought a 1924 Dodge, used, in spring of 1929. But when the Depression hit later that year we couldn't afford to drive. No one could. Gas cost 25 cents a gallon, and we were only making about a dollar a day. So we put the car up on blocks in the barn. The kids could walk to school and church, and if Pete needed something for the farm, he could ask Mr. Roney to borrow his truck. I hadn't learned how to drive yet, so it was no great loss to me.

One 4th of July, in the thick of the Depression, the kids so pestered Pete that he took the car out of the barn. After futzing around with the choke, the carburetor and the spark plugs, he started it up. We took it to Wicker Park, Munster, for the 4th of July picnic. Every year the Christian Schools from Lansing, Highland, and South Holland would put on a 4th of July festival there.

Before the 4th came along a man dressed up as a clown went up and down the streets, Pied Piper like, trying to get our kids to come to Lansing's 4th of July festival. We didn't let our kids go to that one though. We told our kids stay to with us and our church people. No telling what they might pick up at those secular picnics.

Kids from our area schools would meet up there at Wicker Park. At school they would ask each other "Are you going to the 4th?" Everyone knew what that meant. There were lots of games. One was ring throwing. You tried to throw rings over bottle tops. If you did, you won a prize like a small stuffed animal. The men played a game of strength. They would go over and hit a rubber pad with a giant mallet. Hitting the pad caused a clapper to go up like a thermometer. At the top of the inverted thermometer was a bell. The goal was to ring the bell by smashing the pad so hard the ball in the thermometer hit the top. Only the strongest men could do it. I can still remember Don Moes and John Zwart ringing the bell; they were both over 200 pounds, and construction workers.

And then there were the "nigger babies." I cringe to say it now, but we thought it was natural back then. They were pins that balanced on a board. They were painted black, with eyes, nose, and mouth. If you threw a ball and knocked one off the rail you won a prize. There were also races; foot races, and gunny-sack races. My brothers and sisters and their kids were all there too. The racing they all did at home or at Ma's house on

Sundays paid off on the 4th of July. They knew how fast everyone in the family was, so stood aside and let the fastest one in the family represent them in each age group. Lin once won a foot race for girls in the 2d and 3d grades. She got a prize: a blue ribbon and a quarter. Boy did the kids hang on to their quarters! We saved a little bit ahead of each 4th and gave each our kids a quarter for the day. They instantly became professional economists.

"What is the value of an ice-cream cone versus that of a horse-back ride?"

"If I buy a hot dog, can I also get a soda, and still have enough for a ride?"

My brother Al sold fruit, usually oranges brought up from Florida. Boy were they good. The money went to the Christian Schools.

Firecrackers were everywhere. There was no law against them then, and I think it gave the young guys a sense of power. They'd take a whole string of firecrackers, light them at once, and then throw the whole string. It went bam, bambambam, sixteen times. Sometimes those crazy kids would throw them close to us, just to scare us. Once, a naughty boy threw some just a few feet from a little baby. That poor little one cried and cried, but thankfully didn't get hurt.

Chicago had a fair of its own in 1933 and '34 and was it BIG! It was the *Century of Progress* which celebrated 100 years since the city of Chicago was incorporated. Admission was 50 cents. We scrimped and saved, so finally Pete and I could go. I'm sure Stan and Al would have liked to come along, but it was too much money.

It was amazing. The colors were spectacular. Building after building was painted or lit in bright colors. There were dinosaurs with little electric motors in them which made them move and seem alive. There was the "Sky Ride," that went hundreds of feet overhead, giving anyone who could afford it a view not only of Chicago, but of Wisconsin, Indiana and Michigan as well. The ship that Admiral Byrd had used to visit the Antarctic was harbored on Lake Michigan. There were airplanes, dirigibles, and blimps overhead. Mr. Edison showed off many of his new electric devices. All these amazing things made me think of Psalm 8.

> *When I consider thy heavens, the work of thy fingers, the moon and the stars, which thou hast ordained;*
> *What is man, that thou art mindful of him? and the son of man, that thou visitest him?*

Now Everyone is Poor

*For thou hast made him a little lower than the angels, and hast
    crowned him with glory and honour.*
*Thou madest him to have dominion over the works of thy hands;
    thou hast put all things under his feet:*
All sheep and oxen, yea, and the beasts of the field;
*The fowl of the air, and the fish of the sea, and whatsoever passeth
    through the paths of the seas.*
O Lord our Lord, how excellent is thy name in all the earth!

Sundays in Lansing

After our families moved back to the Illiana area, most of us also went to the same church, the First Christian Reformed Church of Lansing, Illinois. When we first came back, the services were still held in Dutch. But some of the younger families, ours included, lobbied the consistory to change to English, since we knew that we could never keep the young people in the church if we didn't speak the new language. Our services were usually around an hour and a half long. First came the *Call to Worship*:

> *O come, let us worship and bow down: let us kneel before the Lord our maker. For he is our God; and we are the people of his pasture, and the sheep of his hand.*

I always liked this call to worship. We are God's flock. I'd known quite a few sheep from our days in Montana, and they are helpless creatures. If they fall when their wool is full, they can't get up. They are prey to wolves, coyotes, or mountain lions. They can find grass on their own, but need to be led, lest they wander. So it's nice to think that I'm a sheep, and God is my shepherd. Then a song, usually a musical call to worship.

> *Come thou Almighty King, help us they name to sing*
> *Help us to praise, Father all glorious, o'er all victorious;*
> *Come and reign over us, Ancient of Days.*

Singing in our church was good. We weren't worried whether we sounded beautiful; we just opened our mouths and sang with full voices. Then, some women picked out the alto line, and men the tenor and bass. Pretty quick it sounded like a choir. I pity kids these days who don't feel they can sing, or never even get a chance. Then, the welcoming benediction:

> *Grace and Peace be unto you from the Lord Jesus Christ.*

Yes. It would sure be wonderful to have more grace and peace in our lives. Perhaps there were a few announcements here, and then we read the law, almost always the 10 Commandments.

I admit I often blanked out when the law was read. It was the same thing, week after week, and since I hadn't committed murder or adultery in the last week, I felt pretty safe. I would often use this time to check what was going on around me. I remember once seeing Mrs. H. sitting in the pew in front of me. Like the rest of us, she sewed her own clothes, but alas, she was not a good seamstress. The zipper on her dress looked like it had been laid out over a stretch of bad road. I was thinking what a bad seamstress she was, and that I would never go out in public with a dress like that. At that moment the preacher read the summary of the law: "Love the Lord your God with heart, soul and mind, and your neighbor as yourself." Nuts. Though I hadn't committed murder or adultery, I am pretty sure that what I was thinking about Mrs. H. wasn't love. I had better confess that.

Then the Assurance of Pardon:

If we confess our sins, he is faithful and just to forgive us our sins, and to cleanse us from all unrighteousness.

After that a hymn of pardon, something like "God be Merciful to Me." Then, the meat of the Sunday meal, the sermon.

Pete's second cousin, Daniel Zwier, took a call to be a preacher next door in Munster, Indiana. So sometimes we would go to hear him. He was a good preacher, who wrote out his sermons. He gave me a copy of one he wrote based on the First Question and Answer of the Heidelberg Catechism,

Q: What is your only comfort in life and in death?
A: That I am not my own, but belong in both body and soul, in life and in death, to my faithful savior Jesus Christ.

He preached from Isaiah 40: 1–2.

Comfort ye, comfort ye my people, saith your God. 2 Speak ye comfortably to Jerusalem, and cry unto her, that her warfare is accomplished, that her iniquity is pardoned: for she hath received of the Lord's hand double for all her sins.

Here's what he preached:

The general design of this part of Isaiah's prophecy is to comfort the afflicted people of God, who are contemplated as in Babylon, near the close of the exile. They had been punished for their sins, and the punishment began to bear fruit. They repented. And now the Lord, by the mouth of His prophet, addresses words of consolation to his people. He assures them that their warfare is accomplished and their iniquity pardoned, because full atonement has been made.

Now all this refers, of course, in the first place, to the people of Israel. But is has a further application. In the suffering of the Redeemer ample satisfaction has been made for all the sins of His people; a full atonement. The message of the Lord can be a message of consolation" Speak ye comfortably to Jerusalem!"

This is the standpoint of the Catechism. "What is your only comfort in life and death?" In considering the whole of the truth as revealed in God's Word, different standpoints may be taken. The Catechism aims to be a thoroughly practical book for the people. It combines the devotional element with the instructive. This is a striking question: "What is thy only comfort in life and death?" It is, in fact, the great, vital question of life. It answers to the natural desire of man for happiness. How can you be happy, supremely happy, in life as well as in death?

It needs no proof that the Catechism does not mean to put the happiness of man in place of the glory of God as man's chief end. The Catechism itself will furnish proof abundant. This feature is to be explained from the nature of the Catechism as a practical book for the people.

Comfort, in general, is a state of ease and rest of mind and heart that comes to us when pain, distress, or danger have been appeased or surpassed by the consideration of the possession of some great good.

In comforting, we use a balance. We place something of greater value over against the evil that has befallen us, something that will assuage our pain and grief. Our minds and hearts were disturbed, but by the consideration of some great good we are freed from care and distress, and the mind and heart feels again at rest.

For example: the people of God in the captivity were sore afflicted. By the rivers of Babylon they sat down and wept. But now the prophet comes with an announcement of a great deliverance. The days of weeping will soon end.

Comfort, therefore, presupposes misery. Ever since sin came into the world, man has been subject to misery; the world is full of it, a valley of tears. It matters not, whether rich or poor, old or young, learned or unlearned, we are hourly exposed to a thousand sources of misery. Affliction, in some of its many forms is the inevitable lot of men. The Christian is no exception. Yea, often it seems that he especially has to bear the burdens of life, while the wicked prosper.

Besides, the Christian knows not only earthly sorrows and disappointment as they are the lot of all men, but also spiritual distress. He is troubled by his sins, and tempted by his spiritual adversaries. He knows of doubts and temptations that the world knoweth not. These form not the least of his trials. In such time especially does he realize the need of comfort.

What shall we throw into the scale to outweigh all the trouble of this life? Add to this the fear of death, and the fearful expectation of judgment to come. No there is nothing in this world that can calm our fears and quiet our soul. The only comfort that will outweigh all our troubles is that provided by God! Sin lies at the bottom of all our misery, and no man is able to bear away sin. Only the removal of sin can take away all its consequences. Only the Lamb of God taketh away the sin of the world, and with sin, all its miseries.

The only comfort that meets our need is that provided by God Himself. Our Catechism says that it consists in this: "That I with body and soul, in life and death, am not my own, but belong to my faithful Lord and Saviour, Jesus Christ.

This is the one thing needful. If this is ours, we have perennial comfort. The ambition of natural man is to be his own master. As the cry of the French Revolution proclaimed: "No one above me; no God nor master!" He imagines that happiness will be obtained if he succeeds in throwing off all the fetters that bind him. Hence all the struggle and discomfort in this troubled world of ours. For it is a futile struggle! "I am my own master" means the same as "I am my own slave." I t means to be a tool of Satan! Man cannot be independent. He is a dependent creature. If he is not God's servant, he is Satan's slave, in bondage to corruption. He may imagine himself to be free, but it is a delusion, ending in terrible disappointment and misery.

The Christian knows better, being taught of God. He knows that as long as he is, or rather imagines he is, his own, he must provide for himself, and his cares and sorrows will multiply. But if Christ is his Lord, if he is His property, all cares are taken away, because He careth for His own. This is comfort that outweighs all miseries; comfort that will not fail, even in the face of all foes, sin, devil, and death. It meets every need.

It is a comfort in both life and death. There are many things in which the children of men seek comfort; the lust of the flesh, and *the lust of the eyes, and the vainglory of life. But this world passeth away, and the lust thereof. Death comes. And what do these things avail when death approaches you?*

It is a comfort pertaining to body and soul. Both belong unto Him, are redeemed by Him, will share in the fruits of His work. Man with all his science can alleviate some of the pains of the body, but is powerless to remove the sorrows of the soul. But Christ removes all cares. This gives true rest.

He has fully satisfied for all my sins. He has gone to the bottom of all misery; the only way to effect a complete cure! He has delivered me from all the power of the devil. From the worst slaver, from the most terrible bondage He has bought me with His precious blood, and no one can tear me, His rightful possession, away from Him.

He so preserves me that without the will of my heavenly Father not a hair can fall from my head. Nothing can harm me. He will make all things world together for my good, and make them subservient to my salvation; even those things that seem dark, and seem to be against me.

Finally thru His Holy Spirit, the Comforter, He assures me of eternal life. All the sufferings of this present life are not worthy to be compared to the glory that shall be revealed unto us. And in my sincerity to live henceforth unto Him, He makes this assurance double sure; because this proves that I am not my own bet belong to Him.

This is indeed comfort that leaves nothing to be desired. Is it yours?

We heard two sermons like this, week after week. A lot of our preachers, like him, were intellectuals. They went to seminary and studied Greek and Hebrew and lots of other things. I don't know how all those sermons have shaped me, but I'm sure they must have. To have some aspect of the Bible explicated and applied, week after week, no doubt directed and comforted us, perhaps in ways we will never know. And, hearing Pete's cousin preach like this made me wonder what Pete might have done with more education.

Keeping the kids quiet in church was always a chore. When they were babies, I stayed home with them, but once they were weaned Pete and I took turns. He'd go to the morning service, and I'd go to the evening service. The evening service was usually not till 7:00, since the farmers had to finish their afternoon milking and get cleaned up first. During the sermon we would pass out peppermints to the kids to keep them quiet, and if the preacher went especially long, they got two.

Sometimes the kids would have funny questions about what they heard in church.

"Why is there a bomb in Gilead?"

"What? A bomb?"

"Yes, the song says, "Theeyere is a bomb, in Gileaaad."

"Ah, no, that's a *balm* not a bomb. A balm is like some oil you put on a sore to make it feel better."

Or, "Why did they put Jesus in the gravy?'

"What?"

"Yes, at Easter we sing, "Low in the gravy lay."

"No, no, that's the grave, he, lay. Jesus was laid in the grave."

These questions were cute, but as the kids grew, they got sharper, especially from Al.

"If the world was created in six days, how do you explain those old dinosaur bones they found that are millions of years old?"

He had me and Pete on that one. "Well, maybe they were long days," or, "how can you be so sure those bones are that old?" "Why don't you ask the preacher about it?" But he never did; he didn't think it would sound too good for a teenager to challenge the minister.

Church services usually started at nine-thirty and ended at eleven. After the benediction, we would all file out. The preacher would shake everyone's hand. I can still remember how soft his hand was compared to Pete's. The kids stayed after church to go to Sunday School. While they were there, Ma would rush home to get out the raisin bread, cookies, coffee and tea ready for the whole Recker tribe. The adults (brothers, sisters and in-laws) would come over while the kids were in Sunday School. One of us then had to go back to church to pick up the kids. But we'd often get chatting and forget about them. Thankfully, Ma's house was not too far from the church, so if the kids had to walk it wasn't hard on them. Often, one of us would look at our watch, slap our head, and speed back to church, only to meet the nephews and nieces walking down the street.

When all of us were there, there were 43 cousins! Upon arrival, each child would have to give grandma and grandpa a kiss. Ma and Pa stood, waiting, for each one. The kids could easily reach Grandma Recker at 4' 11". In fact, when they got to be as tall as she was, they always wanted to "measure," back to back, to prove that they had grown taller than grandma. But she would have nothing of it.

"We're not going to measure! I don't care how tall you are. I'm your grandma—now give me a kiss!"

With Pa, they all had to look up, or stand on tip-toes. Before getting to his lips they'd have to navigate their way around his mustache. He knew they were trying to stay away from his whiskers, so he bobbed and weaved like a prize-fighter, getting in as many tickles per kiss as possible.

If it was summertime the kids played outside; kicked the ball, played catch, or rode on the swings. In the winter the kids were usually in the basement, which was unfinished and block, so they could do some fairly rough stuff down there too.

The adults stayed upstairs. We would talk and joke and catch up with each other. One sister-in-law loved to dominate the conversation with tales of what her children were doing. She'd bring pictures, and we all had to admire them. Someone mentioned that their daughter was becoming quite a piano player.

"Ruth, come over here and play that piece you're learning."

"Oh mom, it's not ready yet."

"Well, no one here is going to care, you can show us."

"Dick, is it true you can walk on your hands? That must take a lot of balance."

One Sunday, brother Bill informed us his son Rob felt called to the ministry. When Pa heard this he bent over, shook his head, and fought back the tears.

"Bill, when you were a young man in Montana you wanted to be a minister. But look, God saved that for your son. Wonderful; just wonderful."

The kids always had a great time with all their cousins. Most of the cousins were about the same age as our kids, so they had playmates left and right. In the summer it was especially fun since they could go outside and play ball, or tag, or hide and seek. Once, they managed to get five of them into a forty-gallon barrel. They were squeezed in there like little tadpoles, but happy little tadpoles.

On one of these Sundays two of my brothers-in-law, John and Jake, started to bother Stan about going to work.

"When are you going to get to work, Stan? You're thirteen years old now. You should be helping your Ma and Pa with the bills." I stepped in.

"He's going to High-School. All my kids are going to get a good education. They are smart and can do great things with the minds God gave them."

I wished someone had stepped in for me when I was that age, but times were different from 1912 to the late 1930s when Stan and Al were teens. The whole country was going to school longer since fewer kids had to stay home to work.

One thing we did not talk about on Sundays was the preacher. I know a lot of families had "roast preacher," for Sunday dinner, but not us. Oh, occasionally we might mention that something in the sermon really struck us, but we did not go over the message point by point, searching for heresy, poor logic, or weak delivery. We felt that the preacher was appointed by God, and it was not our place to criticize.

We usually went to Ma and Pa's place, but in later years took turns going from one of our houses to the other. Sometimes it was at my house, and I would have to prepare like crazy on Saturday night. We'd get all the dishes out and find as many chairs as possible. We would set up a special small table for the little ones. Everyone brought something, so I didn't have to do all the cooking. If we were getting together at my house, I would make the main meat dish, one of my sisters or sisters-in-law would make a salad, another would make a vegetable dish, another a dessert, and so forth.

Once, my rotten little sister-in law played a trick on me. We both had the same set of dishes, a nice Dutch blue Delft set of plates, cups and saucers. I had just gotten mine. We had the dinner at her house. As usual, the women did the cleaning up after the meal, and my sister-in-law put the dishes away, hers into her cupboards and mine into the basket I had brought along. Well, when I got home, I opened the basket to put my dishes away and found that most of the dishes were older, and chipped. They weren't my nice new ones, but her old ones. I was so mad, I wanted to go wring her neck!

I'm sure she would have sweetly responded, "Oh Minnie, we both have the same dishes, how was I to know whose were whose?" I fumed. I talked to Pete about it and showed him the dishes. He was not going to get involved in this one. A problem between me and my sister-in-law was not something he wanted any part of.

Our church always supported missionaries too. There was one woman from the Christian Reformed Church named Tena Huizenga, who had gotten us involved with the Tiv tribe in Nigeria. I met her once at a Women's Missionary Union meeting. These meetings were organized by the Classis, so all the church women from the Christian Reformed church in the Illiana area were invited. We had prayer meetings and raised money for our missionaries. The annual meeting was quite a social event, since church women from the whole area got together. We all wore our best dresses; and if we didn't have a good one, we made a new one, or borrowed. We rode together to the church where the meeting was held, in Munster or Highland, Indiana, or South Holland or Lansing, Illinois.

Tena Huizenga dressed up in the native costumes of the Nigerian people, wearing bright, flowing batik robes, and she brought along some of their musical instruments. She played the drums and showed us how. She talked about the church work there. It was very hard going at first, but when the Tiv people learned that we really wanted to help them, they started to come around. When we admitted that their drum music would be better for them than our hymns, they converted to Christ by the thousands. Our church took care of their physical needs too, by sending teachers, farmers, and doctors as missionaries.

We all sang missionary hymns at the meetings, like "From Greenland's Icy Mountain." A few hundred women singing in full voice was beautiful. My own voice is not particularly good, but when added to those of hundreds of others it came off as sweet praise to God. The main goal of the meetings was to raise money. Not many of us had much, so we concocted events at which we could sell things. I made what I must say was a beautiful quilt and sold it at a fair. Others made pies, embroidered, and did hand crafts. The food at the Women's Missionary Union was inevitably tasty. No one would just throw something together for an event like that; we all brought our favorite recipes. Over lunch we could catch up with each other and find out about relatives or friends who had moved. We could also catch up on the romances our kids or grandkids were having.

We were decades away from having women as preachers in our church, but didn't think of it as a problem. We women contributed to the church as much or more than the men did, just in different ways.

L-R. Ahlrich Jr,. Alhrich Sr., Minnie, Lena, baby Alice,
Boudewina Kok Recker, William

Peter and Minnie's wedding photos

Minnie in Montana

Pete in Montana

AUCTION!

As I am going to move to Illinois, I will sell at Public Auction at my place 9 miles south of Rapelje and 2 1-2 miles north-west of the Al Thomas ranch, on

Wednesday, April 14

The following described property, to-wit:

4 Head of Horses, 3 Mules
1 white horse 1520 lb 1 brown horse 1300 lb
1 black horse 1100 lb 1 blue saddle horse 900 lb
1 buckskin mule 1100 lb 1 white mule 1100 lb
1 brown mule 900 lb

11 Head of Cattle
1 blue cow 7 years fresh May 1st
1 red cow 6 years fresh in June
1 red cow 6 years fresh now
1 red heifer 2 years fresh soon
1 yearling steer 3 heifers 3 young calves

2 Hogs
1 sow will farrow May 1st
1 barrow

50 Chickens
2 sets work harness   1 buggy harness
1 heavy stock saddle

Machinery
1 LaCrosse 3 bottom disk plow
1-7 ft Case disk harrow
1 John Sulky plow   1-70 hay rake
1 tandem disk harrow   1 P&O engine gang
1 Emerson engine four disk plow
1 John Deere disk plow   1 garden cultivator
1 wagon with box   1 spring wagon

Household Goods
1 Ideal range   1 heater   1 kitchen cabinet
1 dining table   6 chairs   2 rocking chairs
1 Singer sewing machine   1 dresser
1 9 by 12 linoleum rug   1 high chair
1 baby crib   1 bed stead   1 spring
1 washing machine   100 fruit jars
2 5 gallon cream cans
1 Empire cream seperator 500 lb

Many other arcticles too numerous to mention.

Sale starts at 11 a. m.   Free lunch at noon.

TERMS, CASH.   Nothing to be removed till settled for.

PETER ZWIER, Owner.

M. J. Visser,   W. J. Soderlind,
   Auctioneer.   Clerk.

Auction in Montana

Simon and Peter Zwier

Stan and Al

Don and Irene

Linda

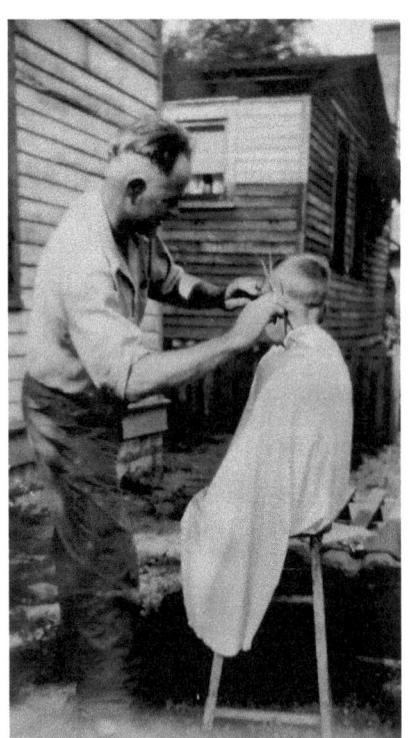

Pete cutting Stan's hair

Boudewina and Ahlrich

After the wedding. Nellie Boxum, Lena Recker, Alice Recker, Dick Recker, Ann Zwier, Peter Zwier, and Minnie Zwier

Rena B

Son Al

Apple picking in Washington

Pete at Minnie's birthday

Harvest. Pete, Al, Stan, Lin in foreground

L-R Dick Recker, Minnie Zwier, Alice Smit, Lena Kikkert, Christine Stammis, Bill Recker, Ahlrich Recker Jr, Front: Ahlrich Recker Sr., Boudewina Kok Recker

Minnie in carriage

Adult children L–R Al and Irene DeVries, Corky and Stan Zwier. Minnie. Don and Esther Zwier. Paul and Linda Van Til

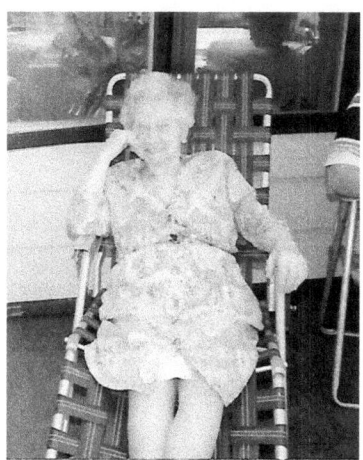

Lawn chair at Stan's

Minnie, months before her death, with baby Marie Van Til

A Woman's Work is Never Done

SEWING WAS A HOBBY for me as much as it was a job. And as I look back on it, it was also probably recreation, and maybe even art. Since it was such a productive hobby, I spent quite a bit of time on it, starting early on. I bought a Singer treadle sewing machine for myself in 1921, a year before we got married. That's the kind you power with your foot. The pedal is about two feet wide and one foot deep and is yoked to a pulley whose belt powers the machine. You move your foot up and down like keeping time to a march. I can still hear the four-to-one stitch-to-pedal sounds in my head from working that machine: dadadada, dadadada, dadadada.

A few months before our wedding I ordered white material from the Sears catalog and sewed my own wedding dress, just as my sister Lena had done. It came out quite nicely: lots of lace and a full-length train. When Stanley was born two years later, I took it apart and sewed a beautiful white skirt for his bassinet. I also used left-over pieces for Pete's shirts. I guess I'm not especially sentimental about such things. I know some women hang on to their wedding dresses for years and years, thinking maybe one day their daughter will wear it. But I really needed that material for other things, so it didn't make sense to put the dress in storage and order new material. Better I should use that nice material for my baby and my husband. I certainly wasn't planning to get married again.

Re-using that dress was only the beginning of my recycling efforts. If Pete wore out parts of a jacket or pants, I would slit the seams, wash the pieces, and lay out a pattern for a girl's dress or a boy's shirt on them. I was always surprised how much material was in a sleeve of a man's shirt or jacket. Split open, jacket sleeves were usually about two feet long and one foot wide, and if there wasn't quite enough material, I would improvise and make a collar or cuff out of a contrasting material. Sometimes

I would even put soft fur collars on jackets for Irene and Lin. They often received compliments on how cute they looked.

When it came to laying out a pattern, and especially using a plaid or print material, everything had to be laid out exactly so it would line up correctly at the seams . . . lots of pinning and basting. When sewing with corduroy, the wale all had to go in the same direction, or it would look like two different pieces of material. Sewing a zipper in the back of a dress also required patience and skill, since it always tended to bunch up.

When we moved back to the Chicago area I tried to get together with my three sisters one afternoon a week for talk, tea, and cookies. Often, we would exchange *Buttrick* patterns or bring along clothing we had sewn for ourselves or our children and talk about our creations.

"Well, Tini, that looks nice," or, "Who'd you make that for?" Or, "Looks like a lot of the dress patterns this year are knee length." Or, "Did one of your boys get that rabbit fur for you?"

Years later Singer came out with a kit to motorize their sewing machines, and Pete was delighted to hook it up for me. "Look here," I remember him saying. "They've got it set up so that the pulley from the treadle fits on the drive of the electric motor. Whoever designed this sure was smart." Now I could plug in the machine and give my ankles a rest. It's the same machine I have today.

Once I made a cape for Irene from a piece of black wool I'd saved. I trimmed the collar with a rabbit fur that Don got for me. He liked to trap rabbits, setting traps all around the farm. When he caught one, he would gut and skin it. We ate the meat, and I was able to use the fur in my sewing. Sometimes Don caught raccoons too, and once he even caught a mink down by the creek. He was able to sell that mink fur in town for a nice price. We let him keep the money from that.

One day Stan, Al, and Irene were heading home from school, and little Irene was running along, trying to keep up with her big brothers' long strides, when her cape fell off. Since she was afraid of being left behind, she kept running and let the cape fall on the muddy path. When she got home without the cape, I immediately noticed and asked her, "Where is that new cape I made for you?"

"Well, Stan and Al were going so fast, I couldn't keep up, and it fell off."

"Stan," I said, "you go back right now and get that cape. I worked hard on it, and Irene needs it."

Thankfully the cape was right there in the path where it had fallen off. Stan brought it back, and I cleaned it up so she could wear it again.

It made me proud when I saw Rene, and later Lin, going around in the nice clothes I made for them. Even though we could never afford store-bought clothes, they were a couple of the nicest dressed girls in their school.

Irene was a giggler. It didn't take much to get her going. If one of her brothers made a funny face at her she giggled. If something funny was on the radio, she giggled. If the dog was wearing a skirt that Lin had put on her, she giggled. Lin, though not so giggly, was also sweet. She was always smiling and never had a harsh word for anyone. I guess she got that from Pete.

Both Irene and Lin were always reading. Every week or two we would go to our little town library, but after a while, they had read almost all the books written for their age, so we went to the big library in Chicago Heights. That got to be quite an outing. We would all get ready, get in the car, and head out. Don would go too. We could easily spend a couple of hours browsing: "Look at this one, Mom. It's a biography of Teddy Roosevelt. Didn't you say you saw him once when you were a girl? Didn't he create all those parks out west?" "This one is about whales and dolphins. Have you ever seen one?" "What's a 'Mohican'?"

We found so many interesting things to read: histories, biographies, novels, stories from ancient times to the present. It was hard to believe that we could get all the books we wanted just by showing our library card. Sometimes the kids took out a dozen books per week, which was the maximum allowed. We gave the librarian our card, and she wrote down all the titles and then stamped the due date on the card that went in the back folder of each book. Lin liked books and libraries so much she eventually became a librarian.

The girls worked hard too. Of course during the school year they had to go to class and do their homework, but when they got home they worked. They never had to find a summer job either, since the farm and the house were everyone's job. Pete and the boys didn't see all the work we did, whereas you could look out at the field and immediately tell what they had done. In fact, I often repeated the saying: "Man works from sun to sun, but woman's work is never done."

But I learned the hard way that being sarcastic about that with Pete didn't really pay off. Sometimes he'd say,

"So, Minnie, what did you do today?"

And I'd answer, "Oh, nothing, just sat around and read."

And then he'd put his hand on my shoulder, smile, and slyly say, "Good for you. Then you probably saved up plenty of energy for bedtime."

I'd rolled my eyes and lift my head to the heavens. What do you do with a man like that?

From early on, maybe five years old, the girls were put in charge of the chickens. They fed them grain, filled their water dishes, and collected the eggs. Back then we didn't have fancy coops in which the eggs came sliding out the bottom onto a rack. You had to reach in and get the eggs from beneath each hen. Usually this meant pushing the chicken off her roost with one hand and grabbing the egg out from under her with the other. But hens don't like being pushed around. They want to keep setting on the eggs, so they would peck the hand that was trying to move them or take their eggs. The girls would often come back from the chicken coop with red marks all over their small, soft hands.

Slaughtering the chickens was a job for the guys, but we all came to help and watch. Pete, Stan, or Al would grab a chicken that was done laying, or a young rooster, bring it to the chopping block, lay its head on the block, and cut it off at the neck with a cleaver. The body of the chicken would fall to one side, and the head to the other. The head would never budge, but boy did the body. It would run wildly, from side to side, and even backwards till all the nerves quit moving. It was quite a sight, and the kids were entertained by it. Then it was clean-and-pluck time, and the women were certainly involved in that. Gut the chicken, throw it in some steaming hot water, and pluck the feathers—a messy job.

Housecleaning was a big job too. We didn't have any electric vacuums early on, so we used a broom on the hardwood floor, and then a mop, which was usually just the same broom with a damp rag tied round the bristles. The men took off their work boots when they came in from the field, but our floors still got lots of dust and dirt on them. I wasn't one of those "Crazy Clean" Dutch women, but I didn't want dirt and dust all over my floors either. Since the windows were open for most of the summer, the dust came in on its own from outside too. So we swept the floors daily, except Sundays, and mopped them weekly.

I often passed cleaning time by singing or humming. I had many hymns and popular songs memorized, so my repertoire was pretty wide. I remember one particularly pretty tune that dated from Civil War times whose words were rather grim:

One wore blue, and one wore grey.
As they marched along the way
A fife and drum began to play
All on a beautiful morning
[Verse 2]
One was gentle, and one was kind,
One came home, one stayed behind.
A cannonball don't pay no mind
All on a beautiful morning
[Verse 3]
Cannonball, don't pay no mind
Though you're gentle, or you're kind.
It don't think of the folks behind
All on a beautiful morning
[Verse 4]
Two girls waiting by the railroad track
For their darlings to come back.
One wore blue, and one wore black
All on a beautiful morning.

The men oversaw the farm, but we took care of the vegetable garden. We planted lettuce and onions when the frost came out of the ground in early spring. Asparagus and strawberry plants stayed in the ground year around and bore early, yielding three or four small harvests each spring. The first green beans then made an appearance by late June, and in good years we got three or four picks per planting. The first pick was the best, when the beans were long and tender. By the third or fourth they got a bit tough, and you could clearly see each seed within the short pod. Tomatoes came in later, in August and September, and we canned bushels of them in quart-sized Ball jars. We added our own green peppers and onions to the tomatoes so we could use the sauce for stews and soups.

Canning tomatoes took some time. First you had to pick them, of course, lots of them. We would typically have a dozen or so tomato plants that yielded a few bushels, so picking was a half-day job. Then you had to rinse the dirt off them and core them with a paring knife. The next step was to boil them in a big pot. (You needed a nice big canning pot that held about four gallons.) Once they'd boiled and cooled you took them out and pulled their skins off. Then you cut them into pieces and put them in the jars along with the chopped green pepper and onions. The jars had to be very clean and preferably warm. Then you put the lids on, which had a rubber seal around the rim, and finally tightened it down with a screw-on cap. You then put the jars in boiling water for about an hour. If the lids sealed, you could hear them make a little "pop" as they cooled. But there was always one or two that didn't seal, so we would either make something with those tomatoes on the spot or try again to seal them. Since we had many bushels of tomatoes, we had to boil pot after pot, starting in August for a few days when the tomatoes first came in and then going on again in September or even October if the frost didn't get to the later ones.

Once we had the jars filled, we put them in the cellar, and during the winter we would go down for something almost every day. With those tomatoes I could quickly make some chili, soup, or spaghetti. We canned the peaches from our tree too, using more or less the same process. I also often made and canned applesauce that tasted far better than anything you could buy at the store.

Raspberries grew along the fence row and yielded two crops each summer. Picking them usually entailed a small loss of blood, thanks to their tiny little thorns. But it was well worth the pain, since we could eat as many as we wanted along the way. We'd clean and bag the ones we didn't eat and put them in the ice box. Of course, while we were canning and freezing I was able to spend time with my daughters. We'd talk about all kinds of things:

"So, Irene, did the girls like the new dress I made you?"

"Oh, yes. They wondered how you got the lace like that."

"Ruth's mom made her one that was pretty too, but in blue."

"So, Lin, you aren't doing quite so well in math. Do you like your math teacher?"

"He's OK. But I just don't like math very much. I'd much rather just take English or History courses."

I count those times as real blessings. I got to get close to my girls at the same time I was teaching them a useful skill. I knew that when they got married and had homes of their own they would continue to do the canning and the sewing and the gardening, just as I did thanks to my mother.

By Thanksgiving we really did have a lot to be thankful for. Our pantry was full and ready for the winter, when there would be no more crops. We weren't completely self-sufficient; we still had to buy flour to make the bread, and oatmeal for breakfast, and molasses, and salt, and many other things, but we always had something to eat. Not a day, not even during the Depression, did we go hungry.

Every Saturday night the girls and I would listen to "Your Hit Parade," on the radio. It played all the popular songs of the day, like "I've Got a Gal, in Kalamazoo," or "Don't Sit Under the Apple Tree with Anyone Else but Me." Neither Rene nor Lin were great singers, but that's OK. I'd listen with them and try to sing along. We also liked to listen to The Lone Ranger or Little Orphan Annie on the radio. They were dramas that always left you in suspense at the end of an episode, so you'd have to tune in again the next week to find out what happened next.

Irene went to Bloom High School during the war years, 1941–1945. Talk of the war dominated everything. Like her, most of the kids had a brother or close relative serving overseas. She was one of the very few Dutch girls there among the largely Italian kids. She got a good education and was a good student. One day she got in a little trouble for talking too much, and the teacher had her stand in the corner with her hands held over her head, a common punishment. Later she heard two of the men teachers talking.

"That little Irene is sure developing nicely, isn't she?"

"Sure is, I think I'll punish her that way all the time."

In those days, men felt it was fine to talk about women that way, but thankfully, it never was more than talk.

When Irene was in High School, she wasn't allowed to go to the dances, since our church prohibited it, and that was pretty tough on her. Some of those Italian guys were pretty good looking and would have loved to teach her how to dance. She did date one Italian Catholic boy—Sammy Bova a few times, which made me extremely nervous. We all knew how horrible it could be if you married a Catholic: the children would all be baptized and raised in the Catholic Church. I was worried.

I talked to Rene about it, and with many tears she agreed to stop dating him. But I had to ask myself: Why am I so wary of Catholics? What I remembered from my own childhood was simple: "Stay away from them!" You can be good neighbors with the Catholics, but don't you dare join up with them in marriage or church. Other Dutch Reformed people had the same feelings, if not stronger.

I did some reading to learn why my concerns about the Catholics were so grave. I discovered that the Dutch have been oppressed by the Catholics for centuries—a long, ugly history. In the Netherlands, the ten Northern provinces are Protestant and the southern three provinces along with contemporary Belgium are Catholic. This was not decided in a committee meeting, but was the result of more than 100 years of struggle, torture, and war.

When the Reformation broke out, the Netherlands was under the control of the arrogant Spanish kings. Spain had established itself in the Americas only decades before and was stealing as much gold from there as it could lay its hands on. It was also spreading Catholicism at the point of the sword, under direct papal orders. In the early 16th century, when Charles V of Spain reigned over the Netherlands, there were only a few Protestants, which didn't bother him. But later in that century, by the time his son Philip II assumed the throne, Calvinist Protestantism had grown rapidly in the Lowlands. Philip vowed to eradicate it, seeing it as his holy mission. He introduced the Spanish Inquisition to the Netherlands, having earlier perfected its techniques on Jews and Muslims.

Philip appointed a Dominican monk, "Torquemada," to root out Protestantism in the Netherlands. Torquemada had free rein, and used it. Over the course of 18 years he had over ten thousand Dutch men and women burned alive. Nearly one hundred thousand others were imprisoned, had their property confiscated, or were tortured. The torture included all of the then popular instruments for inflicting pain—fire, water, weights, screws in fingers, etc. There were no trials, nor appeals. If two people accused you, you were dead. And since the people who accused you got your property, they were highly motivated. Pope Alexander VI officially approved and blessed this "heavenly remedy."

Meanwhile the Calvinist Reformation had been growing in France as well. Jean Calvin was a Frenchman born a generation after Luther. While a law and literature student in Paris he became a convert to Luther's cause, and ruled French speaking Geneva from 1541 to 1564. His political views included the belief that lesser rulers could and even should throw off higher rulers if they had become unjust. Francis I, king of France at the time, felt threatened, and had the French Calvinists, called Huguenots, jailed, tortured, and killed. Over three centuries of sporadic persecution many of these Huguenots fled to the Netherlands.

One of the thousands of these French refugees was my great grandmother, Maria Konje, who married Dirk Kok. She brought her fear of Catholics with her, along with that head of beautiful, black hair which has been passed down for generations in our family of otherwise fair-haired Dutch.

This long-winded story about the history of France, Spain and the Netherlands continues to affect our family, and does so for many Dutch.

As a nation, the Netherlands suffered dreadfully at the hands of the Catholics. And since thousands of Jewish and Protestant refugees from Spain and France kept coming to Holland, they added to the catalogue of bad feelings toward the Catholics with each new arrival.

Since the Chicago area was so diverse, we always had some Roman Catholic neighbors. I tried to put aside my prejudices about them and did get along pretty well. I often talked with Mrs. O'Donnell, who also had five kids. They were getting Marian Catholic School going in Chicago Heights at about the same time our church people we were starting Illiana Christian in Lansing.

"How are your kids doing at Marian?"

"Good, thank you. Mary Claire is in the choir and Steven is a wrestler."

"Oh nice. Are all the teachers nuns?"

"No, a few of them are, but in the High School there are quite a few lay teachers. The grade school, St. Ann's has mostly nuns as teachers."

"Are they quite strict?"

"Some are," she said with a chuckle, "but not as bad as you've probably heard."

We often chatted, and she got to be a good friend. But I always wondered how she could put up with all that Catholic stuff. There are just too many things that strike us Protestants as strange. Like: why don't their priests marry? Most if not all the disciples, and certainly St. Peter, were married, but they don't let their priests marry today. They are supposed to be celibate, but does anyone really think that putting a white collar on a man will neuter him? No man I ever met!

Then there's their view on marriage. For some reason they made that into a sacrament. As a result, Catholics who want a divorce can't get one, since a sacramental marriage is supposedly fixed for all eternity. So instead of divorcing, Catholics "annul" their marriage, even though it might have lasted 20 or 30 years and included half-a-dozen kids. What a trick!

Years later I remember trying to explain Catholicism to Irene's daughter Jackie. She was maybe ten years old, had been attending Lansing Christian School and talking with some of her own Catholic neighbors in Munster. She had questions about the Lord's Supper.

"So when they take communion, they think Jesus is really in the bread?"

"Well, yes," I answered, "they believe that Jesus is physically present in that little piece of bread."

"How does he get in there?"

"They say that when the priest rings a little bell, the body of Jesus comes into the bread."

She was dumbfounded. "Really?"

"Isn't Jesus in heaven now?"

"Yes,"

"So he jumps down into the bread from heaven?"

"I guess so."

"Well what if the Catholics in Lansing need his body at the same time some other Catholics in Africa need it?"

"I guess there's enough to go around."

Jackie was a smart little kid. But she was stumped.

"I don't get it either," I said.

A Dogs' Vocation

Our dogs seemed to think that God created the world for them. And perhaps he did.

We always had dogs on the farm, usually rat terriers. They were little guys, about 12 pounds of fun, fur and fury. They had random spots of black and brown sprinkled over a generally white coat. Their noses were sharp and pointy, as were their ears and attitudes. They walked around as if they owned the house, the barn, and the land; and any person who came on the property had better get their permission to enter. They were also unfailingly playful and loyal.

Whenever I got the broom out of the closet, they thought it meant I wanted to play a game of "Push and Sweep" with them. The rules of the game were: whenever I pushed the broom, they nipped at it and jumped on it. They made games out of everything. Whenever I picked up the kids' toys, they grabbed the toy and insisted on a tug-of-war. Whenever I was cooking, they sat at or on my feet, looking up at me with big, pleading, brown eyes, licking their lips in anticipation of their portion.

We had a dog—Rocky, and a bitch—Junie. And then we had their offspring. Every time Junie was in heat, Rocky took care of business, chasing her around the yard and mounting her in fevered passion. When Junie was great with puppies, the kids would look at her and sing a popular tune, "June is Bustin Out All Over." Three months later Junie would deliver a litter of six or eight puppies. We humans served as the midwives.

Junie would go in the basement, to the box we had prepared for her. We kept an eye on her, and when we knew she was due, followed her downstairs to her box. She would lie down and the birthing would start; first one little puppy nose coming out, then the whole puppy in its thin and slippery casing. We took the birth sack off the puppy with our fingers, being careful to remove it from the nose so the newborn could breathe. We gently pulled on the head and front feet of the next pup to help Junie along. Then another came. Repeat process. Clean off the after-birth and ensure that the new pup was breathing. Repeat five or six more times, depending on the size of the litter.

Once she gave birth to eight puppies. We left her with those puppies nestled at her side, nursing sweetly. When we came down later to see the puppies she had given birth to one more. But since we didn't clean the after-birth from that one's mouth, it died, a sad moment of death on a day of birth.

There are few things more entertaining than a litter of puppies. Once they can crawl and walk a bit, they are a constant, wriggling pile of joy and activity. They nipped at each other, at me, at Pete and at the kids. Their little teeth were like needles. Ouch! They played and played and then slept and ate. Their little noses always led them on new adventures. Once they could get out of the basket they wandered through the whole house. But puppies are hard on rugs, floors, and anything else they can reach with mouth or paw. The pee, the poo and the scratches quickly wore through our flooring, and my patience. But they loved to be held, and having four or five at a time on my lap was endearing. They all wanted to be held and petted at the same time. And they all crawled over me and the kids whenever we let them out of the box. They were easy to entertain. For them, a little strip of cloth was considered a wonderful toy. They would pull on it, chew it, and then carry it off and hide it, as if it were a great treasure.

We let the puppies outside if they were born in the spring or summer, and invited neighbors and friends to come and watch them "run" with their short little legs. Some who saw them inevitably wanted a dog for their own house or farm. There always seemed to be good homes for them. When Rocky and Junie got older, we kept a couple of their pups for ourselves—Junie Jr. and Rocky II.

When Linda was little, maybe four or five, she used to play with the dogs, as if they were her dolls. She would find strips of cloth or elastic and wrap them around the dogs' heads and waists. Around the head they became bonnets; around the waist they were skirts. Now dressed, they were ready to go out. She would put them in a baby carriage and parade them up and down Torrence Avenue. Of course they would jump out or fall out, but that was part of the game. Linda, the good little mother, would carefully re-arrange their "clothes" and put them back in the carriage.

When they were only a month or two old, we would hold them up over the water tank for the cattle. When we put them close to the water their little paws started to churn. They instinctively knew how to do the Dog Paddle.

When we moved, which was often, the dogs were carried out in the last load, riding in the car with us. They would tentatively walk into the new, strange, house. They suspiciously stuck their noses into every corner of every room till they found a good place to lie down. They were content in every house we lived in, since they were with us.

When moving, the boys would use them as "pack hounds," tying an old ice-skate strap around them and then loading them up with stuff. The dogs would look at the packs, clumsily walk around with them on, and wonder what it was all about. They provided entertainment for the whole family.

The boys and the dogs were a delightful match. When the boys were little they would go out and play with the dogs for hours on end. Two boys, two dogs, a stick and a ball were all it took to keep them happy and active. First the boys threw the sticks and the dogs fetched them. Then the dogs ran away with the stick and played keep-away from the boys. Then one of the boys found a long stick and challenged the dog to a tug-of-war. The dog pulled on the stick like his life depended on it. And growl! Wow did they growl. Pull the stick—Aaarrrghhh. Get the ball before the boys could reach it—GGrrrrr. You would think they were trained killers by the sounds they made. They weren't in the least bit tough or mean with us, though. When we called, they came quickly, with tails furiously wagging. They suspected that we had food for them, or a new game to play.

But one day we found out that they were indeed killers; rat killers. Our neighbor Mr. Wiltjers came onto the yard. He lived a few blocks away on a little farm like ours. He asked Pete,

"Can I borrow your dogs one of these days? I cleared out some of the trees on my property last summer, and the wood pile has been lying around all winter. I moved some branches from the pile there yesterday, and out sprang three rats. They must have been nesting in there all winter, and I don't know how many there are. Could you bring your dogs over to get the rats for me?'

"Sure," said Pete. "Why don't we say next Wednesday afternoon? I've got some things to take care of around here this week, but next week should work out fine."

Well, when the kids heard about this the excitement grew and grew.

"When are Rocky and Junie going to get the rats? Wednesday? Can I come? Do you think there are a lot of them? Will Junie be scared of a really big one? They are rat terriers, aren't they?"

Oh yes. On Wednesday they all came with Pete and the dogs. So did I. A fun event like this was not to be missed. We couldn't afford to go to the zoo, so this was the next best thing. We walked the dogs on their leashes down to the Wiltjer house, all in a parade—me, Pete, Stan, Al, Irene and Don (Lin was too little). The kids were excited. We got to their house and Mrs. Wiltjer made us some lemonade and had some cookies for the kids. The kids were as polite as necessary, but could hardly contain their enthusiasm for the big hunt. The Wiltjer kids were primed too. They had two girls and a boy, about the ages of Don and Irene. Finally, the great moment arrived.

"I suppose we ought to let those dogs have a look at the wood pile," said Mr. Wiltjer.

Pete nodded.

The dogs were beside themselves with joy. The very thing they had been bred and raised for was now about to happen. They pulled on the leashes as if they knew their purpose in life lie just ahead of them in that brush. We let them loose. They sniffed, and ran, and barked, and sniffed, and wagged, and jumped. The rats apparently knew when it was not a good time to go out for a walk, so Mr. Wiltjer pulled out a big elm branch. (Many elms had to be cut down because of Dutch Elm disease.) A brown rat came dashing out of the pile. Junie was there. She ran him down and clamped her jaws on the back of his neck. The rat continued to move, but Junie shook it by the back of the head. The neck broke, and that rat would never move again.

Another rat came out, this time a mottled brown one. Rockie was on the spot. The rat ran fast, but Rockie was far faster. Those short little terrier legs could go from a full stop to full speed in two steps. He got this one a little far back on the body. The rat turned and gouged at Rocky, narrowly missing his face. Rocky let go of the back of the rat and dove for its neck. He then shook the rat with such ferocity that I thought the dogs' head might come loose with the rats'. He picked up the rat, wagged his tail, and promenaded over to me. He laid the rat down at my feet as if he were offering me gold, frankincense and myrrh. I patted him on the head.

"Good dog. Good dog."

But it was far from over. Mr. Wiltjer was right. A family, if not an entire tribe of rats had taken up residence in that brush pile.

Now everyone got in on the act. The boys pulled branches out from all sides of the pile. About every third branch yielded a new rat. Junie caught a brown one with a white muzzle. It nearly got back into the pile, but Don shoed it back out with a stick. Junie nailed it. One bite and it was done. Rocky was barking ecstatically. His destiny in life was fulfilled. He was so fast that the rats had no chance. And when it looked like one might be getting away, one of us stood in front of the rat to keep it from going back into the wood pile. As a result, we saw the mayhem right at our feet. First rat, then dog; the quick pursuit, the bite, and then the victorious dog shaking its head so that it looked as if the rat would be split in two. When the action slowed down a bit Rocky and Junie would go back to their kills.

"Did that mottled brown one twitch?" Rockie wondered, "I better give her another good shaking."

"Did I see another one under that branch? Junie puzzled, "I better go dig around it and check again."

"Hold it;" suggested Rockie, "I don't remember whether I broke that one's neck. I better give it another good shake right behind the ears."

Those dogs were happy! The kids were excited too. They had known Rocky and Junie as fun playmates, not as trained killers. We went around and picked up the dead rats, over a hundred of them. Forever afterward this day was known in family memory as "The Great Rat Massacre."

When we got home, they were friendly little playmates again, chasing each other around the barn, catching the ball, and fetching a stick. We fed them an especially meaty supper that night. Mr. Wiltjer gave us a couple of dollars, "for dog food," he said. We never bought dog food, and he probably knew that. Why pay for something in a bag when we had plenty of table scraps in the house? That night, they were tired dogs. They went to their rugs and lay down. Each completed their ritual of sniffing at the rug, turning to the right three times, sitting down, laying down, and putting its head on its paws. Then they each let out a big sigh. They were exhausted, but oh so content. That day they had fulfilled their calling in life.

Pete's calling at the time was plumbing. It could have been carpentry, or masonry, or anything else that was building related, but for a time he was a plumber. One day he was working on a house in town with fellow church member Johnny Kuiper. Johnny was a dozer driver.

Our pastor, Rev. Van Dyk lived just down the street in the parsonage. The parsonage was quite a nice place; the congregation treated its preachers well. There were no fences though, so the dogs, including his chow, "Champ" would regularly patrol the neighborhood. Champ found his way to the construction site Pete and Johnny were working at. They had dug a basement and poured a footing. Johnny was back-filling and leveling, and Pete was putting the pipes in the basement. Champ got as close as possible to Pete and snarled. He stayed at Pete's left elbow, trying to nip him every time he bent over to connect or bend a pipe. Pete kept working with a snarling dog next to him for quite a while, but a dog the size of Champ couldn't really be ignored. After a time, he got sick of it. Pete had a big monkey wrench in his right hand. He moved around, pretending to bend over to get a pipe or something. Champ continued to pester, nipping at his left elbow. Pete quickly swung the wrench around with his right, and hit Champ on the head. He was down for the count. In fact, Champ did not rise after the mandatory eight count, nor the ten, nor the twenty. He would never fight again. Now what?

Well, Johnny was a resourceful little guy, who offered, in his pinched, high voice,

"Let me have him, I'll dig a hole for him over there."

Pete needed no convincing; he grabbed the ex-champion by the tail and swung him over the wall to Johnny, who buried him deeply, if not properly.

Later that day Rev. Van Dyk came by.

"Hello gentlemen, how does your work go today?"

"Fine, fine, Rev., thank you. It's great to be outdoors in God's beautiful creation on a day like this."

"Yes, it sure is. Say, has either of you two men seen my dog, Champ? He hasn't come home."

At the moment, Johnny was standing about eight feet over top of Champ.

"No, I don't see him, you Pete?"

Johnny had cleverly changed the tense of his answer so he wouldn't have to lie to the preacher. Rev. Van Dyk thought that since Johnny was just a dumb dozer driver, he couldn't be expected to speak English properly, so he didn't pursue this grammatical error.

"No, me neither," said Pete, who had also picked up on the change of tense.

"Hmm, that's strange," said the Reverend, "he's usually home by now. If you should see him, please let me know."

"Ah, sure will, Reverend."

"Yeah, that's a pretty dog. Hope he comes home soon."

Rev. Van Dyk walked away, his head down in puzzlement and disappointment.

Pete and Johnny didn't feel too sorry for the dog, or for the preacher either for that matter. Reverend Van Dyk was a prickly and prideful man. He was quite eloquent, and had made quite a name for himself as a preacher, but you usually left church feeling worse than when you went in. Rev. Van Dyk had a way of telling you that you weren't so good, certainly nowhere near as good as he was. He would never openly say that he was one of God's very best servants, but he sure felt it. Every time someone talked to him, they knew that Rev. Van Dyk was going to be right, and they would be wrong. He would explain to them, at some length, that if they had carefully followed the rules, and gone by the correct procedures, they wouldn't have found themselves in this trouble. He was like an accountant who seizes on the smallest bookkeeping discrepancy and treats it like grand theft. Having shown you the error of your way, he expected you to thank him, humbly, for correcting you, and setting you on the right path.

When Pete told me what had happened I tried not to laugh, or to sock him one.

"What are you going to do now?"

"Nothing. Johnny and I aren't going to say a word about this, and you better not either."

By Sunday, the entire congregation knew that Rev. Van Dyk's prized chow, Champ, had run off, and hadn't been spotted for four days. Pete and Johnny well knew he was never coming back, but said nothing. They were secretly pleased with themselves for having rid the world of a malicious critter, and duping a pastor who was too proud for his own good. Pete and Johnny had to wait for years, till Rev. Van Dyk took a call to a church in Grand Rapids, to tell their dead dog story. All laughed; and most felt that both Champ and Rev. Van Dyk got what was coming to them.

Perhaps dogs do have a role to play in the great plan of God. Maybe they have a vocation too. Our dogs were born and bred to be ratters and pets. Champ was born and bred to pull a sled through the snow, not harass construction workers. Maybe Rev. Van Dyk missed his calling too. He should have been a lawyer. He would have been paid well to quarrel, and snarl.

The War

WORLD WAR I STARTED before I turned twenty, and now, before I was forty, they were fighting in Europe again. The Germans had not only been beaten in WWI, but in their eyes, humiliated. They were forced to pay vast amounts in war reparations, and not allowed to re-build their military (though they soon did). Hitler used this sense of resentment to stir up the Germans, especially against the French and the English, who had set the terms of the Armistice. We watched from the U.S. as the Second World War started in Europe, ever since Germany invaded Poland in September of 1939. We, like all Americans, had been watching the news from Europe as it came. Hitler invaded country after country in Europe and then subjected England to a ferocious pounding from his Luftwaffe. We knew that our cousins and friends in Holland had been overrun by the Germans and were now living under their boots.

Meanwhile, though we paid it far less attention, the Japanese had been destroying and occupying a good chunk of China, plus Korea since as early as 1910, and were working their way through eastern Asia. Since Japan was an Axis power, along with Germany and Italy, its attack on Pearl Harbor on December 7, 1941, suddenly brought the U.S. into the war. I think it surprised everyone in the U.S. that the attack came from the east, while we were so concerned with Europe. On that day which "lives in infamy," as Roosevelt put it, the United States officially and quickly joined the war. Everything changed after Pearl Harbor. Factories that were idle during the Depression ramped up into overtime. The pacifist movement went into hibernation, and everyone became part of "The War Effort."

Most of the young guys, including Stan and Al, immediately signed up for military service. Stan was 18 and Al was 17 when the war broke out. Al enlisted in the Air Force, since like about half the young guys in America, he thought he would make a great fighter pilot. But they saw how good he was in the sciences and with physical things, so they made him an airplane mechanic/engineer instead. He went to Amarillo Army Airfield in Texas where he completed aircraft mechanic school and got his certification. He was then sent to Mather Field in California where he quickly adapted to military life and spent all four years of the war fixing planes that came back from the Pacific theater. He never failed to send me Mother's Day and Birthday cards. They were always thoughtful, and signed, "Your loving son, Al." He was such a good son. I kept all his letters.

We wrote quite a lot in those days, cards for various special occasions, and letters for general information. My Ma had sixteen grandsons in the service in World War Two, and she wrote to every one of them. I guess it's not surprising there were so many soldiers in our family. We Recker kids were born through the 1890s and early 1900's, and so had our own families by the 1920s. And for whatever reason, we had a lot of boys, all of whom were all willing to serve. They seemed about equally divided among the services—Air Force, Navy, Army and Marines. When they went to enlist, one officer gave them a tough time.

"Recker! That's a German name isn't it?"

"Yes sir. But we come by way of Holland, sir."

"Can you speak German?"

"No sir."

"Any friends or family in Germany?"

"No sir."

If they had gone far enough back in the Recker family, they would have found that my paternal great grandfather had served in the Kaiser's army. But thankfully, they didn't go back that far, or perhaps they did, but didn't care. If my sons and nephews wanted to serve, the U.S. military was happy to have them.

We went to church every Sunday during the war years, of course. It seemed even more important than usual. Every church had a special flag in the front which included a star for each serviceman that the church had sent. Each blue star stood for a young man from the church who was in active service, and a gold star stood for any man who was killed in the war. Our church had thirty guys in the service, including seven of my nephews, and son Al. We all instinctively knew what the flag looked like with its thirty blue stars. But one Sunday a star was missing. I turned to Mrs. Mulder.

"Did one of our boys get killed? Do you know what happened?"

"No, I don't see a gold star in its place, so I can't figure it out."

The whole congregation was abuzz about that missing star. Everyone was trying to be quiet in church, yet all wanted to know what was up. Finally, Rev. DeJonge took the pulpit.

He spoke the words to the Call to Worship.

"The Lord is in his holy temple; let all the earth keep silence before him."

Then he looked out at his troubled flock, with its many questioning eyes. Leaving the liturgy behind, which was quite an audacious move for a young preacher, he said,

"Yes, there is one star missing. But please don't be worried. When the janitor was cleaning around the front of the church, he knocked the flag over. Without realizing it, he bumped one of the stars off. We'll put it back up this afternoon. All our boys are fine."

You could hear a sigh from some 300 mouths at once.

"Aaaah. So that's it. Nobody got killed or went missing in action."

Rev. DeJonge could then go on with the service. I'm sure that if he had tried to preach without recognizing the "fallen star" no one would have registered a word he said.

During the War even Illinois was considered part of the "Home Front." An Office of Civilian Defense formed in Lansing, as well as other nearby towns. Early on they showed a film that graphically depicted the bombing of London. We had to be ready. The OCD ran drills, ringing the fire siren from the center of town at night to declare a blackout. All the houses had to go completely dark. Volunteers from the OCD would go around from house to house to be sure that there were no lights showing. We didn't want German bombers to find us. There was also a women's division of the OCD. Some women worked in the office of the OCD, and we all collected *materiel* for the war: rubber, steel, paper, etc. At the farm there was always something lying around that could be re-purposed: the iron from a plow we no longer used, a beat-up tin roof, etc.

We were farmers and had our own garden, but the women in town didn't, so they raised "Victory Gardens." They would rent maybe a half-acre of our farmland, and then plant crops that their family could use. They planted beans, tomatoes, peppers, corn, etc., which left more food available to send to the GIs in Europe or the Pacific. We were also required to economize on clothing, so I couldn't make pleated pants or skirts—the pleats were a frill that used up needed fabric. Women also sewed bed jackets, beanies, and bandages for our servicemen. The whole country was involved in the war effort, not just the soldiers.

In 1942 Pete got paid $60 a month and Stan $40 to work on the ranch as tenant farmers in Crete. We worked for Mr. Goodson, who owned the 700 acres we lived on, and ran 168 steers there. We got housing as a part of our pay. Goodson was sure that Pete alone couldn't manage the ranch, so he insisted that Stan also keep working there, even though he was of age for military service.

We didn't realize it at the time, but Mr. Goodson also sat on the draft board, so he made sure Stan didn't get in, claiming his work at the ranch was "Vital to the war effort." But Stan didn't give up. He wanted to serve, and applied to every branch of the military. Finally, when the war in Europe was nearly over, Mr. Goodson relented. Stan could serve, so he joined the Army. He went to Virginia for basic training and was then based out of a New Jersey port. By the time he was fully trained, the war in Europe had ended. His job in New Jersey was basically that of a clerk, checking the men in when they came back from Europe to Camp Kilmer. But looking at passenger lists didn't appeal to him. He wanted to get out and serve more directly, so he spoke to his commanding officer.

"Is there somewhere I could serve that puts me a little closer to the war, sir?"

"Well, the army has more troop transport ships than the Navy does now, and we need radar operators. How does that sound to you?"

"Yes sir. That sounds good, sir."

Stan breezed through a bit more training and became a radar operator on a troop transport ship.

When Stan was about to board his ship, he saw his friends John and Lou in line too. Stan was talking with John. They looked around, and suddenly, no Lou! Where was he? They didn't find him. He had gone AWOL. Decades later Stan was driving in Florida, on vacation, praying as he drove along, and his old friend Lou came to mind. Just then it seemed his car was stalling, so he pulled off the road. A trucker pulled next to him to see if he needed any help. He and the trucker looked at each other.

"Lou?"

"Stan?"

"What on earth became of you? The last time I saw you was thirty years ago, in line to board ship."

"Yeah, I didn't make that ship. I joined the circus."

"The circus? Really?"

"Yeah, I didn't want to go in the service, and the circus took me right in. Since the circus moves around so much, the M.P.s never found me. I'm sure they stopped looking after a couple years. I've been driving truck for the circus for a long time now."

"Well, glad to see you're OK. Do you ever get to church?"

"No, not much."

"Well, I hope you will; this meeting is no doubt providential; God is trying to call you back."

"Could be. Thanks Stan. Gotta Go."

Stan never saw Lou again.

When Stan was on the job as a radar man one dark, starless night, he alerted the captain to another ship that showed up on his screen. The captain saw that their courses might result in a collision, so ordered his ship to a complete stop. Stan's ship held some 2,000 returning GI's, and the other was a three-masted schooner, dead in the water. The captain sent a small boat to find out what was wrong. The ship had masts, but no longer any sails. It held Jewish refugees who had survived the European Holocaust but were now homeless and at sea. They tried to land at various ports along North Africa but were rejected by all. They decided to set sail for the U.S., but their rudder broke in a storm, so they were adrift in the mid-Atlantic.

Stan's shipmates took food, water, and gifts of various sorts for the refugees. They were thirsty and hungry since their ship had been rudderless for some days. Stan's ship stayed in the area to keep an eye on them while the captain radioed Norfolk. A Navy ship steamed out immediately, and towed them to the U.S., where they found sanctuary. I suppose Stan saved lives that day. If those ships had collided, or if the refugee ship had simply floated off . . .

On another voyage Stan's ship broke down just short of Germany, and they needed to get it fixed by the Germans—the same Germans of course, with whom they had just been fighting. Stan and the whole crew were worried. They feared the Germans might be bitter, and try to land one last punch. But there were no hard feelings. The average German seemed to know that they were at fault for having started the war. And as more and more information came out about the concentration camps, etc., the more embarrassed they got. In fact, they were quite happy to help their American conquerors. By post-war standards in Europe, our guys were happy and wealthy, men who ate every day, and wore good, new uniforms. Our guys gave some of the German kids a candy bar, or some other treat, and were in turn treated like heroes.

Sometimes Stan's ship carried German prisoners who had been quartered in the U.S. back to Germany. He could understand a bit of German due to his Dutch, so was able to have some basic conversations with them. Some asked, "What will become of us when we get back?"

"Ich weiss nicht." I don't know.

But in a few cases, he did know. If the prisoners were former members of the S.S. or the Gestapo, he knew very well. They would be prosecuted and executed.

While in Europe many U.S. servicemen got engaged to French, German or English girls. But the U.S. government wasn't going to send a bunch of women on a ship needed by the troops. The soldiers came home first, and then petitioned for their brides or fiancés to follow. One such young woman from Germany was on Stan's ship. When they arrived at port in New York, she frantically looked for her fiancée, from Texas. He never came. The poor girl had to climb back aboard the same ship and go back to Germany. Another time coming back from Germany there were some French women aboard. One called to Stan,

"I've been looking for you, come over to my room tonight."

"No, I think you were looking for someone else."

Stan didn't forget his morals, even while far off at sea.

Stan made sergeant in his tour. He went back and forth across the Atlantic five times, so ten voyages in all, traversing more or less the same North Atlantic route that I had made as an infant. Some of those passages were mighty rough.

Back home, Irene was in High School. In fact, I can always remember which years she was in High School since they were the same as the war years: 1941-45. Don was in Jr. High, and Lin was in grade-school.

During the war we had German POWs come to work on the ranch. They lived in a nearby barracks in Thornton. (Later they would build Illiana Christian High School in those barracks.) I don't know how many of them were in the barracks, but most days a guard would come with six of them to work for us. The guard would be armed of course, and Pete would put the prisoners to work. There was a lot to be done. The ranch had 168 steers, all of whom had to be fed, and watered, and have their stalls mucked out. Most of the time we could understand their conversations, since Dutch is so close to German. We heard them talking about their families, and their girlfriends, and what they hoped to do when they got back to Germany, etc. They were treated well. In fact, they didn't really work any harder than Pete and Stan did, plus, unlike soldiers in combat, they got regular meals. They were taken back to the barracks every evening and didn't have to work on Sunday either.

I kept to my regular routine while in the house—cleaning, cooking, mending, etc. In nice weather sometimes, the prisoners would sit on our porch while having their lunches. When they did, Irene had to be a bit careful when she walked by. They weren't about to try anything with an armed soldier right there, but it was pretty uncomfortable for her. Once, I had just finished making bread, and set it out on the window-sill to cool. One of the German boys was working nearby. In German, he said, "That bread sure smells good. I'd love to have a slice."

"Not a chance!" I told him, in my broken German.

"If you weren't here on our ranch, you'd be back in Germany trying to kill my son or nephews. You're lucky to get whatever the warden gives you."

The gall. The Germans were well known for their arrogance and tactlessness long before WWII. I think they always looked down on the Dutch as sort of lesser, little cousins. I wasn't going to support them while they were murdering us.

One of those cousins from Holland later recounted a story from Easter, 1943. That morning in church the preacher mounted the tall, austere old wooden pulpit and said, with a conspiratorial raising of his eyebrows,

"I have some very good news for all of you."

Well, the whole congregation knew that Rev. Scholten was a leader in the Dutch underground and had access to radio and other sources of information that none of the other congregants did. So, all were raising their own eyebrows and holding their breaths when he spoke of some "very good news." He turned to the congregation, lifted his arms and exclaimed, "He is Risen!" The congregation gave an audible gasp of disappointment. They had hoped to hear of an Allied landing, or that the German troops were leaving the Netherlands, or something of that sort. But he was right. It was and is Good News.

Some of our cousins in the Netherlands also hid Jews from the Nazis. It wasn't just little Anne Frank who owed her life to the Dutch. The Jews had been living in the Netherlands for centuries and were very close to the Dutch. Some had intermarried, and even those who hadn't were generally well accepted. Many good Dutch Reformed people hid the Jews without giving it a second thought. They simply knew it was right. How could they let Hitler kill their neighbors?

During the war, Dutch farmers had a little game they would play with their windmills. A windmill can be tilted in any direction, and its blades can be set in any direction too. The Dutch underground developed a system whereby the farmers would set their windmills in certain directions as signs for the Allied bombers flying overhead. For example, having the blades straight up to the sky and perpendicular might mean that the Germans hadn't moved, whereas turning them in another direction might mean they had gone further east.

One of the guys from our church, Herm De Vries, was part of the liberation of the Netherlands. He marched proudly through the Dutch towns they had freed. Herm was a very good guy, but he had one quite noticeable flaw, which was his very large posterior. When marching in the parade, the little Dutch kids called out, "Look at that Fat Ass!" Without missing a step, he responded in Dutch: "Better a fat ass than a 'kliene klootzak.'" A *kliene klootzak* is literally a little ball sack—a scrotum. For the Dutch, it's a multi-purpose insult, something like "ass-*&^%" in English. Why "little scrotum" is such a serious insult, I really don't know, but Herm got the best of them.

After the war I can vividly remember when the boys from our church came home. One Sunday all the veterans came marching down the center aisle in their uniforms. What a glorious parade! There were thirty from our church alone, and every one of them came back; no gold stars. Granted, some had to be brought to the front in wheel-chairs, and others had arms in slings, or even a missing limb, but they all made it. The whole congregation broke forth into cheers mixed with deeply felt tears. It was one of the rare times when it was considered OK to clap in church. The minister prayed: "Thank you oh great and merciful God for bringing these young men, these Christian boys back to us, to our church, and to their families. We praise you God for your great mercy."

A New Post-War World

When Al came home from the war he went to our church college—Calvin College. I think he wanted to reconcile what he knew about science with his faith, but I'm afraid they didn't help him much. At that time evolution was a taboo subject at Christian colleges, and Calvin's professors were probably afraid of getting in trouble if they said much about it.

He came home from school more confused about it than when he left, three and a half years later. He couldn't finish that last semester: bouts of depression sent him into such a state that he couldn't do much of anything, so he moved back home. Then, instead of trying to finish college in Illinois he just took on some menial jobs, the kind of stuff that anyone could do. He was so smart, it hurt me to see him go to a dull job when he could have been an engineer, or a teacher, or almost anything else he put his mind to. But since he left college without quite finishing, he didn't apply for any professional jobs. And since he was often troubled by depression, he sometimes missed even that work, having to call in sick when he just couldn't get going in the morning. It was painful to see my wonderful son drag himself around. He was such a dear, good, young man, as well as a smart one. I know he didn't ask to be depressed; it just came with his nature. He probably got it from Pete's mom, the one who had been sent to the New Mexican asylum. It turns out that others in that family suffered from depression too.

Many young soldiers died during the war years, but of course old people kept dying off too. My Pa died in 1945, at eighty years old, a proud American father and grandfather. This left Ma alone in her house, so when the lease on our tenant farm job came to an end, we moved in with her. Lin and I helped her out around the house, and we had a free place to live. Ma's house had two bedrooms and one bathroom on the main floor, plus a full basement. Pete and I stayed in one of the upstairs bedrooms, and we rigged up some blankets to create barriers for the kids bedrooms in the basement. We usually ate downstairs. The basement had windows in it, so when we were eating, the neighbor kids could see us. One of them, Jeannie, was a friend of Linda. While we were eating, they would sometimes carry on a conversation through the basement window.

"What are you having?"

"Oh, we had that last week."

"Are you coming out to play after supper?"

"How long will it take you to do the dishes?"

One day Lin was sick and had to stay home from school, so Ma used the time to teach her how to count to ten in Dutch.

"*Een, twee, drie, vier, vijf, zes, zeven, acht, negen, tien.*"

I think Ma was a little annoyed with me for not having taught my kids Dutch. But since both Pete and I had learned English as children, we really didn't speak Dutch around the house. That was intentional. We thought American families like ours should speak English.

Lin was given the job of mopping the upstairs floors. She had to use a heavy mop that had little braided ropes on it, with a bucket of soapy water, and wring it out by hand. She didn't enjoy it, nor could she understand why she had to do it *every week*, when you couldn't see any dirt on the floor. Ma and I made it clear that it had to be done every week, regardless of what it looked like. I suspect Ma thought that making her a good housecleaner would bring out the Dutch in her too.

We did have a scare with Lin one day. She was on her way home one evening when a boy jumped out at her and tried to grab her. She turned and ran and kept running and running till she arrived exhausted at the house. I was irate. Why should a good girl like Lin have to run for fear in our own neighborhood? I wasn't happy with Pete's response either. He put his arm around her and said, "I'm so glad you're alright," and then sat back down in his chair. I said we should call the police, and suggested that he go out and look for the boy. But he just said, "I'm sure he's gone now." It made me as mad as I have ever been.

Don had assigned jobs when we lived with Ma too. The basement had a coal furnace in it, so Don got the job of shoveling the coal and stoking the furnace. This meant shoveling in the middle of the night in winter. Like most houses at the time, this one did not have a water heater either, so every time you wanted hot water you had to boil it. On Saturdays when everyone took baths, we'd boil as much water as we could in our largest pot, bring it to the tub, and add cold water from the tap to lower the temperature. We could boil more water if we wanted to, but it was always a trick: if I boil two pots of water will the first one have cooled off so much that the whole tub is no longer warm?

While in his teens Don and his friend Jake S. apparently had a little Halloween tradition. After singing all the verses of *A Mighty Fortress* at the annual Reformation Day service, they would go out together to play tricks on some of the local farmers. All the farmers back then had outhouses, since no sewer lines had been hooked up out in the country. Most of the outhouses had doors with holes in them in the shapes of the moon or the stars in order to let in a bit of moonlight at night.

Each farmer would put his outhouse a little way in the back yard, preferably far away enough that the smell wouldn't reach the house, but close enough that a winter's run to it wasn't too long a hike. The farmer would dig a good hole, maybe six feet or so deep, and a couple of feet wide. Then, he'd pick up the outhouse on planks and put it over the hole. When the hole was nearly filled, he covered up the hole with dirt, dug again, and moved the outhouse.

Don and Jake thought it was a good Halloween trick to tip the outhouses. If the farmer came out to use it later that night, he might fall in the hole. Or, the next morning he'd have the smelly and nasty job of moving the outhouse back to its original spot or digging out a new hole.

Don and Jake would go out on Halloween/Reformation Day, as soon as it was dark, sneak into the farmers' yard from the back, grab the outhouse and shove it over. They had apparently done this at Harold K's farm for a few years in a row. So one Reformation Day, no doubt before the worship service, Harold moved the outhouse, stationing it exactly a foot to the front of its hole, just a little closer to the house. When it was good and dark, Don and Jake came around behind the house from the field. They stealthily made their way toward the outhouse. They made their final crouch in the dark, ran forward with hands outstretched to tip the outhouse over.

Slip . . . Slide . . . Yuck!!! They were up to their armpits in pee and poop. Oh my goodness did they scream. "AAAHHH! NO! HEEELP!!!"

They couldn't get out, since the hole was nearly full, and the sides were extremely slippery.

Inside the house, perhaps some forty yards away, Harold was reading the latest issue of the *Farm Journal*.

"Hmm, look at this new tractor that Allis Chalmers has come out with," he said to his wife Doris. "I bet I could plow more acreage with that one."

"Aren't you going to help those boys get out?" Doris responded.

"Oh yes," said Harold, slowly flipping the page.

"Hmmm, Ford has a new tractor too, and it looks like they've re-aligned the front wheels."

"Go get those boys out!"

"Ya," said Harold, rising ever so slowly from his chair.

He trekked to the barn, carefully checked over his tractor, and turned the key. He kept it well-tuned, so sadly, it started right up. He went to the wall of the barn and found a chain. No, that wasn't the right chain for this job, so he looked for another. At last finding just the right length and weight chain, he hooked it to the back of the tractor. He drove out to the stinky, slimy hole, filled with urine, feces and two odiferous teenage boys. He tossed the chain to them.

"Hang on boys, I'll pull you out."

Out they came, slithering one by one.

"Don't expect I'll be seeing you around here next Halloween, eh?"

"No sir." They replied in near unison.

Harold dragged them out of the cesspool. They were covered from head to toe. They each trudged to their homes.

Don arrived at our back door around eleven o'clock. Knock, knock.

"Who's there?"

"It's me, Don."

"Well come in; why do you suddenly need to knock on your own door?'

"Well, I, er, don't, um . . ."

"Are you OK?"

By this time I was at the door, and a little worried. I opened the door and was instantly smacked in the nose by the most horrible odor I had ever encountered, and this after having lived on farms for decades.

"Whaaat?!"

"I, uh, fell into an outhouse hole."

"How could you possibly do that? Oh my goodness, stand back, and move over there, down-wind!"

"Get the hose, and hose yourself down."

As he was hosing himself down Pete and I continued our interrogation.

"Whose outhouse hole was it?"
"What on earth were you doing there?"
"You mean he left the hole uncovered?"
"Who was with you?"
"So you both accidentally fell in the same hole?"
"Why did he move the outhouse?"
"Why did he think you would be coming on to his yard?"
"You were there last year too?"
"So for how many years have you had been tipping his outhouse?"
"How many other outhouses have you been tipping?"

"Take off all your clothes except your underpants," said Pete with disgust. Then realizing how awful he still smelled; "OK, you better take them off too." I went in the house and let them finish the rinse job.

Three rounds of soaking, yet his clothes and his skin still reeked. We threw him some rags to dry off with. There he stood shivering and stinking.

"You're going to have to sleep in the barn tonight," said Pete.

"OK" said a very humble Don.

We tossed him some old sheets, rags really, and he brought them out to the barn. He went into the hayloft and made himself as comfortable as possible. I don't know how much he slept. The clothes he was wearing had to be burned. I picked them up with a stick and threw them into the 55 gallon drum we kept outside as a fire barrel. The next morning, we went out to do chores and check on Don. His smell met us well before he did.

"Come on down, we'll have to wash you down some more."

Don sheepishly climbed down the stairs. We gave him some good, strong lye soap, and a stiff brush. He scrubbed and scrubbed, and we rinsed and rinsed. We gave him the worst pair of overalls we could find, and a shirt that the dogs had been ripping at. He put them on, and went about his chores, at some distance from the rest of us. He took breakfast, lunch and dinner in the barn. After three days the smell had abated to the point where we could have him inside for meals, with the windows open. After a week he was back in the house full-time. I had some very good boys, but they weren't angels.

Meanwhile, Pete was working at Thornton Fractional North High School as their yard and maintenance man. He was good at his job, since he could fix anything, and he liked to keep the yard looking good. He came home from work one day and announced rather sheepishly that he had quit his job.

"What!" I shouted. "Whatever did you do that for?"

"Well, the guys are going on strike in order to get better wages."

"Here we go again, I thought, first it was the Ford plant, and now this job."

"Pete, you aren't cut out to be a union man. You go back right now and get that job back. If you don't, you might never work again."

I had worked hard ever since I graduated from grade-school and Pete had labored from an even earlier age. He couldn't just stop working now; we had bills to pay.

"Ya, OK," he said with a sigh.

He was in his fifties, and his better working days were behind him. He had developed a heart problem too. Who would hire a man that age that was known as a union trouble-maker? He went back and was immediately re-hired, thankfully. In fact, that job did turn out to be the one he would hold for the rest of his working years.

By this time, I felt that I really needed to learn how to drive, so I asked Pete to help me. He patiently explained how to put the clutch in all the way when starting, put the car in gear and then gradually let out the clutch. After that, I was to move the stick-shift to another place where second gear was while pressing in the clutch again. I couldn't do it. I got the car started, but then when I let the clutch out the car lurched and bucked like bronco back in the Montana rodeos. After trying on three separate occasions, I gave up, or more accurately Pete gave up on me. He said, "I think I'll keep doing the driving."

On Memorial Day we would drive out to DeMotte to help Bill and Jess bunch asparagus. They had a farm, and acres of asparagus were always ready on Memorial Day. DeMotte seemed like the other end of the world to our kids, but it was really only about forty miles southeast, in Indiana. As many Recker cousins as possible would be called upon to go out and cut the asparagus. Then some of the smallest ones would follow behind with rubber-bands, putting them into bunches. Boy was that a lot of work. Jess, I and another sister or two would get lunches ready while they cut and bunched. It was usually a pretty big picnic lunch: sandwiches, an apple, a homemade cookie, and some lemonade. The grass had sprouted by then, so we could find a nice soft spot to eat on. Since the cousins were all together it seemed as much of an outing as it did a workday to them. When they all got together the cousins sang, "Hail, hail, the gang's all here."

Bill and Jess sure appreciated the help. Bill had kept his taxidermy work going so the kids all went into the house to see Bill's stuffed animals. Going into their living room felt like they were walking into a forest—with fox, squirrels, pheasants, quail, and even a wolf staring at them. At the end of the day we drove home back west down Rte. 30. The kids were always asleep in the back by the time we'd driven a mile down the road.

Finally, My Own House!

AFTER THE WAR, STAN and Al both lived at home, and were both working. The two of them quietly schemed, put some money together, and bought three acres for us in Lansing for $1,250. I was 54 years old and was finally going to have my own house!

Stan, Al and Pete did most of the work (Don was away in the Air Force). After they formed the settings for the concrete setting, the huge concrete mixer came to pour the foundation. Stan and Al then laid out the block basement while Pete tended mortar for them. To lay a block wall, you start out on the corners of the foundation making "leads." You have to make sure it's a perfect, square EL on each corner. You then run a line from one corner to another to ensure that you're going straight from one lead to another, and then you lay the first course of blocks on the concrete foundation. You have to check to make sure the first course is level before you add the next courses. Once one wall is up, it's on to the next lead and repeat. We had a full basement in that house; since it was sitting on high ground we didn't have to worry about flooding. At the top of the basement walls, above ground level, they put in windows, some of which were clear and see through, others of which were glass blocks, and opaque, twelve inches long and eight inches wide like the concrete blocks. With them we had natural light, even in the basement.

They then set a wooden beam that was six inches wide and eight inches thick across the farthest parts of the wall. That would serve as the foundation for the floor joists, which also served as the roof of the basement. After the first year, when that dual-purpose floor/roof was in we moved into the basement. It wasn't elegant, but it worked. They put in a basement bathroom with a shower that stayed there even after the main floor was built. The guys built a couple of interior block walls too, so we could have three rooms, a bedroom, a kitchen/dining room, and a "living room" that also served as a secondary bedroom. We got to know each other pretty well that year.

The next year they put in the main level. Stan did the carpentry work with Pete's help, while Al kept working at his regular job to pay the bills. They set the wooden frame on the block foundation in sections and nailed it in with special nails that would pierce through the concrete block. Then up with the outside wall frames, and inner walls. Then the plumbing, and the electricity and heat. I have really come to love my house. It's nothing fancy, but it has all the modern conveniences: a gas stove, electricity throughout, and appliances to make things go easier. I was sure proud. My house was hardly a mansion, but it was mine, finally, and my own sons and husband built it for me.

I sometimes wondered why we were so committed to the Chicago area, especially in February and March. The winters were harsh, cold, and bitter. In March it started to warm a bit, but it was distressingly ugly. All was gray, the trees had yet to bud, the birds had yet to return, and the sun had yet to shine. There were days on end, and sometimes weeks when we saw no sunshine. That affected all of us. When the skies were gray, so were our spirits. Al, in particular, seemed to get down when the sun didn't shine. It seems that when you get up and see the sun smiling at you, you smile back. You can say, "Thank you, God, for another beautiful day in your world." But without the brilliance and warmth of the sun, it's almost as if we are left on our own. I know that's not true, but the sun and the stars do remind us: God is here.

We had our own phone in the new house. It was a party line with six houses on it. Our ring was one short, two longs. Mrs. Peterson's phone was two shorts; Mrs. Murphy's was long, short, short, etc. The household that had a teenage daughter at home usually got the most phone calls. Sometimes we'd listen in on each other. You'd hear the ring, and know it wasn't for you, but just out of curiosity, pick up the phone to hear what was going on. It seemed like everyone else had more interesting lives than we did. Once I was talking to my friend Rose.

"How are your boys? Is Steve's hand healing up?"

"Yeah, he's doing fine. Have to keep him off that two-wheel bike for a few days though."

"Ah, good. Well, got to get going; need to head to town to get a few things."

"See you later."

Then, before I could get the phone hung up I heard another voice.

"Hello Minnie, this is Sophie Peterson. I hear you are going into town. Could you please pick me up some flour? We've run out and I want to bake some bread."

"OK. Regular flour or wheat?

"Regular."

"I'll pay you as soon as you get it."

I did buy it and she did pay for it. I didn't get mad at her either; it's just how we got along. I think we were less private in those days. We knew everyone on our street, and we all chatted whenever we saw each other. If I could help her out by picking up some flour, why not? I'm sure she'd have done the same for me.

Things got trickier though, when Rev. Eldersveld and his family moved to our street. As a pastor, he made calls that people shouldn't listen in on. One time he was on the line and knew there were other people listening in, including myself. He had a big bass voice.

"I know there are other sinners on this line right now, and unless you want all of *your* sins to be made public, I suggest you get off the line, and never listen in again."

Click, click, click.

Our new house was at the end of a little gravel road that never got plowed by the city trucks. Pete decided that we should have a road grader to level off the street when the ruts got too deep, and to plow the snow in winter. He didn't ask me about it, he just turned up in the driveway with a road grader behind the truck one day.

"What's this?" I asked.

"Well, it's a road grader."

"I CAN SEE it's a road-grader! But why did YOU buy it?"

"The road's getting mighty rough."

"Of course the road needs grading! But why did YOU get the road-grader?

"Well, I can do a good job of it."

"Neh! Pete! The neighbors use this road too. They could have helped buy it."

"Yeah, well, but now I bought it."

"Yes, you sure did. I guess that means I won't be buying any new furniture for the new house." That man and money was a bad combination. Why on earth couldn't he have gone around to the neighbors, made a proposal, and gotten everyone to pitch in? He seemed to feel that since he could do something by himself, he should do it by himself. From then on though, we had a nice, level, gravel road.

Our little road also crossed over a creek and a railroad track. Later on we later had grandkids falling in the creek, though I'm not sure they really tried too hard not to. There was a wooden bridge over the creek made of heavy boards. In fact, they were more than boards; they were old railroad ties, so every time a car crossed it you could clearly hear the babababap of the wheels hitting each board. No one ever snuck up on us.

Once a neighbor got hit by a train on that road. The train track didn't have a gate where it met our little road since the crossing was so inconsequential. When a train was coming you could hear the whistle blow, but since there were trees on both sides of the road the train seemed to come out of nowhere. Evidently the driver was listening to his radio, or not paying attention, and BLAM! The train knocked his car hundreds of feet down the tracks and into the creek. The driver died on the spot. When you have a car versus train collisions, the tie always goes to the train.

One thing I appreciated about the house was that it was easy to have my family over on Sundays now. We had kept up this tradition for decades, even after Ma and Pa died. Most of us still lived near each other, and with one exception, wanted to see each other. The one exception was my sister-in-law, the same one who stole my nice dishes decades back, and pretended not to know any better. For years and years she had been going on about her kids, her husband, her house, her fine things, etc. Any time we got together the rest of the family quickly ran to find a seat far away from her, since if you sat next to her you were doomed to an afternoon of hearing her brag. She never let anyone else say anything while she brought out her pictures and insisted on showing them.

"See, this is when my son graduated from High School. He got very good grades . . ."

Well, I had one son who was a valedictorian and another who was a salutatorian, but according to her I wasn't allowed to say anything about them. Only her children mattered.

"Here's where Dick and I went for our last vacation. See those springs?" They say the water there is some of the purest in the state . . ."

I'd had enough.

"Nellie! You just shut up. I've heard enough about you and your family to last me for three lifetimes. You think you're the only ones who have done anything?"

"You think you're the most important person who's ever lived?"

"Pete and I and everyone here are at least your equals, and if you talk about being a Christian, probably your superiors. If you ever want to come to this house again you will bring no more pictures. You will not speak one more word about your family. And you will return my dishes!"

I haven't seen her for a few years now.

Both Irene and Lin were there and heard the whole thing. They were pretty surprised, never having seen me erupt like that. They knew how I felt about Nellie though, and I think the whole family was relieved that I told her off.

We were finally able to take a vacation or two once we moved in. One year we went to Starved Rock, on the banks of the Illinois River, only 100 miles from Chicago. Eighteen beautiful canyons line a four mile stretch of sandstone there. It got its name from a legend about the Indians. The story goes that chief Pontiac, of the Ottawa tribe, was killed by a warrior from the Illini tribe. To get revenge, the Ottawa chased the Illini down the riverbanks to a precipice between a canyon and a waterfall. The Illini held up there, but couldn't get past the Ottawa for food, and so starved among those sandstone rocks. All this may just be legend, but it's plausible. Lin climbed around among the rocks with Jeannie, pretending they were Indians. It was July, so we showered in one of the waterfalls. God must have smiled when he created places like this.

Toward the end of 1956 we took a bigger trip that I had long desired to make—New Jersey. I know it's not the world's greatest tourist attraction, but I wanted to meet our relatives—the Koks—who had welcomed our family nearly sixty years earlier. Only one or two of that generation was left, so I hoped to see them before they went to their reward. Pete, Lin and I took a train, reversing the direction that Pa and Ma had taken so many years earlier. Since the trains had improved so much over the years, our journey took less than a day. The Koks had lived in Paterson for three generations now and were well established. We had written to each other a bit over the years, and so were not strangers. They had Americanized their name from Kok to Cook, but were still faithful members of the Christian Reformed Church, and welcomed us as if we were long lost friends.

They took us into "The City," New York. What a treat! We only made it into Chicago on rare occasions, so getting into New York was a pretty big deal. We climbed up into the Statue of Liberty, the beautiful lady who welcomed us, and millions of others to our land. We saw the Rockettes.

Wow could those girls kick and dance! There must have been twenty of them in a line, and every movement was perfectly coordinated. They kicked their legs up to the level of their eyes, and then back down and up with the other leg. They must have been in great shape! The clothes they wore were a little too revealing—I wouldn't let my girls go out in something like that—but they sure were attractive. I kept my eyes on Pete. I think he enjoyed it.

We were in New York City on New Years' Eve, 1955. We stood in Times Square, with thousands of others, waiting for the ball to drop. I loved to watch not only the ball, but the people. We Americans sure come in a lot of shapes, sizes and colors. What a beautiful country, and people. When the ball fell, Pete and I had a nice little kiss. We said a little prayer of thanks for what God had done for us in the past years, and another asking for God's blessing in 1956.

My Sweet Pete

I'VE SOMETIMES WONDER IF Pete would have married a horse, if he could have. He sure did like them. The horses were draft animals, to be sure, but some were with us longer than our kids, living up to twenty-five years. Each horse had a name—Barney, Julie, Fritz, etc.—and each had its own character. When Barney was young, for instance, he was quite a playful fellow. He'd run and prance around like he was showing off for the girls. Fritz was more of a somber horse, always looking like he needed cheering up. Julie was a bit lazy, so we usually paired her with Barney to keep her going. When Pete would yell "Heeya," Julie would wait for Barney to make the initial pull to get the implement moving, and only then take her first step. The guys called the horses by name, and the animals knew their voices. Many times I saw Pete call to one of the horses and watch it come to him.

Same with the cows. If one was acting up and didn't want to be milked, Pete would come over, lay his hand on her and say, "Now, Bessie, you be a good girl and let Stan milk you." I'm quite sure Bessie didn't understand the words, but his voice usually calmed her.

When the crops came in the fall, we dropped everything else and got out the harvest. The boys stayed out of school until mid-October or so, since they were needed to work in the field. To hay, we pulled a cutter alongside the horses that was like a long arm with a blade on it, which cut the stalks. It went to one side of the horse while Pete sat on the other side, driving. After the hay was cut the horses pulled a rake, which gathered the hay onto rows. Finally, we would come along with hand rakes and throw the hay up onto the wagon.

When the guys were haying, I would make them lunches: a sandwich, an apple, and perhaps a bar of something I had baked. I packed it up in a basket and sent Rene or Lin out with it. When Lin was little, she thought it was quite an honor to go out into the field and deliver lunches to her dad and big brothers. She was a dozen years younger than Stan, so by the time she was five, Stan, Pete, and Al would all be working outside, waiting for her. She'd grab the lunch basket firmly with both hands, as if she feared the big bad wolf might try to get it. Off to the field she'd go, where dad and big brothers were working. She'd walk straight up to them, often clambering over little mounds to reach them, and proudly announce, "Here's your lunch!"

"Thank you so much, Lin," Pete would say, and the boys would chime in with "Yes, thank you." Her dad and brothers made her feel quite important. Then they'd invite her to stay and have lunch with them. I'd always pack something extra so she could join. They'd look for shade in hot summer days, but at midday in the summer that might mean just sitting in the narrow dark strip thrown by the wagon. Then Pete would pray, as he did before every meal:

> *Our gracious God and heavenly Father, we come to you in the noon hour of this day and thank you for your many blessings, for the good gifts of the earth, for strength and health to labor in your fields, and for our good country that gives us peace and freedom. We know that many in your world go without good food, and shelter, and we ask that you be with them, and provide them with what they need. And now we pray, again asking for the forgiveness of our sins, in Jesus name, Amen.*

This was his common prayer. We lived every day in the presence of God, and prayed before each meal. I'm sure the practice went back generations, to times when people weren't at all sure when they would have their next meal. So it was a good reminder.

Corn had to be picked by hand, since we didn't have the big mechanized harvesters yet. You had to wait for the corn to dry out good, which sometimes didn't happen till early November. You'd grab an ear at the top, strip down the husks, and then break the ear off the stalk. Then you'd toss the ear on the wagon, preferably without hitting your son or brother on the head with it. A horse slowly pulled the corn wagon, which had a makeshift wall nailed to one side of it, so when the guys threw the ears, they wouldn't go flying off the other side of the wagon. When the wagon was full the driver carted it off to the granary.

Some corn we wouldn't pick. Rather, we'd cut the whole stalk off when it was still green to be chopped up as silage and brought into the silo, which was over fifty feet tall. The cows ate from that silage throughout the year. Since the silage started to ferment, it emitted a funny smell, but one I kind of liked. In the summer, since the wind couldn't pass through, it got dreadfully hot in those silos. Since the corn was decomposing and letting off noxious gases, the temperature inside could get well over a hundred degrees. There were some sad stories about kids falling into corn silos. Sometimes they would climb to the top, curious to know how far out they could see, then lean over too far, and fall in. Most wouldn't survive the fall; if they did, they likely suffocated.

In the 1940's a lot of farmers started getting tractors, whose great selling point was: "Once you're done for the day, or the season, you don't have to feed and water the tractor. You just park it in the barn." Our fellow church member John Z. thought that was a great idea, so he bought one, and his first ride was a wonder—having that loud, powerful machine beneath him felt good. When he drove the tractor into the barn he cried "Whoa," just as he had done for decades with his horses. The tractor paid him no heed, continuing into and through the other side of the barn.

I'm glad that Stan, Al, and later Don could help Pete, since by the time he was in his fifties, Pete had developed a heart condition. Maybe it was a natural thing, or maybe he got it from delivering coal. I don't know exactly what it was, but the doctor said that he should rest as much as possible and not eat fatty foods. For Pete that resting was nearly impossible. Even after he'd had a minor heart attack in his fifties and was retired, he'd get up every morning, have something to eat, fix himself some tea, get in his car, and head out, usually to do some good deed. Oftentimes he'd come home with someone and say,

"Minnie, look who I found wandering around town. You remember John X, don't you? He was in our church years back, till they moved to Michigan. He's back in town for his uncle's funeral. I told him you always make an extra plate for supper." I often did, since I knew Pete might well drag someone home with him. So we'd have John over for dinner that night and grill him with questions: "How old was your uncle?" "He went to Munster Church, right?" "Wasn't his daughter the same age as Irene? What have you been doing in Michigan?" If Pete didn't bring a guest for dinner, and there were leftovers, he'd observe, "Enough there yet for a hungry man," as if to prove that he should invited more people over.

Pete's best friend was his step-brother—Joe Smit. They'd go out for coffee, help each other with little household projects, and shoot the breeze. They even gave each other haircuts. None of them were too stylish, and some of which were really bad, but then men usually don't care much about that kind of thing.

When we finally had in our own house in Lansing, Pete pulled a fast one that sent me back to work. When Al and Stan returned from the service, they both lived at home and paid me some rent. Stan got married shortly thereafter, but Al stayed on for quite a while. One day I asked him, "Aren't you due to pay me this month's rent?"

"Pa told me you weren't going to charge me anymore."

That surprised me, so when Pete got home I grabbed him and asked, "Did you tell Al not to pay us any rent?"

"Well, ya. You know he's having a hard time.

"But I need that money!"

"I'm sorry, but now I gave him my word. I can't go back and say I changed my mind."

I wanted to kill him, but with that not really being an option, and since we still had bills to pay, I went back to work. One of the guys from our church who owned a couple of office buildings in town hired me to clean them. I was in my fifties, going back to the same job I'd had when I was fifteen.

On his days off, and later on in retirement, Pete liked to go to the hardware store. Not only did he sometimes find some tools he'd liked to have, but he got to hear and tell stories with his buddies. Gus Bock, who owned the store, always loved to have Pete come in, since it was like having another salesman on hand.

For example, once when Mr. Heerspink came in and needed something to fix the leak in his bathroom, Pete showed him what he needed. When Widow VanderLaan came in complaining that her back door was stuck and the screen door slammed, Pete told her, "Here, buy these screws and hinges, and I'll come by with my tools later to fix it for you." Sure enough, Pete got his toolbox, made sure he had what he needed, went to Mrs. VanderLaan's house, and fixed the doors. A few hours later he returned and said,

"Ah, the poor lady is struggling without her husband, and her only son lives in Michigan."

"Good that you could help her. Did she pay you anything?"

"Nah. She gave me a nice piece of apple pie, though, and told me to take the rest home."

I liked apple pie as well as any, but we needed the money. Pete never made a big salary, and I was always cutting out some little thing from the budget to keep us going. It never seemed to occur to him that he should charge someone for the work he did. He just figured that if God had given him the abilities of a handyman, he should use that gift, especially if the person in need was a fellow Christian. I admired him for that, but it upset me too. Here I was scraping pennies together to pay the bills every month while he was going around doing charity work for others.

Pete went to the hardware store and hung around with some of the characters who showed up there like Hank O. and Bill K. Both could really tell a story, though usually fictitious. Whatever you said could be transformed into a comedy. I'd sometimes go to pick up Pete and overhear them. For example, Mrs. Schumann, the wife of the lawyer in town, came in one day at just the wrong moment. Hank was saying, "You hear what that George Schumann charges for an hour of his time? Fifty bucks! And that's before he actually does anything. Fifty bucks just to hear about the problem!"

"Wow, I listen to your problems every day, and don't charge a thing," Bill kidded back.

"Maybe I should start."

"Ha! The advice I get from you is free, and that's twice too much!"

'Ah, hello Mrs. Schumann. How are you today?"

"What are you looking for today?" asked Hank, nodding slowly and respectfully.

"Well, the sink is leaking, and the water has dripped through the flooring into the basement. My husband told me to pick up some things to fix it."

"Ah," nodded Bill. "That could be a bit of a job."

"I suppose, and George is not really much of a handyman. But he thinks he can fix it himself."

"Sure, sure, he's a smart guy. He'll get it . . . Here, you're going to need some new pipe joints and connectors . . . And you said it leaked through the floor? Then you're going to need another piece of flooring and some caulking to replace it . . . Is it leaking from the top of the sink or just the bottom? . . . Ah, then you'll need some new gaskets for around the spigots too."

Then Hank had an inspiration. To look at him you'd have thought he'd just understood how to make an atom bomb. "Is George right or left-handed?"

"Left."

Momentarily, Hank had a peculiar sparkle come to his blue eyes, but Mrs. Schumann didn't notice.

"Aah, then he's going to need some new tools."

Now Bill caught on. "Yaa," he nodded, with all three chins rising and falling in solemn accord.

"Oh, yes," Hank said, sadly shaking his head.

"Most of the tools we have here are for right-handers. But over there on that wall is a special section of wrenches, screw drivers, and other tools for lefties. They're a little more expensive, but they're worth it."

Bill confirmed this with a solemn grimace, deeply sorry that the wife of the $50 an hour attorney would have to spend so much money on new tools. They loaded that poor woman up with a couple of hundred dollars' worth of stuff like "left-handed wrenches and screw-drivers." Oh, my goodness! I guess if she was dumb enough to believe them she deserved it.

Those guys were just always on the lookout for some trick to play or mini-conflict to start. One time, Bill asked Mr. Bultman, "So, is your son is graduating from Hope College, over there in Michigan?"

"Yes. He'll be a teacher," Mr. Bultman replied proudly.

"Oooh," said Hank, his sad chins sloshing from side to side.

"Didn't Hope lose its accreditation for teaching last year?"

"Ah, yah, I read that too," chimed in Bill.

"What do you mean!?" Responded an agitated Bultman.

"Yeah, something about not enough classes in elementary pedagogy," nodded Bill, somberly. (Both were both pretty well read, so this kind of language came all too quickly.)

"Yeah, I think the students are okay if they stay in Michigan, but they can't get away with those low standards here in Illinois."

"No, no, standards here are a bit higher."

"What do you mean? My son is going to come home and be a teacher here!"

"I hope so, Mr. Bultman. I hope so."

"Me too. I just hope he doesn't get caught up in that accreditation problem here in Illinois."

Bill and Hank knew just enough about most things to be dangerous. They knew a little about colleges, plumbing, cows, and feminine hygiene—always just enough to give someone a hard time. The fact that they were both originally from Sheboygan, Wisconsin, can't be coincidental. Up there in Wisconsin they have a tavern on every corner, and when Hank and Bill were kids you could start drinking beer legally at age sixteen. Up there it gets so cold that there's really not much to do all winter except drink beer and tell stories. So Hank and Bill had probably been practicing their craft since they were teenagers, schooled in the fine art of BS. Here's an early example:

"You know ole Jim Dipschitz?"

"Who?"

"Jim. Dipschitz."

"No, can't say as I've had the pleasure."

"Yeah, so Jim Dipschitz goes to the judge, says, 'Judge, I really want to change my name.'"

"Ahh, that Jim Dipschitz."

"Judge says, 'A wise decision Mr. Dip . . . er, um, Jim. Have you considered what name you might like to take instead?'"

"Sure, I always liked the name Harry."

Today, if you were starting a University of BS, you couldn't do better than to have Hank as your Chancellor and Bill as Provost. They knew the fine points: Where is the soft spot of every person who comes in the shop? How can I exploit what they just said? How far can I push it before they realize they've been had? My, oh my, they were good. I couldn't blame Pete for going to the hardware store when those guys were around. The entertainment value was priceless. We couldn't afford to go to the shows in Chicago, and the programs on TV were OK, but the Gus Bock BS-ers performed week in and week out for free.

After he retired Pete would fix a few things around the house and take care of a couple of chickens or dogs and the yard. But by age 60 he couldn't work anymore; his heart just wouldn't let him. One afternoon, the neighbors' goats got loose so Pete naturally leapt from his chair and went out to corral them. He walked into the field, suddenly fell down, and never got back up. His sweet heart just stopped. He was only 61. It was 1960.

Al found Pete, picked him up, and brought him home. We had seen enough dead animals by then to know a lifeless body when we saw it, and I cried outright, without hesitation or restraint: "Pete, oh, Pete, you wonderful, sweet man. I wanted to grow old together."

At the funeral visitation I couldn't believe how many people came to express their sympathy. Some I didn't even recognize, but they all had nothing but wonderful things to say about Pete:

"Your husband was such a good man, he helped me with . . ."

"I'll always thankful for Pete. He talked to me when he was the yard-man at the high school when no one else seemed to care."

"He was the best driver we ever had."

"When Pete was yard man at the high-school he was the only one who could get that mower going."

I had to learn how to live without him, but it wasn't easy. We had been married for forty years and had never hurt each other, at least not intentionally. He was a kind, gentle, and loving man from beginning to end. We were different of course: he was a practical man who worked with his hands, whereas I lived a good share of my life through books, and in my own head. But we always got along, and I never once wondered if he would be there for me. I missed him dearly. I just longed to have his arms around me, holding me, knowing that he would always be the dear husband I had wed and loved.

A month or two after he died, I was in bed, crying, feeling alone and abandoned. Then, slowly but surely, I felt as if he *were* holding me. I could hear a voice speaking clearly, in masculine tones, though not Pete's, "Minnie, you know I will never forsake you." I had been touched by God.

Such A Good Son

STAN WAS MY ELDEST, and I couldn't have asked for a better kid. If he'd have been trouble, I'm sure it would have been much more difficult raising the younger ones. But Stan set a good example, without my having to tell him to. That is not to say that he was quiet, or dull. He had a sneaky sense of humor that I appreciated. As a little boy, for example, he would come home from school with silly riddles: "What's the biggest ant in the world?"

"An eleph*ant*."

"What's black and white and red all over?"

"A newspaper."

Not long after Stan was born in Montana my sister Christine (Tini) was pregnant too. She had married John Stammis, a good Christian Reformed man. During her pregnancy she had the German measles. Though it wasn't so difficult for her—she just had a rash and a fever—it affected the baby, Arnold, terribly. He looked a good bit like Stan, but the poor child never was whole. His body grew all right, but his mind never caught up. So while Stan grew in body, mind, and spirit, little Arnold just grew physically. It hurt to see my dear sister struggle, but she and John cared for that boy with all the love and care that anyone possibly could have. I often think that parents of handicapped children must have a special place set aside for them in heaven.

Stan and his brother Al were together quite a bit. They were only two years apart, both smart and hard-working. Stan was a bit better with his hands and Al a bit better with the books. They played outside all year around, making things with wood or bricks, or "campfires," etc.

When we lived on the farm in Lansing, Stan did a bit of hunting. We got him a Benjamin BB gun when he was 12. With it he shot some squirrels and rabbits around the farm. Then when he was about sixteen he got himself a 20-gauge shotgun—an Ithaca pump that expelled the shell casings from the bottom, which is helpful since it almost never jams, and your eyes are not distracted by a shell casing flying off in your peripheral vision. With that he could go rabbit hunting, or duck hunting, or pheasant hunting, not only around the farm, but also on some neighbor's properties who had open fields. The boys liked to trap animals too and then bring them into town to the furrier, "green," which means—untreated. I'm glad they didn't try to tan the hides themselves. That would have made a real stink.

Don loved to go out hunting with his big brother. He'd see Stan putting on his boots and getting his gun and ask, "Can I come?"

"I don't want you to get in the way."

"I won't get in the way. I'll walk off to the side, a little behind you, just like you told me."

"But I always worry you're going to get too close. Then when you kick up a rabbit, I'll turn and shoot you."

"I won't get too close!"

"OK. Put your boots on."

Thankfully, Don never did get too close, and no one was ever hurt with the guns.

We lived not far from one of the biggest flyways in America, the Kankakee Valley and Willow Slough. The whole area was low and marshy, and each spring and fall thousands of ducks and geese would migrate through. There were little buffleheads that looked as if they were wearing a white raccoon mask on their heads, while their white bodies floated like cotton balls atop the water. Scaup passed through too, both the greater and the lesser. All three types of mergansers dropped in: the hooded merganser with its round head and white splotch, the common with its pure green head and white body, and the red-breasted with its fluffy and scruffy looking hairdo. They were all diving ducks. The mallards with their fluorescent green heads didn't dive and were resident year-round.

Some guys from out east used to come to our area to hunt each fall. They were rich guys, very rich. They came from New York or Boston and killed hundreds of ducks in a matter of a few days. Who said they could do that? The ducks were coming from Canada, heading south, right through our backyard, and these guys who lived miles away came and shot them by the hundreds. It galled me. They had a lot of money and used it to kill off the ducks that were traveling a thousand miles from their homes. We had next to no money, so could only hunt the ones who happened along our pond. It's probably always been that way all through history, the rich taking the best for themselves and leaving only what they don't want for the rest of us. But it's not right! God made the ducks, and he made them to inhabit particular rivers and marshes. The people who lived nearby should be the ones who could hunt them. But instead, the rich men from far away shot them, their money trumping both God and nature.

During the Depression I was often worried if we would have enough food for the children. It got so bad that I had to ask little Stanley for help. When he was a little boy in Montana, Pete's mom gave him a silver dollar. That was a big deal. But after the church paid for our little baby Kenneth's funeral, I felt guilty that I couldn't even put a nickel in the collection plate, so I asked Stan, who was maybe thirteen years old, if I could have that silver dollar to put in the plate when it was passed on Sunday. He was sad, and looked down, but without saying a word, went to his dresser, took out the dollar, and gave it to me.

Stan was a lot like Pete—handy, able to use his abilities to work around the house and farm, but he was more like my dad in size, growing over 6'2" tall. He never played basketball, but did join the school baseball team, which won its division. Like many teenage boys he was gangly—his torso seemed to be on a spindle that swung at one rate while his long legs and arms moved at another. In his twenties he filled out a bit, but since he always worked hard, he never got fat.

I made most of Stan's clothes, as I did for all the kids. He had two pair of trousers, one for work and one for church and school, plus maybe three or four shirts. He went to Munster Christian Grade School, and then on the Thornton Fractional High School where he graduated second in his class. He didn't even think about going to college though, since we had no money for it, and like his father, he wanted to work with his hands.

In those days we didn't tell kids much about sex, or childbirth, so Stan only learned that his little sister Linda was going to be born on the day of her birth. It was a Sunday, and Pete told him we wouldn't be going to church. He was stunned—we never skipped church—and asked, "Why not?'

"Ma is going to have another baby."

"Really? Is that why she got so fat?"

I don't know why we were so secretive about it, but everyone acted that way back then.

Stan was a good worker around the farm and then the ranch. It was usually his job to milk the cows and goats. There were acres of empty land nearby to graze them, so they had to be corralled before they could be milked. That usually wasn't a problem, but when the weather was nice they sometimes wanted to stay outside, so Stan had to go round them up. When we were on the ranch during the war years Stan did that on horseback. He had visited Al while he was a flight mechanic in Texas and brought back a big cowboy hat for himself, so when rounded up the cattle he looked like a real cowboy. The German POW's saw him and looked on with raised eyebrows and wide eyes, saying:

"Ein Kowboy!" I suspect the tale of Stan on horseback with his cowboy hat was told in many a post-war German household.

After the war, in 1946, we moved off the ranch and into Grandma Recker's basement. Al was in college then, so it was Pete and I, plus Stan, Don and Lin at home. (Irene had married in '47). Stan was in his mid-twenties, Don in his late teens, and Lin in her early teens, twelve years younger than Stan. After he got back from the service, Stan worked as a carpenter, and when he came home, he liked to leisurely enjoy a nice meal. But Lin always wanted to get going because she had homework to do or was going out with friends. Stan was a notoriously slow eater, so when the rest of us were all done, he would still be sitting at the table. Since Lin had to clear the table and wash the dishes before she could go anywhere, she would hover around Stan and pester him to get him to finish up:

"Are you going to need the catsup yet?"

"No."

Lin would whisk it away.

"How about that salad dish? Finished yet?"

"Yes, thanks."

Lin would swoop in and take that to the kitchen sink, and she'd continue to whirl around, putting this away and washing that until Stan had finally finished his meal. Sometimes, on hot summer days, Stan would stop on his way home from work and pick up a pint of Ice-cream. Ah, now that was a wonderful treat. If some berries or peaches were in season, we'd put them on top. Delicious.

Stan taught me how to drive. It seems that sons are far more patient than husbands. The fact that a lot of cars now had automatic transmissions made them much easier to drive too.

Stan didn't date much. Oh, a little in high school, but when he came home from the service and started working as a carpenter, he found it hard to meet good Christian girls. He was out on his job during the day, and eligible young women were either at home or at their own office jobs. In the evening there wasn't much to do, so we'd play Rook, or Caroms, or some other board game together and listen to the radio.

Stan had a nice voice, not great, but good enough for a choir, so he joined the Illiana Chorale. He would ride into Munster with his friend Cory Morlock for a two-hour rehearsal. They did Handel's *Messiah* every winter and one of the other oratorios, such as the *Elijah* or Verdi's *Requiem,* in the spring. In the middle of rehearsal, the conductor would give them a break. During one of these breaks he was talking with some of the sopranos, one of whom was a Christian Reformed girl—Cornelia Schaap (known as "Corky"). She was tall and had a beautiful voice. She was from the next town over, South Holland, but since she and Stan had gone to different high schools they'd never met. He ended up courting her, and they were soon married—a very good Christian young couple.

After marriage Stan changed jobs, becoming an installer for Roseland Draperies. It takes some skill to get curtains put in just right, especially on a bow window, or a series of different sized ones. Stan could do it though, since he was a good carpenter. He was also a strong Christian witness on his job, as occasion permitted. When he was in a home for an installation, he would strike up a conversation, usually with the lady of the house, and if she was interested, he would talk about his faith. He carried around little meditation booklets that our church produced, and gladly provided them to whoever showed interest. He even struck up a friendship with some priests at a local rectory that needed new draperies. He got to chatting with them and found they were quite interested in our Protestant tradition. He talked freely with them, and they with him. I'm glad things have improved between our two branches of Christianity.

But not all the women were that easy to talk to, especially some of the richer women on the North Side. They gave him instructions but wouldn't allow him to talk. The most they might say was,

"What's your name?'

Stan would politely answer, "Stan Zwier, from Roseland Draperies."

"Before you come in you better take your shoes off."

"Well, ma'am, I'm carrying a special pair of shoes I use for installing in this bag. I keep them very clean, and my feet really need the support when I'm climbing the ladder and kneeling."

"No shoes in my house!"

"Yes, ma'am."

"And I better not have to clean up one speck of sawdust when you're done. You sure did pick a rotten day to come. I have to go to Jennie's house in an hour. How long is this going to take?"

"It should be about three hours. You have some nice windows, and they'll look good when I'm done."

"Oh no! My kids will be coming home, and you'll still be here. Just try to stay out of the way." Stan would shake his head. When he got home, he'd often say about the women he'd had to deal with, "I don't know the man that woman is married to, but I sure pity him. I think I'll nominate him for sainthood."

Stan and Corky had three children in the mid 1950's—Randy, Diane and Rodney, all of whom were born Caesarian. Then in 1960 Corky was pregnant again with their fourth, whom she hoped to deliver vaginally. She was about eight months along, and the baby was nearly ready for birth. One day at that point in her pregnancy Corky felt a terrible pain inside her that was not a normal labor pang. Something deep inside of her was hurting badly. She later learned that the incision from the previous pregnancies was letting loose. She was lying on the floor in her kitchen, in pain, when she called me.

"Ma, the baby is coming, and something terrible is happening inside me."

Her uterus had ruptured, so even speaking took a heroic effort on her part.

"I'll call the ambulance. You stay put."

I called the ambulance, then got in my car and headed over. The ambulance and I arrived at about the same time, and by then she was bleeding badly. They got her up on a gurney and drove her off. I contacted Roseland Draperies, and they found Stan, who met us at the hospital.

When we were together in the Emergency Room, the doctor worked on her for a couple of minutes before the anesthesia took effect and shook his head. "We're losing her, Mr. Zwier. Her whole abdomen is infected. You are certainly not going to have a live baby, and you'll be lucky if you have a wife by the end of the day."

Stan prayed, I prayed, and the doctors worked. The baby was stillborn and Corky was critical. Randy, Diane and Rodney had been called home early from school and were with a babysitter, but Stan picked them up and brought them to see their mom, wondering if it would be their last time. They arrived while Corky was still knocked out, looking white and frail. I can't remember ever seeing any more sad-faced kids.

"Is she going to die?" Randy asked.

"We don't know. The doctors have done their work. Now we have to pray that she gets better."

I think the prayers of children might be the most powerful instruments on earth. They come straight from the heart, without any of our adult fears or shame to hinder. Those prayers worked for their mom. She recovered, came home, and returned as a happy mother of three.

When they got a little older, each grandkid would spend a night or two with me. Little Rodney loved to sleep over, and I always liked having him. Rod thought it was a real treat to go outside and burn the garbage, since I had a kind of a fireplace/pit outside. Of course they weren't allowed to burn at their own house in town. Everything just went into a can in the garage—pretty boring. On the other hand, walking outside with the trash, lighting matches, and starting a fire was exciting for a little guy like him.

Diane came over too. I was now in my sixties my hair was turning gray, as were my eyebrows. When Diane was over I'd say,

"Diane, get the tweezers and come pluck the gray eyebrow hairs out."

She'd sit right in front of me and carefully pluck them, one by one. The next time she was over, I asked her to do it again. She said,

"Grandma, if I pull out all the gray eyebrows you won't have any left!"

Why do we teach kids to always tell the truth?

Pete had planted an apricot tree—as well as a few other fruit trees—in the backyard, and the year after he died, it was covered with blossoms. One day Diane called me over and showed it to me. I said, "How I wish Pete could see these. I sure hope you have a good husband like him some day."

When the grandkids were over, I figured that they could pretty much do whatever they wanted around the house, just as long as they didn't hurt anything. So, among other things, they felt free to snoop through my fridge and pantry. Sometimes they found some cookies or fruit they wanted, but other times they found things in the back of the fridge that I had forgotten about. I can remember more than one occasion when they would pull out a container, open it, and let out a sick, rotting odor. They would proudly bring it into the living room to show, tell, and smell. Their parents and I would snort at it in disgust and tell them to throw it outside on the compost pile.

Randy liked to do art projects when he was in high-school, some of which struck me as strange. I remember a bust of a man he made from clay that looked like a badly misshapen monster to me—the nose was ajar, the eyes didn't line up, and the mouth was an ugly grimace.

"Thou shalt not make graven images," I told him.

"I'm not. I'm trying to make something like Picasso."

"Who?"

"Pablo Picasso, the great Spanish artist."

"Well, why don't you try to make something more like Rembrandt van Rijn, or Johannes Vermeer instead? Those Dutch painters made pictures that look a lot nicer."

He didn't follow my advice.

Stan was always fixing things around the house and so always going to the hardware store. A girl at the check-out counter looked at his hands and said, "Ouch, what happened there?"

"Ah, it's just a blister," said Stan.

"I had one of those once," she said empathetically.

When Stan told me of this conversation, he bent over and shook his head.

"She had *A Blister, Once!*," he marveled.

"I've never added up my blisters. If I had, I would have lost count decades ago. I'm not sure this young generation really knows how to work."

It was true, in a way. Most kids today don't know how to work with their hands, even some of my own grandkids. Stan's son Rodney became a heating and cooling guy, but I don't think Randy or Diane ever learned which end of a screwdriver meant business.

Stan and Corky picked me up every Sunday morning for church, and I'd stay at their house in the afternoon till the evening service. Corky could really cook, and Sunday was the day she showed her stuff. Her specialty was pot roast. She'd get a nice chuck or shoulder roast, put bacon around it, holding the strips in place with tooth-picks. Since the meat was kind of tough, she'd put it in the broiler before leaving for church and cook it at a low temperature for a few hours to tenderize it. (If the preacher went too long, he'd hear about it from the women.) She'd put potatoes, carrots and onions around the roast and add seasonings—rosemary, thyme, salt, pepper, etc. It would all cook together, slowly, in the roaster. When she took it out she'd make gravy with the meat juice, put the veggies in a separate bowl, and then cut and serve the roast. She'd even manage to find a way to use sunflower seeds with the veggies sometimes. For dessert there was ice-cream or pie made with strawberries or blueberries when in season. I'd help with the dishes afterward.

After dinner in the summer, we would all sit outside in the lawn-chairs and have some iced tea. The kids would play around, and occasionally a ball would come rolling or flying by. After the evening church service, they'd take me home. Though I only lived about a mile away, my place was still like a farmhouse, alone on the three acres. When I left on Sunday morning I'd lock the house, since I would be gone for the whole day, and hang the key on a nail in the crook of a big oak tree in the backyard. In the evening Stan and family would sit in the car in the driveway, watch me get the key out from the tree and open the door. When they saw the lights go on in the house, they knew I was safely inside. Of all my kids, I spent the most time with Stan and Corky. They lived closest to me, and my oldest son cared for me deeply.

Stan and Corky even took me with them on vacation out west one summer. I was so happy to see the mountains again! But the trip wasn't all that pleasant, all six of us were together in their station wagon in the heat of July. There was no air-conditioning in our cars back then, so we took some towels, soaked them in water before we left each stop, and held them up to the open car windows. The wind would blow through the towels and cool us down a bit. Then we'd take the towels and wrap them around our necks. I'm not sure that we really reduced the temperature, but at least it seemed like we were doing something to keep cool.

The drive out there was longer than I remembered. When you start in Chicago, it seems like once you hit the Colorado state line from the east you should almost be to the Rockies. But, nope, you still have nearly 200 miles to go from Kanarado, Kansas, to Pikes Peak. You can see Pikes Peak off in the distance not long after you cross the state line, and it looks like you should be there any minute, but it just grows bigger, little by little. Midwestern distances just don't compare.

I remember going to the "Cave of the Winds." We saw stalactites and stalagmites—I can never remember which ones top-down and which ones are bottom-up. It was a very long cave, and windy, as advertised. I just looked around in awe: God is quite an architect. We hiked around in the springs and gorges nearby. I was now in my mid-sixties, so hiking around at that altitude really took it out of me. Randy and Rodney ran around like mountain goats, but the thin air even eventually took its toll on them too.

We went to an Indian store where I saw some things I hadn't come across since I was a girl at the fair in Montana. I bought a nice turquoise ring there, and when Diane got older I gave it to her.

Since Stan and all the other kids eventually got married, it got to be just Al and me at home. Al worked at his easy, menial job, and then went to his room to read after supper, while I did my reading in the living room. Al was rarely happy, but whenever Stan came over, he cheered up, remembering the good times they'd had when younger. I would make tea, and then call Al to come have a cup and some cookies, and chat with Stan and me.

One evening I called up to Al, "Stan's here. Come join us for some tea." But no answer.

"Maybe he's playing music on his radio. I'll get him," offered Stan.

A couple minutes later, Stan came out of Al's room, crying like a little boy who had lost everything. "He's gone, Ma. He's done it this time."

Al had taken pills, a lot of them, and left a little note next to his bed: "I've had enough. I can't see the point of staying on this earth any longer."

Stan held me in his arms while I sobbed bitterly.

"Oh, Alton, Alton, my son, my son. Oh, my son Alton."

Coping After Al

AL HAD TRIED IT once before, putting a plastic bag over his head, and taking some pills. That time, Stan found him on time, got him breathing, and pleaded with him to live.

In retrospect I should have known that Al's life would end this way. He always struggled with depression. He'd never married, so never had a wife to care for him, and enjoy life together. Back in college he had episodes of depression that left him unable to finish his classes. He came home without graduating, even though he made it through three and a half years. When he returned, he took jobs that were far beneath him, the kind that someone with a fraction of his ability could have done.

I suspect that Al felt free to end it all after Pete had died. He must have known that Pete's tender heart would never have recovered from such a loss. I guess I have to thank him for showing mercy to his father that way. I just wish he could have done the same for me.

What could I have done? I don't know. I tried to be a good mother. I certainly never hurt or belittled him. To the contrary—I thought he was as wonderful a man as there ever was, and was proud to call him my son. But could I have stopped him from suicide, or cured his depression? I doubt it. I think it was just part of his nature. I knew he was lonely, and that his job was no challenge for him. But he never opened up to me or to Pete. He just kept to himself, and read those books of his—Nietzsche, Freud, and I don't know who. I couldn't understand them, but he read them like they were his Bible.

Maybe if he'd have married, he would have been happier. He had a girlfriend or two when he was younger, but never after he got out of the Air Force. One of those girls, Jennie, wrote him while he was in the service and said she couldn't marry him since she really didn't know who he was. What a perceptive girl! Who, indeed, was Al? He was our son. He was brilliant, introverted, and kind. But he had terrible bouts of depression like his grandma—Pete's mom.

Al was born in Montana, not long before we moved back to Illinois. As a little boy Al was sensitive and had worried about things that most children don't. He felt things deeply, but darkly. One summer he had the job of watching the sheep for Mr. Schultz. He woke up one night, crying from a nightmare.

"Al, Al, what's the matter honey?" I asked, rushing into his room.

"I'm afraid the sheep will get out, and I'll lose them!"

"Don't worry about those sheep. You just go back to sleep."

He did, but since he was so afraid something might go wrong, we asked Stan to take over as a shepherd.

Another time, when he was just a little guy in Lansing, he got sick, badly, with whooping cough. He coughed and coughed, and the snot ran out his nostrils till it nearly touched the ground. It was terrible to see him in that shape. We couldn't do much of anything for him. We just had to wait, hoping and praying he'd recover. I now wonder if he might have been better off dying as a child so he wouldn't have had to suffer so later in life.

He was the valedictorian of his high-school class. One of his teachers said that he had never had a better science and math student: Al was doing trigonometry in the 9th grade. He could do anything when it came to math and science. Like Pete, he was good with his hands, too.

I think when he got older, he couldn't get past that evolution thing. When he went to Calvin College after the war, he thought he'd get his questions answered. Instead, he got more confused. Could God create the world like it says in the Bible, and at the same time have evolution be true? He felt he had to choose between the two.

We named him after my Pa—Ahlrich, but he looked more like my brother Al. Interesting how that turned out. I had planned to give him Pa's name when I first got pregnant, hoping, I guess, that he would be something like Pa Recker. But he really didn't turn out much like him. Pa wasn't brilliant. Pa smiled a lot. Pa went to church.

He never went to church when he came back from the war and then from college. He had been baptized as an infant, and made profession of faith in our church, just like all our kids. I don't think he ever quit believing in God, but he just saw no use for the church. Of course, that didn't make us very happy. We wanted him to be a part of church though we finally stopped asking him if he would join us. It got to the point that some elders came to see him, but he wouldn't even talk to them. They called and called, and he ignored and ignored, so they started church discipline. Finally, they went forward with his excommunication. Elder DeYoung called me the week before they were going to announce it in church. That way Pete and I wouldn't have to be there to hear it and feel the sad stares from our friends and family. What a terrible thing. Excommunication claims that someone is no longer a child of God. That's what they said about Al.

I pray that God is more merciful than the church. In fact, I cling to that belief. God is merciful, and his mercies endure forever. When we baptized Al as an infant, we declared that he was a child of God's covenant, that we would raise him as a Christian, and that the Spirit of God would be within him from day one. We kept our promises, and I believe God kept his. Later, when he was 16, he made profession of faith, accepting the promises God made to him in baptism. How could he not be a Christian anymore?

Not only did he confess the right things, he did the right things. He was not just a good man; he was a very good man. He really did nothing wrong. He did good for others. He never spoke a harsh or ill word. And now he was gone. What was God doing here? Why couldn't God have come closer to Al and given him the strength to live?

God made Al the way he was. God made a sensitive and brilliant man who suffered from severe depression. Do you think God is then going to condemn him after having made him that way? I can't believe that. I know Pete's mother had deep emotional problems, and I later learned that another member of her family also committed suicide. So clearly there were some inherited traits that made Al who he was. But Al didn't choose them, and I didn't choose them for him. Al just had ideas and feelings he couldn't live with. I wonder if the right person, maybe a scientist who understood evolution and the Bible, could have helped him. I don't know how those things work, but why couldn't someone at Calvin College or elsewhere have talked to him?

Al did so many good things. After his death I learned that he even paid for Lin's college tuition. When she was thinking of going to college, he told her, "Don't worry about the money. I'll lend it to you." He was earning a little money from that dumb job that someone with one tenth of his intelligence could have handled. But after Lin graduated and tried to pay him back, Al wouldn't take a nickel from her.

"No, I don't want that money," he told her. "You need it. Don't worry about it. Glad I could help."

I'm going to believe that Al was a Christian to my dying day. In fact, I'm going to count on seeing him someday in the glory of heaven, free from his depression, and free from his doubts. I don't accept that his depression and his brilliance could undo what God did for him in Christ.

Pete was a good dad to him too, holding him while little, playing with him, and then teaching him how to make and fix things when he got older. His brothers and sisters looked up to him for his intellect. Were it not enough that he were so smart, Al was also the most athletic of the boys, becoming quite a good diver after years of practice in the local rock quarry. Don looked up to Al so much it was almost as if Al were Don's father, rather than his older brother. Don followed Al right and left, talking with him all the time.

I loved Al in a way that perhaps only a mother can love a son. I saw his flaws, but they didn't matter. He was my child, God's gift to me, one whom I had given the gift of life. How could someone who was so dear to me simply be gone? Like for all my kids, I prayed for him, ceaselessly, beginning from the day I learned I was pregnant. No wonder I felt such deep sorrow at his death. Only deep love could yield such pain. I can almost understand how the Father must have felt when Jesus cried out,

"My God, my God, why have you forsaken me?"

The pastor from our church didn't even visit me. I suspect he felt so awkward about the suicide that he didn't know what to say—and, he knew full well about the excommunication. What could he have said?

"Alton Zwier, a brilliant man, turned sour on the church and was excommunicated. Later, he committed suicide." I'm sure that's what it seemed from the outside.

I had to suffer on my own, since Pete left me only two years earlier. The other kids grieved too, of course. Stan, in particular, was close to Al and knew of Al's bouts with depression, perhaps even more than I did. But Stan had his own family to take care of and couldn't spend loads of time with me. When we were together, we'd try to console each other.

"Ma, Al was sick," Stan would say.

"I know, but it wasn't a sickness you could see, or cure."

"No, it was all inside."

"He sure suffered."

"Ya, but now it's us who suffer when he's gone."

Dr. William Rutgers, pastor of a neighboring church, came for a visit when he learned that our own preacher was too embarrassed to do so. He reminded me of this passage in Romans:

> *For whom he did foreknow, he also did predestinate to be conformed to the image of his Son, that he might be the firstborn among many brethren.*
>
> *Moreover, whom he did predestinate, them he also called: and whom he called, them he also justified: and whom he justified, them he also glorified.*
>
> *What shall we then say to these things? If God be for us, who can be against us?*
>
> *He that spared not his own Son, but delivered him up for us all, how shall he not with him also freely give us all things?*
>
> *Who shall lay anything to the charge of God's elect? It is God that justifieth.*
>
> *Who is he that condemneth? It is Christ that died, yea rather, that is risen again, who is even at the right hand of God, who also maketh intercession for us.*
>
> *Who shall separate us from the love of Christ? Shall tribulation, or distress, or persecution, or famine, or nakedness, or peril, or sword?*
>
> *As it is written, For thy sake we are killed all the day long; we are accounted as sheep for the slaughter.*
>
> *Nay, in all these things we are more than conquerors through him that loved us. For I am persuaded, that neither death, nor life, nor angels, nor principalities, nor powers, nor things present, nor things to come,*
>
> *Nor height, nor depth, nor any other creature, shall be able to separate us from the love of God, which is in Christ Jesus our Lord.*

It just doesn't get any better or any clearer than that. God's love is unstoppable, and unending. No sin or flaw of man can undo it. And I believe to this day that the love of God was poured out in the life of my Alton. He once confessed it, and he lived it.

Thankfully, this was about the time when we started a new church, so I wasn't stuck with that pastor who wouldn't visit me. It was hard to go to that same Lansing church that had excommunicated Al and then failed to help me when he died. Lots of families were moving further south, and a new church was starting. Stan and Corky, Irene, and other families were going there, so I went too. I needed a new start.

When Al was in the Army, he sent me a letter that said:

> *I have come to realize more and more as the days, months and years pass just how much my religion means to me. Don't ever worry, Mom, that I will forsake what I have been taught. Perhaps I don't agree in all the details, but I know how meaningless this life of ours is if we don't believe in Christ and his love. Sometimes I wish I didn't have to wait all my life before I can go to heaven. It seems so long to wait.*

Perhaps he'd just decided couldn't wait any longer.

Some told me that I should move on or forget the past and just concentrate on the future. Neh! What nonsense! Impossible! How could I forget the wonderful husband I had married forty years earlier? How could I forget the son whom I had birthed, raised, and nurtured? Such advice was nonsense, and maybe even blasphemy. I would go on with life, but it would be a far different life, a life with a very different shape than my married life, and life with son Al. I would have to live without Pete, and with the sheer wrongness of Al's suicide. Death is an enigma, a surd. No one will ever be able to explain it. I can only take comfort in the truth that Christ overcame it.

I feel like Job. He argued and argued with his friends, telling them that he had done nothing wrong, and that God had treated him unfairly. That's how I felt too. What had I done to deserve this? What does God have to say for himself?

In Job, God responded in a nearly crazy way; he gave Job a science quiz:

Tell me about the hippopotamus. Could you have invented or tamed him? Where are the storehouses of snow kept? Why don't you lead out the stars one by one, in order, and by name?

This is hardly the kind of answer that Job, nor I, find satisfying. But then at the end of the book it's strange: Job repented. After all that had happened to him it was Job who repented. Why? The Bible says that he saw God, then repented in "dust and ashes," saying,

"I have spoken like a true fool. I didn't understand a thing. But now that I have seen God, I recognize that my questions and accusations are silly. I have been shaking my fist at God. At God! And I am but a worm of a man. Forgive me, Lord."

It's a crazy ending. But it must be true. Knowing God must somehow consign all our grief, all our complaints and all our questions to the footnotes. Seeing, knowing, and even being loved by God apparently makes all our human problems and follies stand out for what they are—insignificant tripe. I don't know why Al had to die, but I do know and believe "that my redeemer liveth, and that he shall stand at the latter day upon the earth. And though worms destroy his body, and my body, in my flesh shall I see God."

And I earnestly pray that I shall see Al too.

Irene Moves Back West

My remaining four children were all doing well. I thank God for each of them even as I remember the losses of Pete, Alton, and even little Kenneth.

Irene was born shortly after we got back to Illinois from Montana, in 1927. After two boys it was so nice to have a little girl. My brothers and sisters had all married early, so Irene had a lot of older girl cousins. She thought they were sooo pretty. I personally thought they were kind of average, but I guess when you're five or six, girls who are in their teens do look pretty nice. Some of those older cousins like Beulah and Cynthia Recker and the Kikkert girls liked to stop in to play with Irene. They got out dolls that I had sewn and some half-broken tea sets and had a nice time having "teatime," and playing "house."

"Would you like some tea, ma'am?"

"Why yes, thank you. What lovely dishes you have."

"Thank you, they're from my grandmother."

"Care for a cookie?"

That was part of the fun—Irene got to bake cookies with her big cousins. They would use my oven and ingredients and usually made oatmeal cookies. I supervised the process pretty closely, since I didn't want any mishaps in my kitchen.

My brother Al always gave our kids a penny on their birthday. He usually did it after church on the Sunday nearest their birthday. On Irene's birthday, Al pretended as if he had forgotten, while little Irene anxiously followed him through the foyer. Finally, he turned to her.

"Why Irene, how are you today?"

"Fine, but don't you know it's my birthday!"

"Oh my, I forgot," he said, clasping his forehead in mock horror. "I hope I have a penny. Ah yes, I happen to have one right here."

He gave it to her, and got a kiss from a sweet little girl in thanks.

In her teens, Irene was glad we weren't as strict as a lot of Dutch Reformed families. For example, we let our kids play outside and ride their bikes on Sunday, and we didn't go to church for every imaginable event. Some of that might have been due to the fact that we lived way out in Crete, some 15 miles away from church. We didn't feel we had to set strict curfews for the kids either, since they knew well enough to be home at a reasonable hour, especially on school nights. I had a little tradition of emitting a cough when I heard them come in late at night. That way even though the house might be dark and Pete asleep, they knew I heard them when they came in.

When we lived in the house in Sauk Trail as tenant farmers, we had that family of hillbillies living with us. There was a man, a wife, plus three little kids—two boys and a girl. When Irene was about to graduate from High School, she prepared some hand-made party invitations to send to all her friends and family. Without her knowing it, those two little boys followed her when she took them down the lane to the mailbox. They snuck behind her, took all her beautiful cards out of the mailbox and threw them in the mud. We would have liked to kill those little rascals!

In high-school Rene had the hardship of being Al's younger sister. Al got straight A's without much effort, while taking the hardest classes he could find. So, when sister Irene Zwier turned up in those classes a couple years later, the teachers assumed she would be a bright and shining academic star like her brother. Irene was no dummy, but she was some distance from Al intellectually. One day she came home in tears.

"I got a B+ in Algebra. Mr. Schmidt asked me why I couldn't be more like Al." Thankfully, she was unlike Al in temperament too, with a cheerful smile ready at all times.

Whatever books Rene brought home from school, I read. It was fascinating to see what they were getting in their classes. She read "Lord of the Flies," and "A Separate Peace," and "East of Eden," so I did too. Sometimes I didn't have time to read them while she was studying them, so I'd go to the library and borrow my own copy later. I read the geography, the history, and the civics books too. Such lucky kids—they got to go to High-School and learn all that stuff.

Irene had a long bus ride every school day. The bus went way around all those country roads and took nearly an hour each way. Since she had to take that same bus home in the afternoon, she couldn't join any of the after-school activities. She suspected that the boys didn't ask her out much since they didn't want to travel all the way out to the ranch to get her.

Rene was in high-school during the war years—1941–1945, so she saw all the German prisoners as they worked in our fields. I think she was a little frightened by them. Sometimes she had to navigate her way past the prisoners just to get in the house. There she was, at age fifteen, walking past half-dozen or so German soldiers who were just a few years older than she was. She didn't know any German, thankfully. I could understand them and wasn't happy about the way they talked about her.

She had a brother and lots of cousins in the service, and she knew they were the enemy, so it was a little disconcerting to her to see how well they were dressed, and treated.

"Look at those guys—they are wearing nice rings and watches. How can they be prisoners?"

One day the U.S. soldier who was guarding the prisoners happened along at the bus stop when Irene was getting off. He gave her a ride. That was quite a treat for her, riding with a handsome soldier in his uniform in an Army Jeep.

Irene was the first of our children to marry. She married Al DeVries when she was just 19 years old. Al was a WWII veteran from our church who had served as a Marine in the Pacific. Al's younger brother Adrian was the same age as Irene, and had been with her all through school, so we knew each other's family. Their mother asked Al why he didn't take Irene to a dinner for returning servicemen held at church. He did, and a couple of years later they married.

During the war, everything was rationed, including gas, so we never drove. One afternoon shortly after the war we were all outside while Rene was getting ready to go out with Al. We saw a new car coming down the lane. Who could that be? It was Al. He had spent most of his military severance pay on a car, so now he and Rene could go out in style. Rene was pretty impressed.

Al DeVries was a little guy, maybe 5' 6". But unlike most small men, Al was never bitter, or carried a chip on his shoulder about being short. You know how some small men can be—they let you know very quickly that they are *Quite* important, no matter their size. You never got that feeling from Al. Maybe he gained so much confidence in the Marines that he never felt inferior to anyone.

When the war started in 1941, Al was 17, one year too young to serve. But he so badly wanted to go fight Hitler that he got his mom to sign for him at the recruitment office. He got into the Marines. I now marvel that guys like him were sent all over the world to defend our country—he looked like such a little boy when he left. But neither size nor age really tell you much about a man—what goes on inside the heart and the head is far more important.

When they sent him to the Pacific, he had to take a troop train all the way from Chicago to Los Angeles. I think that while crossing the long, wide prairies, climbing up mountains and coursing through dry canyon territories he fell in love with the West. He always loved the West, and many years later he and Rene moved to Denver.

For many years he didn't talk about the war much, except for a few funny stories, like taking showers on Saipan. As soon as the rains came the guys would all strip down, find some soap and lather up. But then, suddenly, the rain would stop, leaving a few hundred guys with soap all over them, dripping wet, with no way to rinse off. They looked at each other as if to say, "Why not? Everything else in this war is screwed up."

In later years he told more serious stories of the battles he was a part of in Saipan and Okinawa, two of the bloodiest in the Pacific. He was among the men who were spit out of those troop carriers into the sea, wading ashore under enemy fire. I shudder to think. He scrambled up those atolls looking for any little bit of cover. On Saipan his commanding officer, General Buckner, was shot and killed no more than two feet away from him.

Though he was a little guy, he carried around a heavy machine-gun. He hauled that big gun around, set it up on a tripod, and got the shells lined up for firing. He did his duty. I suspect guys like him killed dozens of Japanese. Years later his son Jerry moved to Okinawa, so he and Al toured the area where the battle occurred.

> *Our big ship was in the ocean over there somewhere. The landing craft must have come ashore about there. I had to hunker down for a while and couldn't do much—just tried to stay alive. The bombers had been at their job for over a week, but the Japs were on their own territory now, so they were going to fight to the death. We managed to creep forward; it must have been over there somewhere. Finally, we got to that ridge and I was able to get my machine gun set up. I tried to keep my head down when loading. Then when I got a clip of shells in, I rose up, peered through the sight, and fired away.*

When more than a million men come home from the service, they needed work, and housing, and they wanted to start families. Businesses grew, churches grew, and not long afterwards, schools grew. Al's first job after the service was as a plumber, working on the many new houses that were going up all around us.

Irene dreamt of being a nurse but she, nor we, had any money for college. Guys who were in the service could go to school on the G.I. Bill, but the girls who stayed home couldn't. And since Pete and I could count our assets by emptying our pockets, Irene even had to pay for her own wedding. She worked at Hoekstra's grocery store as a checkout for a couple years after High-School so she could save up some money. We were at least able to provide her with a place to live while she was saving up for marriage. Rene even bought Pete's white shirt for the wedding at the last moment. While she went to the Minas store to buy it, she met Stan coming out with an ironing board, his wedding gift to her.

Irene didn't learn how to drive till later in life either, so Al or Pete had to take her around. Pete drove her into Chicago to look for a wedding dress. I think he was happy to be able to do that small thing for her. Like most weddings then, the service itself was in the church sanctuary, and then the reception dinner was in the Christian school cafeteria.

I know my girls saved themselves for marriage. That was assumed for them as it had been for me. I never lectured them, or worried about it. The only time I even raised the issue was when one of their cousins got pregnant before marriage. I looked at them, waved my finger, and said with fervor.

"Don't you girls ever do that!"

But times were changing in the U.S. I can still remember the first time I saw a picture of a woman wearing a bikini in some magazine in the early 60's. The young woman was a model on the French Riviera. I thought,

"I'll never see that in America."

Boy was I wrong. I saw women on the beaches of Lake Michigan wearing them just a few years later. By the 70's my own grand-daughters were wearing them at the public pool. Wow.

After their wedding in '47, Al and Irene lived upstairs with her in-laws, which seemed to go pretty well. She never complained that her mother-in-law meddled or bothered her about house-keeping or anything. After two and a half years of marriage I got a little worried that they might not be able to have children, since this was in the days before birth-control when the babies came pretty quickly. But she never worried: she thought that since her mother and cousins all got pregnant with no trouble, she would too. She delivered our first grandchild in

1950—Jackie. Her kids would be a part of the "Baby Boom" generation, born in the decade or so after the war.

That little Jackie was a cutie, and a smarty, and tiny, since both of her parents were small. I still remember when she had the "Welcome Speech" at our church Christmas program. She must have been about four. She walked briskly to the pulpit then climbed up two extra steps that had been set up for her. At three feet, two—and one-half inches her head was barely visible. With great assurance, and with a strong, clear, voice, she said,

> *I'm so glad to see you.*
> *I'm so glad you're here.*
> *We wish you a merry Christmas,*
> *And a happy New Year.*

I helped her memorize her little speech. In fact, so did Pete, and her uncles and aunts, so at family gatherings we would all recite it together, mimicking her fervor.

After Jackie came Jeff, and after Jeff—Jerry. I don't know why Rene was so committed to the letter "J," but the names were fine. Jerry was the first of three grandsons born that year—1958. First came Jerry DeVries, then Rod Zwier, then Kent Van Til. They all ended up in the same class in High-School.

I remember when those boys were all about five or six and we were at Stan and Corky's house one Sunday afternoon. Stan had planted a nice orchard in his yard, just as we had in ours. The apple tree had blossomed, and the little apples were about golf-ball size in early summer. For some reason, unknown to me still, those little guys went out and knocked all the green apples off the tree. Had they been given another couple of months they would have been great for eating or baking. But no, the little destroyers did the job. Stan gave Rodney a spank, and Al DeVries and Paul Van Til gave their boys one too. Why would they do that? Why are people, and especially boys, so destructive? If they see something they can take, grab, and wreck, they do it.

Pete and I would often babysit for Rene and Al when they visited friends or went to church events. I played with Jackie, and Pete played with the boys. He always had something that they could "fix." He'd take the wheel off their tricycle and then help them put it back on. He'd look around for some wood or bricks and then help them design a "house."

Jeff and Jerry were quite the boys. They often got in a little trouble when they came over. They would wander down to the creek to look for crabs or frogs, and inevitably fall in. When they came back to the house all soaked and muddy Al or Irene would yell at them, and then get them cleaned up. It got to the point that Irene kept a spare set of clothes at my house, just in case.

The boys loved to be at my house and play on the road grader, letting the blade go down, and then cranking it back up. Once Jeff nearly let the blade down on little Jerry's toes. Now that I think about it, I can't believe we let them play on that machine.

Pete kept all his tools in the basement, and the boys thought that was their own special playground. Pete had a grinder/wheel that you had to turn by hand to sharpen things. The boys thought that was the best toy in the world. They would get an old screwdriver and hold it on the grinder till it was worn down to a fine point. One of them would turn off all the basement lights so they could see the sparks fly.

Just for a joke, my son Al once took Jeff DeVries and Diane Zwier with him to the tavern when they were about eight or nine. He went in, sat them down next to him, and said "Belly up to the bar, kids." He then bought them a Coke.

Well that was pretty big stuff for two little kids. They came home and reported every detail to the rest of us. Irene and Al kind of shrugged it off, shaking their heads at their brother and brother-in-law. But Corky got all upset.

"How could you bring little children into a tavern?"

"What do you think people will say?"

In 1962 Al and Irene had one more boy, Joel. He was born in good health, but he had a sudden and terrible onset of pneumonia at only 20 months. I remember it was a Saturday, and Irene was home with the kids and Al was working overtime. Little Joel was running a temperature and not feeling well. Irene called the doctor, who said she should give him some medicine that he would call in to the pharmacy. Irene ran to the pharmacy and got the medicine, but it didn't help little Joel. Another call to the doctor resulted in a trip to the Emergency Room, where they immediately took him for an X-Ray. No sooner had they taken the X-ray than that dear little boy died. Irene knew it right away, saying "He's gone," and sobbing her way out of the X-ray room.

Rene and Al were devastated, as were we all. This kind of thing was happening way too often in our family. I had the baby Kenneth who lived for only a couple of weeks, Stan and Corky had a still-born, and now Irene had a dead toddler. I think it was the worst for Rene and Al, since Joel had lived to twenty months, was walking and talking, smiling, and showing his own delightful personality. Why would God let him die? Was Joel destined to suffer from the same debilitating depression that so troubled Pete's family, making his death a merciful act that spared that spared another terrible loss later in life like son Al? I can't say. I can say that we all grieved deeply with Al and Irene. Nonetheless I believe that God is good, and his mercy endures forever. The song that Casey Van Til sang at the funeral displayed that faith.

> *When He cometh, when He cometh,*
> *To make up His jewels,*
> *All His jewels, precious jewels,*
> *His loved and His own.*
> *Refrain:*
> *Like the stars of the morning,*
> *His bright crown adorning,*
> *They shall shine in their beauty,*
> *Bright gems for His crown.*
> *(2) He will gather, He will gather*
> *The gems for His kingdom,*
> *All the pure ones, all the bright ones,*
> *His loved and His own.*
> *(3) Little children, little children,*
> *Who love their Redeemer,*
> *Are the jewels, precious jewels,*
> *His loved and His own.*

Al DeVries was something of an amateur naturalist. His favorite magazine was the National Geographic, and he really loved the outdoors, so he and Rene would often sneak out for little hikes in our area. They took me along to Pokagon State Park in Indiana one Sunday afternoon, since they had gone there the year before and thought I would like it. I certainly did. It was a cheerful spring day, and the flowers were all coming out. I recognized most of them: the Ladies Lockets with their flowers hanging downward from the stem, a row of pink flowers with little white petals on the inside, the butterfly weeds that certainly weren't weeds, but beautiful clusters of yellow, orange and vermillion flowers, and then Lenten Roses, standing up even when there was yet snow, with five or six speckled petals of white or red, purple or pink.

When we got back to Lansing Irene said,

"I think we're too late for evening church."

"I think we had our worship outdoors today," I replied.

When they were in their fifties, Irene and Al moved to Denver. By then Al was a supervisor for a heating and air-conditioning company, and there was plenty of work for him out west. Their eldest son Jeff had moved to Denver right out of High School, following a favorite teacher from Illiana Christian. Not long thereafter, their second son Jerry moved to California. So later in life, Irene and Al decided to go west too. I told her,

"You're going to like it out there."

But I sure missed Irene. I was in my early eighties and she was in her early fifties, and in one sense she was leaving home for the first time. She had moved out of my house of course, but only a few miles away. She was always there to talk with, and help out, but now she'd be far away. It seemed right, somehow though, that they were going out west. Pete and I had met in Montana sixty some years ago, and now Rene and Al were completing the circle.

I was able to visit them in Colorado—my first trip on an airplane. Wow is that an experience. By then Chicago had its second big airport—O'Hare Field. What an octopus of a place that is—just getting around inside the airport was a journey in itself. Then to takeoff you get going fast, while the plane shudders a bit, then you feel the wheels leaving the ground, look out the window and see the ground falling away.

It was terrific to be out West again. I saw flowers I hadn't seen since I was in my twenties. I woke up and was greeted by mountains. I watched as the clouds clung to the mountains, and life just seemed happier. It was March, yet I could wear a summer dress by early afternoon.

They joined a Christian Reformed Church there, and once they were established Irene was elected as a deacon. Imagine that! My giggly little Irene was on the consistory! I sure was surprised. In our church in Lansing we didn't have any women deacons yet, though "women in church office" was a hotly debated subject in our denomination. But as I thought about it; why not have women as deacons, or maybe even elders and preachers? Women are certainly as capable as men at doing those things since we are filled with the same Holy Spirit as the men. Why not use women's gifts in the church? In a way, since I visit the sick, help the poor, and encourage the weary, I have probably been a deacon in our church, without the title

When Jerry was in California, he met a girl, Mary, and got engaged. He called me with the good news.

"You remember me telling you about Mary, the girl I've been dating? Well, we're going to get married."

"Jerry, is she Dutch?"

She wasn't, but she seemed quite nice, nonetheless. I flew to sunny California for their wedding, my second trip on an airplane. It was hard to believe the weather could be so nice in December.

Don
Christian, Agnostic, Jewish, Divorce

Don was born in 1930. With two older brothers and one older sister we were a growing family. Though she is only two and a half years older than Don, Irene claims to remember that on the day of his birth Ma Recker came over, as well as my sister Tini. Irene says she noticed when they came over, and then heard a baby cry. I can't say whether it's really possible that a two-and-a-half-year-old could remember something like that. Maybe she heard me talk about it later, but maybe she did remember.

Don was a sweet boy, but a picky eater. Decades later he told me that he didn't have enough to eat when he was little. I couldn't believe it. Though poor, we always had oatmeal and bread and potatoes around. I think the truth is that he didn't like the food choices we had, or the goat's milk that was always available on the farm. I doubt Don really went hungry, since he grew to be a full-sized man, with a good mind.

Al was Don's hero. Don followed him around like a puppy, trying to imitate him. Since Al was so smart, Don felt he had to do well in school too, and he did. Al looked after Don, helping him with school-work, taking him out trapping, and talking with him.

There was a pond behind the farm in Crete where the kids would like to go play. They found tadpoles in the spring and fish in the summer. There were usually turtles, and a pair of mallards who stayed year around. The grass near the pond was tall, the willows hung down to the water, and the cool water from the bottom of the pond fizzled up to the surface. One day Don spotted a snake as he and Rene were coming home from school. He was about ten and Irene maybe twelve. Don told her:

"Stay here. Follow that snake. I'll go get a hoe."

Rene followed the snake at just the right distance—close enough to keep a constant eye on it, and far enough to keep from getting bit. It stopped next to a big rock near the pond. Don came back.

"Where is it?"

"Right there."

Don came with the hoe, sticking it out with the metal end toward the snake, a big old rattlesnake. He held the hoe as far out as he could with one hand and the snake struck out at it. Don then grabbed the hoe with both hands and whacked it. He hit it somewhere in the body, causing the snake turn in on itself for protection. Don hit the body again, but as it was now wounded it couldn't lung back at him. The snake tried to slither away, but since it was badly cut in two spots, that wasn't possible. Don quickly got behind it and hit it in the head. Now the snake was in its death throes, squirming and writhing, still trying to escape. Don and Irene stood back, waiting for the end. When the snake stopped moving, Don came along and kicked it. No response.

I was in the kitchen when Don came in and proudly showed me the dead snake. It was a timber rattler, now rare in Illinois, with six pairs of rattles on its tail. They could have been killed! But no, it was just good sport.

Don was a good student. He tended to the humanities and literature whereas Al was more of a scientist. Don knew he wanted to be a teacher ever since he was a little boy. I'm not sure if one of his teachers at Lansing Christian inspired him, or perhaps in High School at Thornton, but I couldn't have been prouder. Don went to Calvin College straight after High School in 1949 when Al was still there, having started in '46 when he came back from the service. I don't think either of them liked Calvin very well—it was too strict for them.

While there Don really did suffer from hunger, so Al had him come over for meals now and then. By 1950 Don could see that a war in Korea would likely be starting up, so he decided to enlist in the Air Force before the Army could draft him. Since Al had been in the Air Force Don thought that was for him too, and by enlisting in the Air Force he could be sure that the Army didn't send him to the freezing cold Korean peninsula. His plan worked; he never did get sent to Korea. After basic training the Air Force sent him to Washington D.C. where he worked for the "NSA." We never really figured out what he did there, but he stayed for the entire length of the war. While in Washington he met a young woman who worked at the Canadian Embassy.

Her name was Esther Lightstone. Yes, she was Jewish. She had moved to Washington, D.C., and was renting a room in a Y.W.C.A. They were introduced to each other by mutual friends and dated for some time. We knew Don was dating someone named Esther Lightstone, but not much more than that. Then one day, out of a clear blue sky, in February of 1955, we got a telegram:

ES AND I MARRIED THIS MORNING. VERY HAPPY. DON.

I could have killed him. A telegram! No engagement announcement, no bringing her home to meet us, and no church ceremony? BANG! We're married! That was it. I hopped around the house for days, sputtering right and left. That stinker. Since Esther was Jewish, Don no doubt recognized that a church wedding would have been impossible. But why didn't he bring her home and introduce her to Pete and I and the other kids? That's what he should have done. Though she had been married for five years herself, Irene was especially upset. She and Don were close in age, and had grown up doing all kinds of things together. She didn't sputter or yell, like me, but she felt hurt that her dear brother didn't introduce her to his fiancé. Pete, as usual, took it in stride. He shook his head, and then shook it some more, and then read the Bible, and while reading, shook his head again: "That Don."

When we did meet Es later that year we were delighted. She was quite young, almost the same age as Lin and just a few months shy of her 20th birthday. At 25, Don was married and discharged in the same year. Having nowhere to go, they came back to Lansing and moved in with us while Don applied to colleges on the G.I. Bill. It was great to have them around. Es was such a pleasant, vivacious, and bright young lady. For me it was good to have another daughter in the house again. I think she liked living with us too. It seemed like she was always at my elbow in the kitchen.

"How do you make the gravy?"

"What kind of apples are those?"

"Do you need to use lard, or will any fat or oil do?

I guess her mom didn't have time to teach her much, being occupied with five older brothers. But having her around gave me a chance to get to know her, and hear her story, which was a tough one, redolent of anti-Semitism.

She was born in Ottawa, Ontario, Canada on April 5, 1935. Like me, her mother was an immigrant who arrived around 1900; she from Poland. Her father was born in Canada in 1897 of Russian immigrant parents. They were affiliated with a conservative branch of Judaism, though I don't know its name.

These days, I think of Canada as being a big, open-minded and welcoming country, but for most of its history it was a pretty anti-Semitic place. For years it was even legal to refuse housing to Jews in Canada, and they were barred from many professions, public places, and institutions. It was a tough place to grow up for little Esther, and that anti-Jewish sentiment left a lasting impression on her. She remembered being chased home from school by some French Quebecois kids who threw rocks at her, taunting her with shouts of "Dirty Jew" or "Christ Killer."

Though her family was conservative, Es really hadn't been saturated with Jewish customs and beliefs. I suspect that since she was the only girl in her family they worried more about insuring the boys maintained the tradition. Her parents, Sam and Libbie Lightstone, moved their family to Ottawa after being kicked out of some little town in Ontario. One day, the local minister there had rallied the community to expel them, the only Jews in town. The whole Lightstone family of five boys and one little girl trudged down the railroad tracks all the way to Ottawa, and remained there.

Esther's father was a jeweler and a watchmaker by profession, his family trade. During WWII, he repaired the dials on the control panels of the Royal Canadian Air Force's aircraft. He eked out a living as best he could as a jeweler, but like us, they were poor. Her mom was a homemaker with a beautiful singing voice, and spoke perfect Yiddish, as well as Polish, French and English. They found a beat-up piano somewhere and managed to get it home where several of the kids learned to play, though without any formal instruction. Es excelled in music in spite of those limitations, even learning to play the cello. I'm not sure where or how such a poor family acquired one, but she managed well enough to join her high school orchestra. Like her mother, Es also had a beautiful alto voice and sang in the high school choir. Music was a big part of their family life, as it had been in ours.

Growing up in Canada required that the kids find some way to have fun during the long, cold winters. For Es, that meant ice skating on the Rideau Canal. She used her brothers' hand-me-down skates and put cardboard in the ankles for supports. In spite of the condition of the skates she became an excellent figure skater. I still remember watching her do a "sit-spin." one day when we went skating on our pond. She squatted on both legs, then stuck one leg out, and began to spin on the ice, faster and faster. My jaw nearly dropped!

She said her family was so poor that they would sometimes go to the Salvation Army to get items from their food pantry. In order to get a box of food they all had to sit through a sermon and then come up to accept Jesus at the end. In order to maximize the amount of food they got, each member of the family would sit in a different location so each would get their own box.

Es was bright and talented: she was fluent in French, a fine musician, and the valedictorian of her high school class. She once bitterly related the story of her High-School graduation ceremony. She was seated on stage with all the classmates who were to receive awards. Her valedictory award was to be presented last, as the grand finale. An esteemed teacher had long held the special honor of presenting the valedictorian with his or her award each year. Unfortunately, this teacher was also an infamous anti-Semite. When the time came in the program for Es to receive her award, the woman simply refused to call her name, and went on to the next item in the program. No one intervened, though everyone in the building knew the valedictory award should have been made then and there. The program rolled along, and there sat Esther, empty-handed, in tears, with no recognition for her considerable achievement. That clearly stung, even years later when she told me about it.

We sure liked Esther, or Es, as we always called her. She was a little firecracker, with a witty comment for any and every occasion that kept us on our toes. Not long after moving in with us Don got accepted at Northern Illinois University in DeKalb where he took a degree in U.S. History and obtained his teaching credentials. I wish I could have done the same. While Don pursued his degree at NIU, they lived in a little trailer somewhere off-campus while Es worked at Sinclair Oil as a secretary. Pete and I visited them once in DeKalb, where they seemed to have a nice life as a young, married, American couple, complete with friends and social events to attend. They ended up in Libertyville, IL, on the north side of Chicago when Don took a teaching job there in 1959. As it turned out it was the only job he ever had. I'm sure those kids were well taught. I remember him saying that he had to teach a new class one fall, and to prepare for it he read fourteen books on the subject.

Pete died in 1960 and so did Mr. Lightstone, Es' father. Don and Es' first child was born In December of that same year, bringing a new life into a year of death. Their baby "Roxanne" was a little girl who seemed as much a carbon copy of Es as a daughter. Her whole head was covered with dark, black, hair that looked as if it had been growing for years. It was hard to believe she had any Dutch blood in her. Their second daughter, Marcia, arrived in December of the following year. She was a little cutie too, though more of a cross between Don and Es in looks. In June of 1966 they had their last child, a little boy—Bret. Three such nice-looking little kids, and smart! Of course, I think that of all my grandchildren.

Es stayed home as a wife and homemaker, while also teaching piano lessons in her home. The wages she earned from teaching piano eventually paid off the mortgage on their house, which they bought in 1959. Had they bought it much later the mortgage would have undoubtedly been unmanageable, since houses on the north side of Chicago got to be expensive. Es joined things: a Junior Women's Club, service projects, and a group of young moms in town. To satisfy her musical interests she also joined a local community chorus and took roles in Libertyville's musical theater. She had a part as a "Pick A Little, Talk A Little" lady in a local production of *The Music Man* held at St. Mary of the Lake Seminary in Mundelein. Es invited the whole alto section from the chorus over to practice at her house and was part of a woman's trio.

The children filled the house with their own music. Roxanne and Marcia both learned piano from their mom, and while little Bret never took an interest in piano, he seemed to have come from the womb with a pair of drumsticks in his hands. He banged away on everything, so at a very young age Don and Es got him a drum-set. He would sit with the radio going and play along. The girls also took ballet. Imagine that! Our church had once prohibited dancing, and now Roxanne and Marcia were studying ballet in one of those fancy North-Side studios. With the girls practicing, Bret banging away, the piano students, the chorus singers, and the stereo, their house was never quiet.

When they first married, we wondered what would happen to them religiously. Would Don convert Es to Christianity, or would Es convert Don to Judaism? As it turns out, something else happened. Many years later Es did become a Christian, but shortly after he came back from the service Don became an agnostic. To this day I don't know why.

While they lived with us after they first got married, Don participated in prayer and Bible reading at the dinner table as always, but once he got out of our house he never went to church again. And when they had children, he didn't want them raised in any faith. I never understood what turned Don off from gospel, though I suspect it wasn't so much the gospel he didn't care for as it was the church. And, he looked up to Al for everything, almost as if Al were his Savior. So when Al started asking a lot of questions about evolution and faith, stopped going to church and was excommunicated, Don too turned away. If the Christian faith was not strong enough to stand up to the questioning of his brilliant older brother, why bother? I have been praying for Don since I became pregnant with him, and my prayers have never ceased till this day. Perhaps I'll see him return to the faith before I die.

When Don and Es moved to Libertyville back in '59, there were no Jews there, a fact of which Es was keenly aware. She looked for a synagogue. She looked through the telephone book to find Jewish sounding names. She looked in the market to find kosher food, but found nothing. In fact, a friend later told her that in 1959, when they first moved in, realtors would not even sell or rent housing to Jews in Libertyville. I don't know if anyone suspected Es of being Jewish at the time. Or if they did, they let it slide, since Don's name was on the loan. But Es always seemed fearful that someone would find out about her Jewishness, and the miseries of her childhood would be revisited upon her children.

I remember a game that Es came up with called *Magic Magazines* that we would play at family gatherings. She would lay nine magazines out in a square on the floor. Es would say, "When Roxanne comes back in the room, she is going to magically choose whichever magazine you all decide on." The cousins together chose one of the nine magazines. Roxanne was then called back into the room.

"Is it this one?
"No."
"How about this one?"
"No."
"This one?"
"Yes!"

The kids were just amazed, and so were some of the adults at first. Then the secret leaked out: when pointing to the first magazine with a stick, you point to the part of the magazine that corresponds to the location of the chosen magazine. So, for instance, if everyone chose the magazine in the middle of the nine, you pointed to the middle of the first magazine. More and more of the cousins got to know the trick, and more wanted to play. But you can't play tricks forever when everyone knows the secret.

Brett was the youngest of the cousins. Since he was a sweet, sensitive little boy his older cousins and sisters picked on him a bit. When we got together for holidays, the older kids would gather around Brett in a conspiring circle.

"Is it your birthday, Brett? Shall we sing for you?"

"No! No! No Happy Birthday!"

But sing they would, lento, and somehow in a dreadful minor key.

"Happy Buuuurthdaaay, too yoooo. Happy Buuurthday to yeeeww."

"No, No, Stop!"

It was amazing to hear how bad Happy Birthday can sound when a bunch of kids are trying their worst.

Finally, Don overheard it. By about the second "Buuurthday" he was on the spot.

"Stop teasing him, you kids!" They did. I wonder if Brett even remembers that anymore. I hope not.

Seeing Don fall away from the church was painful. And it got even more painful when he and Es started having problems. I am sure that an often-sullen Don was no picnic to live with, while dynamic little Esther was always 200%, full-steam ahead with her own plans. When their kids were teenagers, they could stand it no more, and divorced. I guess they had lived in different rooms of the house for a while and tried to kind of stay out of each other's way, but you can't live like that forever. I had always thought that divorce was something that happened out in Hollywood, among those decadent, glittering stars, who seemed to change marriage partners the same way they changed furniture. But no, it happened in our family too.

Shortly before the divorce Don and Es were invited to one of my granddaughter's weddings, I think maybe Kim's. The family, minus Don, came in separately and was seated on the bride's side. When Don came in his nephew Rodney, proudly ushered Don to his family, not knowing that they had come in separate vehicles in order to avoid each other. When Don saw where his nephew was leading him, he quickly ducked into the pew behind his family. I suspect that Es could feel his blazing gaze, drilling through the back of her head during the whole service.

After the divorce, Don acted like Esther had never existed. He couldn't understand why I would go to visit her and the children or invite her over.

"I'm your son, she's not your daughter," he said with indignation. "Why do you have to keep seeing her?"

"Don, she was a part of my life for over twenty years, and her children are my grandchildren. I didn't divorce her, you did."

He didn't like that a bit, but he was far too respectful of his mother to prevent me from seeing them.

Each child lives his own life. I'm afraid both Al's and Don's were difficult.

Lin Completes the Circle

Linda was our baby, a sweet one. She had big blue eyes, but dark hair like me. She came into the world an easy birth and lived as a mild and pleasant child. Nonetheless she was a bit of a tomboy. Don was four years older, and taught her to play baseball, and a little basketball. She climbed trees and would sit up in the branches reading. One day on the ranch in Crete she cut through the field and a steer started to chase her. It was frightening to see, a little girl being chased by an 800-pound steer, but could that little girl ever run! From then on, she walked only on the lane.

Lin started school in Lansing Christian in 1940 when she was just four. Her first-grade teacher scared her to death, so I decided to take her back home and let her start school again the next year, hoping for a little more maturity on her part and perhaps a different teacher. When we moved to Crete, however, the local Lutheran pastor came over and talked to us. "Why send your kids way back to Lansing Christian School," he asked, "when we can take them in our Lutheran school here?" So, Lin went to the Lutheran school and learned the Lutheran Catechism instead of the Heidelberg Catechism. The Lutheran Catechism always asked,

"What does this mean?"

Decades later Lin could still quote it. For example:

> *The First Article: I believe in God the Father Almighty, Maker of heaven and earth.*
>
> *What does this mean?*
>
> *I believe that God has made me and all creatures; that He has given me my body and soul, eyes, ears and all my members, my reason and all my senses, and still preserves them; that He richly and daily provides me with food and clothing, home and family, property and goods, and all that I need to support this body and life; that He protects me from all danger, guards and keeps me*

from all evil; and all this purely out of fatherly, divine goodness and mercy, without any merit or worthiness in me; for all which I am in duty bound to thank and praise, to serve and obey Him. This is most certainly true.

Isn't that a beautiful answer? Too bad that the Reformed and the Lutherans couldn't get together in one church—we have so much in common. I guess the sticking point was the Lord's Supper. Calvin said, "Yes, God's Spirit is really present in that bread and wine." But Luther pounded his fist on the table and repeated the Bible text which reads, "This *IS* my body." Hard to believe that an argument about something no one could see could keep the two sides apart.

There were only a few kids in each grade of that tiny little Lutheran school, so when they finished the material for one year, they just opened new books for the next one. By the middle of third grade, Lin was doing fourth grade work, and by the end of the following year she had finished both fourth and fifth, making it through three years of material in two years. When we moved back to Lansing some years later, she joined the same class she had started as a four-year-old.

When we lived on the ranch, we had no indoor plumbing, so at night we would set out a "slop bucket" in each bedroom to catch the pee or poo that came out at night. Each morning we would go outside and empty it. Lin must have been about seven and Rene about fifteen when Lin discovered blood in the slop bucket. She feared that Rene was sick and dying. When she asked about it, Irene explained to her what happened when girls got older.

"Why?" asked Lin.

"Well, it's so that we can have a baby."

"Really? How?"

Irene gave her the short version of making babies, and Lin was stunned, thinking it was quite a dirty business.

"Don't tell Mom," she said.

"I think she already knows," responded Irene.

Rene took Lin under her wings. She knew how to cook, clean, sew, get the eggs, etc. I hardly had to teach Lin a thing—she just did what she saw her big sister doing. Occasionally I would ask her to do something, and she would just keep on chatting, or reading. Then I'd grab whatever it was that needed doing and take care of it myself. It usually only took a minute or two till she saw me, felt embarrassed, and got busy.

Unlike Stan and Irene, Lin went to college. She had encouragement from her brother Don, and as I later found out, money from her brother Al. She wasn't the smartest of my kids—none of them could compete with Al—but she was plenty bright, especially in the humanities. She wanted to be a teacher. I wonder where she got that from. In those days you didn't need a four-year degree to teach grade school. A two-year certificate was enough. Since Calvin College was our church's official school, she only applied there, and of course she got in. While at Calvin, she did the one wrong thing I ever heard about. The girls there lived in "Coops"—homes that had been re-modeled as dormitories for women, each with its headmistress. Lin's headmistress was a widow whom the girls called "Aunt Caroline." Every night each girl had to sign in before ten, to prove she hadn't missed the curfew. One night one of Lin's friends, Carol, called the one phone in the house, and Lin answered.

"Is that you Lin?" Carol asked.

"I'm not going to make it back on time. Can you sign me in?"

"OK, I guess so," Lin answered, not particularly sure just what she should do.

When Carol came in much later the headmistress caught her, but when "Auntie" looked at the sign-in sheet she noticed that Carol had already signed in. She asked,

"Who signed you in?"

"Uuh, I asked Lin to."

"Lin, come down here," Auntie called up the stairs, and when Lin complied asked,

"Did you sign Carol in?"

"Yes," Lin meekly replied, nodding.

"Both of you are going to be on K.P. all week next week, and you are not leaving the Coop at all this weekend."

Lin told me this story when she came home that Thanksgiving. I hardly needed to scold her. She had already paid a pretty heavy price for that slight misdeed.

When Lin graduated with her teaching certificate there was a shortage of teachers. Lots of the GIs had come home from World War II in the late forties, gotten married, and were having children in the early fifties, so by 1955 when Lin graduated the grade-schools were full and growing. One day out of the blue, the principal of Lansing Christian School, Mr. Yff, called me and asked,

"Mrs. Zwier, Lin will be coming home with her teaching certificate, won't she?"

"Why, yes, she graduates in another month."

"We need her here at Lansing Christian. Please use your influence to get her over here to teach. We know she's a wonderful Christian girl, and she'll make a fine teacher. Please, Mrs. Zwier, talk to her."

I guess I didn't realize how badly they wanted her, and I didn't feel comfortable "influencing" my adult daughter, but when she came home, I did talk with her. One night after dinner I asked, "Do you know where you are going to teach this fall?"

"No, Mom. The schools usually don't hire till summer."

"Well, I know they have an opening at Lansing Christian."

"Really? That would feel weird! It seems like I was just there!"

In a way, she had been, since she'd only graduated from there as an eighth-grader six years earlier.

"Well, I happen to know they'd like to have you back."

"OK. It sure wouldn't hurt to talk to them."

She did talk to them, and started teaching there that very fall, when she was just nineteen. I was so proud, she would be a teacher. I only wish . . .

Those little kids loved her, but she sure didn't get rich. Teaching grade school has never been a lucrative business, and teaching in a little Christian School virtually required a vow of poverty. But since she lived with us—Pete, Al, and me, she could keep her expenses down.

Lin had plenty of friends, and when she was in high school, she dated quite a bit. I was happy for her—they were all good kids, and I really didn't have to worry. Teenagers from Illiana Christian would go to some event together—a picnic, or (finally) a movie, or a ballgame, etc. They weren't necessarily in love; they just did things together. One time Lin would be Francis's date and Paul would take Lin's cousin Ruth. Another time, it would be the reverse.

Paul Van Til was the same age as Lin, so when Lin went to Calvin, Paul was drafted into the service, both in 1954. Paul's uncle was the same Jake Van Til who'd given me my first kiss when we lived in Highland some thirty years earlier. Paul's dad Reinder had immigrated with his wife at the turn of the century, like us, and had lost his spouse in the Spanish Influenza of 1918. To calm his grief, he'd moved to Michigan with seven boys, and two girls. After some years in Fremont he married a woman who had lost her own husband to the Influenza—Sena Bush

Breuker, who had had three girls and one boy. The marriage of the widow and the widower produced three more boys, including Paul, making him the youngest of sixteen. By the time Paul was born in 1935 some of his older brothers and sisters had already married, moved out of the house, and had children of their own. So Paul was an "uncle" the day he was born.

Paul had blond hair as a boy, but it turned quite dark as he grew older. He too was a farm kid. With all those brothers and sisters there was no way they could all sleep together in a little house, so the boys slept in the loft of the barn. It really wasn't that bad, since heat from the cow's bodies kept it fairly warm in the winter, and in the summer, you could leave a door or a window open for ventilation. One night, though, when Paul was a little guy of about six, his brother Cal got him in trouble.

"Do you know that Mr. Nutter saw a wolf in the woods last week?" Cal baited Paul.

"It was a big one. What would you do if you saw a wolf, Paulie?"

Little Paul, who saw his father as a stern saint and fearless protector quickly said,

"Why, I'd yell for Pa."

"*How* would you yell to Pa?

"Why, I'd turn toward the house and yell as loud as I could, 'PAAAAA!'"

Reinder was 54 years old when little Paul was born, and had worked in the fields almost every day of his life, so when he was roused from a sound slumber by his six-year old at age 60, he quickly put on his pants, slipped on his boots as fast as he could, and ran into the freezing cold night, fearing that mayhem had befallen his dear, youngest, little child. When he got to the barn, Paul was quite fine, and his Pa asked,

"Why did you call me?"

"There might be a wolf."

"What?"

"Well, if there was a wolf, I would call you."

"Did you see a wolf?"

"No."

"Of course not! We haven't seen wolves around here in decades. You mean you just screamed in the middle of the night and called me out to the barn to see how fast I would come!?"

"Well, I . . ."

"Ach, you miserable kid!" Pa concluded, and then pow, pow, pow, on the rear end of little Paul, while his brothers nearly choked, trying to keep from laughing. Poor little guy. Growing up in that big family with all those boys couldn't have been easy.

From the time he was a young boy Paul would spend the hot summer days bent over in the fields. He would turn over the soil with a horse-pulled plow, plant with a one bladed sower, weed by hand, and harvest by hand. Every year, as a member of the 4H Club, he'd show some animals at the Lake County Fair. Lake County, Indiana included all the cities and towns just into Indiana from Chicago—Gary, East Chicago, Hammond, and then a dozen or more little towns further south where there were still numerous farms. The fairgrounds itself was large, maybe fifty acres in the county seat of Crown Point. It had permanent buildings set up for the crafts, plus cow, horse, hog, and rabbit barns, and a tent city that sprang up during fair week. There were also games, food trucks, and side-shows. By age ten, Paul was staying overnight at the fair to take care of the animals they showed, cleaning their pens and feeding them. He slept next to them in the straw, like *Charlotte's Web*. He loved it. Fair week was his favorite week of the year.

Paul came to court Lin the winter he was home on leave from Ft. Leonard Wood, Missouri. It wasn't hard to see why she fell for him. He was a good-looking guy with lots of dark hair, though forever contoured in an Army brush cut, a strong jaw, a straight nose, and clear blue eyes. He was six feet tall, and his body was chiseled by the hard work on his father's dairy farm and the service. Like our boys, he'd rarely started the school year until late October, after the crops were in.

Pete had developed heart problems and wasn't able to work anymore, so he had to stay at home and rest. One evening when Paul's uncle Reimer, who was an elder from our church, came to pay a visit, read Scripture, and pray with us. At the same time his nephew Paul came over to pick Lin up for a date. Reimer, always a wit, said,

"I'm here to visit the sick. What's your excuse?"

"I'm here to visit the healthy and good-looking," was Paul's quick reply.

Paul courted Lin every time he was on leave from the service in 1955 and wrote plenty of letters while away. One day his older brother Cal, a bigger and better-looking version of Paul who was married with two kids of his own, came over to talk with us. When he came walking up the driveway, he made quite an impression. He said facing Lin, Pete, and me,

"Lin, I know you have been seeing my brother Paul off and on for some time. I want you to know that he is very serious and has good intentions for you. You know he is a good Christian man, and I'm sure that when he finishes his time in the Army, he will want to marry you. I say this to you too, Mr. and Mrs. Zwier, so you understand Paul's intentions."

"Do you love him?" I asked Lin.

"Of course! I want to marry him!" she responded, almost indignantly. They were engaged the following Christmas, and shortly after he was discharged from the service, they got married.

All my sons and sons-in-laws were veterans: Stan had been in the Army, Al the Air Force, and son-in-law Al DeVries had been a marine in WWII. Don had served in the Air Force during Korea, and then Paul Van Til served in the Army during the peace between Korea and Viet-Nam. I was proud of them, and still am. No one in my family ever shirked his duty, they were all quite willing and able to serve their country.

Paul's two older brothers Cal and Case stood up as groomsmen at the wedding on a hot, cloudy, summer day. The organ played all the typical introductory music and then the "Bridal March": Daaa datata, daaa daaa taataa, and there came the bride. But at the very moment that Pete and Lin took their first step down the aisle, a loud thunder-clap crashed, sounding as if it had broken the inside of the sanctuary. Case and Cal looked at each other and grinned like they had swallowed a mouse and were trying to keep it down. Most of the congregation had a little smile on their faces too, and there was a slight titter. Perhaps thunder isn't a great omen to start a marriage with, but they stayed together despite it.

Paul and Lin lived in Highland, not far from where I had been a teenager, and gotten my first kiss, decades before. They had a nice little house and kept it up well, Lin on the inside and Paul the outside. They made a nice-looking couple. Paul looked like he'd never left the army. Not only did he keep his hair in a brush-cut, he acted like a soldier too. Everything was pretty much black and white for him, but he genuinely tried to do the right thing, including marrying Lin for love. There's an old saying, I forget where it comes from, that goes,

> *The solution to many problems in life*
> *Is to find yourself a very rich wife.*

That surely wasn't the case for our girls. We had no riches. But they were both pretty, and sweet, and pious, and hardworking, and charming, and I'm sure I'm forgetting some of their other qualities. I'm their mom, so I know them best of all, and I feel safe saying these things about them. They were terrific.

I think my girls kept their husbands happy at bedtime too. I remember going over to Lin and Paul's house once when it happened to be their anniversary. Paul had gotten her a skimpy little negligee that included only a few frilly and diaphanous strips of cloth. Lin took it from the box and politely said,

"Thank you."

When I saw her open that box and pull out that see-through wrapper I couldn't stop laughing. Imagining my little girl in that skimpy thing was too much. There's an old story, maybe true, that after she had sex the first time, the Queen of France said, , "Isn't that too good for the commoners?" No, it's not. We like it every bit as much as the royalty do, thank you very much.

By the 1960's the city of Chicago had swallowed up much of the land to its south, and the remaining farms farther out were far too expensive for all but the richest to buy. Since Paul was unable to farm, he made up for his love of it in his yard and garden. His lawn always looked like a putting green, and the garden was a work of art. All the plants were in very neat rows, each, as Scripture says, "according to its kind." Lin used to tease him,

"You should have married the farmer's daughter."

But he'd grin and say, "That's not the only reason to get married."

Lin named her kids "Kent, Kim, Kevin and Kristy." I don't know why she was so stuck on the Ks. Perhaps since her big sister had done such a nice job with the J's (Jackie, Jeff, Jerry, Joel) she thought she should continue down the alphabet. They built a house on what had once been Reinder Van Til's pasture, only a half-mile from where I had lived. Now a suburban subdivision, the pasture, and its cows, were long forgotten.

One day their eldest, eight-year-old Kent, was sitting at the table with his mom. when he asked, "What shall I do?"

"Why don't you draw something?" Lin suggested.

"What shall I draw?"

"How about a cow?"

"OK."

Kent drew a very rudimentary picture of a cow. It had enormous horns, but Lin could tell it was a cow, and not a bull, because of the udders. The udders, however, were situated to the front of the cow. This must have made sense to Kent. The breasts of a woman are front and center, so wouldn't a cow's udders be there too? Lin chuckled. Young Kent had never seen a live cow.

Paul, however, was troubled when he saw the drawing a little later.

"Kent, did you draw this?"

"Yes. It's a cow."

"I see. Did you put the udders in the front?"

"Yes."

Paul shook his head, looking downward in amazement mingled with sorrow. By the time he was eight he'd been in a cow barn dozens of times, and by the time he was twenty he'd milked hundreds of cows, hundreds of times. Now his own son didn't even know which end of the cow meant business.

Plans were made the following summer for the Van Til family to make a pilgrimage to Waupun, Wisconsin, to visit Lin's old coop-mate Carol, now Greenfield. The Greenfields had a farm of some 200 acres and a dairy of about 80 cows (whose udders were all situated to the rear). The Greenfields then had four kids too, about the same ages as the Van Tils', and they could all play in the barn, which provided constant joy and temptation. Kittens, cows, calves, mice, and barn swallows provided live entertainment, and the mow with its mountain of hay was seemingly designed for sliding. There were steps going up into the silo, and others out to the fields. One round of Hide-and-Seek could last twenty minutes or more.

Harold Greenfield milked the cows every morning at 4:30 and every evening at 5:00. He was a strong man, and after years of milking, his patience with the animals fell far short of everlasting. He kept a tool with him euphemistically called a "come-along." It was really a long, heavy, crow-bar. If a cow was slow to come in, or belligerent, Harold would give it a "tap" with the "come-along." The cows learned to obey, promptly. One morning, when one cow was especially recalcitrant, Harold went after it and bade it "come along" with a blow to the head. But the cow did not come along a bit; it lay down, dead. For years afterward, Harold's wife Carol would see him off to the barn in the morning with the plea, "Don't kill them, Harold!"

During that Wisconsin week Paul got to be a farmer again. He milked the cows, now with electronically controlled milking machines, he cleaned the barn out, and fed the pigs. He also drove a powerful tractor, backing the wagon into a parking spot in the barn with only inches to spare on either side. Meanwhile Kim and Kristy gave milk to the calves with bottles. These calves were then named after them, keeping those honorary names forever. Another summer a neighbor lent his ponies to the party. Two kids, usually the boys Kent and David, or both Kevins: Greenfield and Van Til and got to ride them for an hour straight, all over the place, not like the silly little county fair rides where they'd walk a few ponies around a spindle for a few minutes.

Back home Paul had a job as a meat salesman. He went from store to store, seeing which meats the butchers needed, and then sent his orders in to the meat-packing plant in Elkhart, Indiana. Every year his company leased a new car for him to make his calls in, usually a Chevy Impala. In those days, that car had an 8 cylinder, 350 cubic-inch engine, which was strong enough to pull their camper, one of those pop-ups that looked like it had wings. They were loyal Hoosiers, so they camped at various Indiana state parks—Brown County, Shakamak, McCormick's Creek, Turkey Run, etc.

Paul was an organizer. In the Army he had worked for the Warrant Officer and had even thought about re-enlisting in that role. But when he got discharged, he put his skills to use around the house and the camper. Lin would pack food and clothes for the family for the whole week, some going in the camper, and some in the trunk. Paul would stand outside in the driveway with the camper open and the trunk up. The kids would form a fragile chain, delivering boxes, bags, and suitcases from the house to the driveway, and Paul would pack them in tightly and neatly. Typically, about half-way through he would start grumbling.

"How much more does your mother have? I'm not packing a semi."

"A few more suitcases," Lin would yell from the house. "I still have to pack the kids' clothes."

"Grrrr. I don't know what she needs all this stuff for."

At last the car and the camper would be packed, neither with an inch of free space. The trunk would be full and the trailer hitch sagging to an uneasy three or four inches off the ground. Backing out of the driveway and down the curb was the first test. If it passed that with no more than a minor scrape, they were good to go.

Upon arrival, corporal Van Til had the entire set-up system ready. He'd level the trailer on the chosen spot. Using jacks and by moving the trailer left and right so the bubble on his level would be dead center. Once in place and level, the whole cadre would join in. He and Linda would go around the pop-up, loosening the snaps, and then Kent and Paul would each stand on a side and hoist the roof. Lin and Kim would push up the braces so the walls went up, and then climb into the box of the trailer while Paul and Kent stayed outside on one wing. A small push from the women inside made the straps for the wings accessible on the outside. Paul and Kent would pull the wing/bed out while Kevin and Kristy grabbed the support rods. After sticking one end of the rods in the camper frame, they'd wait till instructed to put the other end in the casing on the bottom of the wing:

"OK, now!"

The little ones would scramble to aim the poles while Paul and Kent tried to keep the wing balanced, and lined up.

"Good. Next!" And repeat process for the other wing.

"Good. Snaps!"

Four out of six family members would go around the camper and snap the canvass to the frame. The remaining two, Kim and Lin, would begin to unpack and organize the interior of the camper. Shortly thereafter they would acquire a picnic table. The canopy had to be hung from the front of the camper over the table to keep the rain off and provide some shade. This awning was supported by the camper roof on one side, but the other side needed rods and tent stakes. Kent and Kevin were assigned to the rods. The girls would hold the lines that went from the top of the awning to the ground, and Paul would grab his hammer and pound in the stakes. This entire process should take them no more than 8.5 minutes.

They did do quite a bit of camping. I'm sure it was Lin who insisted on it. She'd had a total of two vacations her childhood, and I suspect that Paul had had none. They would enjoy their family and their state. I went along on one or two of their trips, and later took a few of my own.

Taking Care of the Next Generation

I NEEDED TO KEEP going after Pete and Al died. My Social Security check was small, and the little three-acre farm was certainly not going to support me, so I had to find something else to keep body and soul together. I suppose if I had needed to I could have moved in with one of my kids, but I didn't want to do that. They had enough going on in their own households, and none of them had in a great big house. At age 63 I was still in good health, could do things for myself, and could keep my own house.

One thing I knew how to do was to raise kids, so I got the word out in our church that I was available for long-term babysitting. There were some families like the Kamstras and the DeVries' who had some money, and little children. When the parents took vacations or went on business trips without the kids, they called me to babysit. At first, when I walked into their big, modern houses I thought, "Wow, they've really got it made," but after staying there for a while it seemed pretty normal. They had nicer things in their houses than mine, but I too had bedrooms, and bathrooms, and appliances just like they did. And being good church people, they never made me feel out of place—they were just glad to have someone they could trust staying with their kids.

Mr. Kamstra made his money with Amway. His Calvin College friend, Rich DeVos, started a business that sold household goods and cleaning materials door to door, so each salesman kind of had his own business. Once you got a route going, you tried to recruit other people to sell Amway's products too. Then whoever you recruited had to give you a share of their sales. Kamstra recruited quite a few Dutchmen in the Illiana area who were, as always, eager to make another dollar. Then Amway broadened out and sold all kinds of things, so the salesmen had a lot to offer.

The Kamstras had two children, a boy and a girl, both adopted. The little boy, Brian, was quite a character, and got into everything. He played rough with his little sister, once even kicking her! I really yelled at him: "You can't do that to your sister, or to any girl! You want me to kick you? If you do anything like that again, I'm telling your parents, and they will give you a good licking." He didn't do it again and grew to be a very good young man. I came back to babysit at the Kamstras' house quite a few times.

I had my own grandkids over too. Little Kristy Van Til would come for a week each summer. What a nice girl. We'd wake up and have some breakfast, usually cereal, or perhaps bacon and eggs and orange juice. Then we'd go out for a morning walk, first greeting Old Ned, the horse who lived across the street. His working days were long over, but Mrs. Cordula let him live out his later years in her little field. He'd see us coming and trot on over. Kristy and I would pull some long grass by the side of the road and hold it out to Old Ned. I showed Kristy how to hold her hand flat, so Ned wouldn't accidentally bite her. Watching that huge horses' nose coming down to that tiny little hand, with his lips sopping up the grass, was charming.

Later in the day I'd usually say, "It's time to go to the market." Ernie Van Til had a fruit and vegetable stand right on Ridge Road in Lansing. Kristy would ask, "What are we going to get?" I answered, "Whatever looks good!" Since she'd grown up with refrigerators and freezers, it didn't occur to her to go to the market day after day and buy only a few things for the next day. She and her mom just went once a week. But I still liked to buy fruits and vegetables that were as fresh as possible—strawberries, lettuce, and asparagus in the early spring, green beans, cukes, and raspberries in high summer, and then the plethora of peaches, tomatoes, peppers, blueberries, cherries, cauliflower, and peppers that came in the fall. What riches!

I also babysat for Rich and Jan DeVries. They had one girl, Dawn, the oldest, and two boys. They were all smart, especially Dawn. Every time you talked to her she had tough theological questions:

"Why is the devil so bad?"

"Can God make him better?"

"Does God love Jesus more that he loves me?"

I couldn't answer all her questions, but I tried as best I could. She once saw me on my knees, in prayer, at the side of the bed, and asked me, "Why are you praying like that?" I told her, "I kneel before the maker of the universe, who made me, and loves me. I hope you will too." When she grew up she went to the University of Chicago and studied theology. I hope she got some of her questions answered there.

With both Al and Pete gone I had no man in the house, which meant I had no say in our church's congregational meetings. In those days, the early 1960's, women couldn't vote in church, since it was assumed that the man, as head of the household, would represent his family.

My life had been given to Christ early on, and I had always been a member of the Christian Reformed Church, so I couldn't stand the idea of having no say in church matters. I made an appointment to meet with the Consistory—17 men—eight elders, eight deacons, and the preacher. I was scared to go before all those men, many of whom were known and respected in church and in town. They treated me with honor knowing I had lost both my husband and my son. They also knew how much I had done for the church throughout the years—a couple of the deacons had even been my students in Sunday School. I stood at one end of the long table, and delivered my prepared speech:

As you know, I no longer have any man at home. I am a professing member of this congregation, and a life-long member of this denomination. I'd like to be allowed a vote in the next Congregational Meeting. I have no man who can represent me, and I believe I should have representation here in church, just as I do in the political vote.

It was 1964. They looked at each other, and then at me.

One of them said, "That means that all the other widows should probably get a vote too."

"Yes, I suppose."

I hadn't talked to anyone else about it but could quickly think of three other women who would be affected too.

"Thank you, Mrs. Zwier. We will get back with you shortly."

And a week later they did. I got a nice letter from the consistory:

> Dear Mrs. Zwier,
>
> We thank you for meeting with the consistory at our meeting last Monday. You have been a Professing Member of the Christian Reformed Church for decades and have contributed to the ministry of this congregation in many ways. We recognize that given the loss of your husband, and now your son, that you have no one who represents you in our official gatherings. Therefore, we believe it is fitting that you vote in the next, and all following Congregational Meetings.
>
> Signed,
>
> Council Clerk

That was good for enough me, and it was good for the other church widows too. We formed a group of friends, nothing formal, we just got together week after week, usually to read a book, and discuss it. I loved that. After my kids had left home, I was able to spend a couple of hours each day reading. I had read most of the James Michener novels, as well as those of Leon Uris and Pearl S. Buck. I recommended one of them to the widows—I think it was Michener's *Centennial*. Not everybody liked it since it got bogged down in details you really didn't need to know. Michener tends to start out telling you about the soil and the rocks and the changing of the tectonic plates in all the places he wrote about, which is fine, but if you're not an amateur geologist, it gets a little dry, so I told them to just skip those parts.

We would switch houses, and whoever hosted would bake something. We always put our best plate of baked goods forward: the cookies, the *banket*, the pies. I know I worried about what to make, so I baked it the day ahead of our gathering, being sure to leave enough time to try something else if my first effort failed. We were gracious to each other, and always complimented each other on the food, but all knew it was a little competition.

Some of us would also get together for Scrabble. Wow were those old ladies competitive! We secretly got out our dictionaries at home and memorized all the Q words, especially the short ones that we could squeeze in anywhere. I remember once when Harriet Eldersveld nearly leapt out of her seat when she saw she could use her Q on a triple-word-score blank.

I'd also babysit my own grandkids when their parents had to go out to an event at church, or to a concert or something. I always looked forward to spending time with my nearly perfect grandchildren. I remember when I babysat for Lin and Paul, those silly little kids wanted to keep their socks on when they went to bed. I'd ask, "Why? It's not cold out."

"We want them on!"

"But don't your feet get sweaty with those socks on?"

"We want them on!"

"OK, suit yourselves."

I taught them a prayer that I had learned as a child:

> *Jesus, tender shepherd hear me,*
> *Bless thy little lamb tonight.*
> *Through the darkness be thou near me,*
> *Keep me safe till morning light.*

It had been set to music, so though I was never much of a singer I was able to teach them the tune.

Then they added the "God Blesses":

God bless mommy and daddy,
And grandpa and grandma,
And our teachers, and the president,
And God bless Bernie and the boys in Viet Nam.
May they come home soon and not get hurt.
Amen.

That certainly was the prayer of many of us in the late 60's and early 70's. Along with tens of thousands of others, their cousin Bernie was fighting in Viet Nam. As the war there went on and on, we grew less and less sure it was a good idea to be there in the first place. Was Ho Chi Minh an evil communist who had to be stopped before he took over all of Indochina? Were the Vietnamese leaders we were supporting corrupt dictators? In any case, should our young men suffer and die for something we weren't too sure of, half a world away?

This war was not as all-consuming for America as WWII had been for us, but it sure did affect the younger generation. You had to choose sides—for or against the war. Lots of kids got college deferments or ran off to Canada. Some thought the boys who ran were cowards, while others saw them as heroes. It divided families. I think most of us who lived through WWII assumed that the U.S. military was automatically right. If the U.S. declared war, it meant there was good cause. And since our church wasn't a pacifist denomination, we accepted the government's decision. But then more and more information came out, and it was not good. The turning point was probably the Mai Lai Massacre, where some of our soldiers killed women and children. They apparently felt that all the Vietnamese were enemies, and in mad frustration killed everyone in that little village.

What a bad business. Thankfully none of my grandsons had to go. They were a bit too young, though Randy Zwier came close. I think he might have even had a draft number, but the war was over before his lot was called.

The other extraordinary event during those years was the Civil Rights Movement. I have to admit, it took me by surprise when Dr. Martin Luther King Jr. started marching. I had no idea that down South

Negroes couldn't vote or serve on juries. And apparently, it wasn't even that much better in Chicago!

When we'd arrived in Roseland back in the first decade of the 20th century there were only a few Negroes in Chicago, living in the area south of Harrison and west of Wabash. When we came back to the Chicago area in the twenties the Negroes kept trickling up from the south, and after World War II that trickle became a flood. There was a bus line that ran up from Mobile, Alabama, way down there on the Gulf of Mexico. It ran from the Gulf to Lake Michigan, with stops along the way in Alabama and Tennessee. Thousands of Negroes came up on that bus. Since there wasn't much work, or at least not good work for them in the south, it was mostly the younger black people who migrated north, in a big, continuous caravan. When they got to Chicago, they found work in the factories, or in some low status jobs as porters or maids. I heard the bus ride north was like a moving picnic, with baskets of fried chicken, slaw, beans, chitlins, etc., providing a rich aroma for the ride.

By the 1960s more and more Negroes had moved to Chicago, and our original American home area of Roseland was changing. Negroes had to have some place to live, and Roseland was the next white neighborhood available. The Dutch and other whites didn't want to move out, but real estate agents known as "block-busters" made it just about impossible to stay. They would come to the white people in Roseland and say, "Look, the Negroes are only six blocks away, on 87th Street. The property values over there have gone down by two-thirds. You'd better sell now, before the value of your house falls through the floor too."

Since they had raised families there, and started businesses, churches, and schools, they really wanted to stay. But as Negroes moved closer, it became scary.

Al DeYoung told me why his family moved out: "My boy Jay couldn't ride his bike down the sidewalk anymore. If he did, some Negro kids would push him off and steal it from him." The first time that happened, Al bought little Jay a new bike, but the second time they had to try something else. Most of what were then second or third generation Dutch went west to Oak Lawn or Orland Park, while others came south to Lansing and South Holland, Illinois. One entire Christian Reformed congregation even packed up and moved from Roseland to Lynwood, 25 miles to the south. I know it sounds bad, as if they hated black people, but they just wanted to stay safe.

When Negroes moved up north to Chicago they were only allowed to live in certain neighborhoods. Banks wouldn't lend them money to buy a house in a white neighborhood, and insurance companies wouldn't cover the houses if they did. We whites forced all those poor, migrant Negroes together into a few congested neighborhoods and then wondered why they didn't behave. Few of them got a decent education, and most of the jobs they found were hard labor. I know a lot of whites look down on them, thinking and saying,

"What's their problem?"

"Why can't they hold a job?"

"They must be lazy."

"Those women all have children with different men."

But I think that to understand people you have to understand their families, and I suspect most whites don't understand what most black families have been through.

Roseland Christian School, the same school that I went to decades ago with generations of Dutch Reformed, is now full of Negro children. Academically it's the best school in the area, with loving teachers who do a fantastic job. Since it's not a public school it has to charge tuition, but since most of the Negroes who live there are poor, the same Dutch families who moved out of Roseland now pay their tuition. Some give quite a bit of money, while others humbly serve as aides in the classrooms, or do the cleaning. Though I don't have much money myself, I too give a little something to Roseland Christian School every year.

As a family, we never had any problems with Negroes. All our family's stories with the Negros are positive. When Stan was a little boy in Lansing, he once went to the hardware store with Pete. While Pete went to look at something nearby, he told Stan to wait for him a minute. Stan waited, then turned and saw what he thought were Pete's trousers to his left, put out his hand and held on to them. After a minute, a large, black hand patted Stan on the head. When Stan looked up he saw a kindly Negro man who was wearing trousers just like Pete's. Stan was surprised, and his eyes lit up with fear. But then he saw Pete coming from another aisle and ran over to him. Pete and the Negro man exchanged smiles. Pete told me this story that afternoon with his usual friendly charm but laughed when he mentioned how surprised little Stanley was. Decades later Stan still tells this story, chuckling and shaking his head as he does.

It makes me proud to hear stories like that. God says that all mankind was made in his image and that includes Negroes and Indians. Our kids had apparently learned that lesson, but our nation had not.

Lin didn't meet many Negroes until she went to work at J.J Donnelly & Co. in Chicago, the summer after high school. She took a long bus ride from Lansing up Stony Island, and the further north she went, the more Negroes got on. At Donnelly she put together the catalogues and phone books that made it the biggest printer in the nation, and she had Negro girls working right next to her in the factory, and though she was sometimes amused by the way they talked, she got along fine.

When son-in-law Paul Van Til was stationed in Texarkana, Texas, he also had an experience with Negroes. On Friday evenings after payday, he and the guys in his unit would put on their dress uniforms, go into town, and have a nice dinner. Since they had eaten at the mess hall all week, they were more than ready for a change of menu. There were six of them, one of whom was their Negro friend, Will, who worked nearby. They got to the restaurant and the hostess asked them what they needed.

"Table for six," was the answer.

They waited their turn. Then they waited a little longer. Other groups came in after them but got seated ahead of them. The groups were of different sizes, some of which included other GIs. Finally, Paul went to the hostess and asked, "What's the problem? Why haven't you gotten us a table yet?"

"Well, the five of you are welcome to sit down any time you want, but I can't serve your friend over there," and she pointed to Will. Paul told the others what the problem was.

Will said, "You guys go ahead. I'll grab something at that diner down the street where I've been before."

But no, Paul and his friends wouldn't have it. "If you can't eat here, we're not going to either." They all left the restaurant and went to the diner.

The race problem has probably been the toughest issue in U.S. history. I am tempted to say that we were never part of the problem, since our family was in the Netherlands before the Civil War, and to my knowledge neither I nor any member of our family has ever acted like racists. We never called Negroes bad names, let alone got involved in lynchings or burnings, like they did in the South. But I recognize that I am a part of the white race that took advantage of the black race. Even that is enough to make my conscience tremble a bit.

The Negroes were forcibly brought here, and then abused as slaves. They had their children taken from them and weren't allowed to live in most neighborhoods.

How different our family's experience in America has been! We freely chose to come here. We were welcomed by friends and family. We were offered appropriate jobs. We moved into whatever neighborhood we wanted to. We migrated to the frontier and claimed government land. We sent our children to good schools. No one told us we couldn't live somewhere, or get a loan, or insurance. No one said "our people" weren't wanted there.

I praise God for what America has given us, but I sure cringe when I recall what it has done to the Negroes.

A Few Trips of My Own

By the 1980's, which were also my eighties, I had outlived Pete by over 20 years. I was pretty used to being a widow. Remarriage wasn't really an option. There were very few widowers around, but with kids, grandkids, church, and friends, I didn't need the company. Being single also gave me time to do some things that I probably couldn't have done if married, like traveling.

I took elder trips that were arranged by a local travel agency. I'd go with Mrs. VanderWoude, another widow from church. Her daughter Jeannie was Linda's childhood friend. One of the most beautiful trips was a "color tour" of New England one fall. We got on the bus in the evening and slept all night while the driver got us to Massachusetts. We drove up the Connecticut River which separates Vermont and New Hampshire, just as the trees were changing. There were maples; sugar and red, and birch, and ash, all adding their unique hues of ochre, yellow, red, and orange. It sure was lovely. We got out and took little hikes where we could hear the birds and smell the soil. We also took day trips. I remember going to a pottery factory in Elgin, Illinois. Grandson Randy had made some pots in art class, but I had never made one, so it was interesting to see how it was done. They had to be fired in a kiln. You really can make some beautiful pots if you know what you're doing.

The most memorable of the elder trips was to Hawaii. First, we had to fly, and that was only my third time on an airplane. We flew from Chicago to San Francisco, and then on to Honolulu. What a place! It was hard to believe that there was one state in the U.S. that was such a tropical paradise. We went in March, leaving a gray and weary Chicago that still demanded winter coats. When we got to Hawaii the weather was perfect—80 degrees during the day, and 60 at night. I walked along the beach, seeing all the sun worshippers who come in from the cold. I saw a couple of young guys surfing too. Wow. How did they stay standing on those boards? We went to Pearl Harbor and saw the U.S.S. Arizona memorial. It was hard to believe that only some 30 years earlier Japanese bombs had destroyed it.

In 1969 we witnessed the first man walking on the moon. I can still see the picture in my head. Neil Armstrong got out of the lunar module, climbed down the little stairs, and upon taking his first step on the surface of the moon, said,

"That's one small step for man, one giant leap for mankind."

I'll say it was. What an incredible event! When I lived out west, the fastest way of getting around was on the back of a speedy horse, and we had continued to use horses on the farm till the 1950's.

When I was only four, the Wright brothers made their famous flight from Kitty Hawk, North Carolina. And now, sixty some years later, we would land on the moon! In my lifetime travel had changed more than it had in all previous history. Amazing! It's hard to imagine what might happen in the lifetimes of my grandchildren.

I still lived in my house with my three acres, but housing subdivisions now surrounded it on all sides; one across the creek, and another across the street. I couldn't stand to let the acreage sit idle though; it was good farmland. There were still a couple of farm families in church. Their farms were further south now, but they kept at it. I asked John Brink if he would like to farm those three acres. He said,

"Sure, how much do you want per acre?"

"Nothing; I just want it put to good use."

"No; I should pay you something."

"That's OK; you just keep it clean and raise something."

"Well, Mrs. Zwier, that's really too generous of you."

Maybe it was, but that's the way I saw it. I had some good land that I couldn't farm, so someone else should use the wonderful gift of fertile soil that God gave me. Maybe a few families would eat from the corn John raised. Pete's view of vocation and money apparently stuck to me: the love of money would never be my downfall. To thank me, John Brink did bring me a beautiful gift every year. Once it was a basket overflowing with fruits and chocolates. Once it was a rug that someone had gotten from the Middle East. I don't remember what else. But I do remember happily looking out my window year after year and seeing healthy corn growing six or seven feet tall.

Epilogue

MINNIE ZWIER SPENT HER last years in the Holland Home, a rest-home in neighboring South Holland, IL. While there, she continued to sew, and read. She saw her life like her sewing. In both you only see the outside stitches, the events leave their marks on us: you move; you marry, you graduate; you give birth, etc. But the real living happens on the inside, between the stitches. You get up in the morning and put on the coffee. You smile at your husband and give him a kiss as he heads out the door. You work in the kitchen and think,

"This soup didn't turn out as well as the last batch; but it will have to do."

You daydream and sing while your hands are busy doing some mindless task. You wonder if the Puritan society described by Nathaniel Hawthorne was really as grim and strict as he relates. You pray; quickly before supper, or endlessly during a long tribulation, when it feels as if prayer is a wrestling match with a large, muscular foe.

Minnie's name never appeared in the newspaper because of something she had accomplished. She made no discoveries, wrote no books, nor created works of art. God didn't call her to such things. God called her to the life of an immigrant, a settler, a mother, a widow, and a church-goer. Throughout it she followed God. God set out a pattern for her, and she stitched it up. At time she lost sight of the pattern or wondered if it was there at all, but not a day passed in which she failed to pray to the One who made her.

In her last week, Rene came to visit her from Colorado.

"How are you, Ma?"

"Oh, you know."

"Yeah, I know. But you're feeling okay?"

"I guess."

"Irene! Hear that?"

"No. What?"

"The singing; there are fiery-looking men on rooftop next door singing."

"Really? Are you sure?"

She smiled. "I'm sure. I'm very sure."

Minnie Zwier died a few days later, on December 20, 1992, weeks after her 94th birthday.

"These too lived by faith . . . of whom the world was not worthy."

Hebrews 11.

www.ingramcontent.com/pod-product-compliance
Lightning Source LLC
Chambersburg PA
CBHW070736160426
43192CB00009B/1458